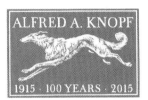

A House of My Own

A House of My Own

Stories from My Life

Sandra Cisneros

ALFRED A. KNOPF

New York

2015

THIS IS A BORZOI BOOK
PUBLISHED BY ALFRED A. KNOPF

www.aaknopf.com

Knopf, Borzoi Books, and the colophon are registered trademarks
of Penguin Random House LLC.

Grateful acknowledgment is made to the following for permission
to reprint previously published material:

Arte Público Press: "I Salute the Dead (Darkness Under the Trees)"
from *The Sadness of Days* by Luis Omar Salinas, copyright © 1987 by
Arte Público Press, University of Houston. Reprinted by permission
of Arte Público Press, University of Houston.

Princeton University Press: Excerpt from "Ithaka" from *Collected Poems*
by C. P. Cavafy, copyright © 1992. Reprinted by permission of Princeton
University Press, administered by Copyright Clearance Center, Inc.

Page 383 constitutes an extension of the copyright page.

Library of Congress Cataloging-in-Publication Data
Cisneros, Sandra. [Essays. Selections]
A house of my own : stories from my life / Sandra Cisneros.
First edition.   pages cm
"This is a Borzoi book" — Verso title page.
ISBN 978-0-385-35133-1 (hardcover) — ISBN 978-0-385-35134-8 (eBook)
1. Cisneros, Sandra—Homes and haunts. 2. Cisneros, Sandra—Family.
3. Mexican Americans—Mexico—Biography. 4. Mexican American women
authors—Biography. 5. Authors, American—20th century—Biography.
I. Title.
PS3553.I78Z46 2015   813'.54—dc23   [B]   2015007520

Front-of-jacket photograph by Diana Solís
Back- and spine-of-jacket image:
Mingei International Museum / Art Resource, N.Y.
Jacket design by Stephanie Ross

Manufactured in the United States of America
First Edition

Para Tey Diana Rebolledo, *fe*

Carla Trujillo, *ánimo*

Ruth Béhar, *inspiración*

Macarena Hernández, *corazón*

Josie F. Garza, *devoción*

Y para iluminación, Norma Alarcón

The pearl is the oyster's autobiography.

—FEDERICO FELLINI

Contents

A House of My Own

My desk in my Chicago Bucktown flat when I was writing
The House on Mango Street

Introduction

A long time ago, which was yesterday, I could tell time by the typeface on my manuscripts. I mean yesterday BC—Before Computers. I owned a variety of manual typewriters and only gradually and reluctantly moved into the electronic world without somehow ever managing to get ahold of the Rolls-Royce of typewriters—an IBM.

I roamed about the earth and borrowed typewriters in Greece, France, the former Yugoslavia, Mexico, and throughout the United States. My manuscripts were sheaves of paper with holes from where the placket struck the page too fiercely. And everywhere I went, the poems or stories or essays I typed, with their mismatched typefaces and consistent typing errors, reminded me, like passport stamps, where I'd been.

Sometimes I was living on a grant. Sometimes I was living in a borrowed house or guest room. Sometimes I convinced myself I was in love, but most of the time I lived alone in a space that wasn't mine with bills that flared like small fires. That meant I passed through a lot of houses, loves, and typewriters, never quite finding the right one.

I am writing this now on a laptop in central Mexico, in a region where my ancestors lived for centuries. My office is a leather *equipal* table and chair on a covered terrace. On either side of me, a Chihuahua snoozes. Next door a palm tree rattles like a maraca, and down in the town center a church bell gongs the hour.

In my last house in San Antonio, Texas, I worked in a two-story office in my backyard and lived with a flock of dogs that followed me about like Mary's little lamb. I still own dogs, and I still have a lot of typefaces on my manuscripts; some files I can't open because the computer is long gone and so is the software. I count the passing of time by the purchase of writing machines.

So I'm gathering up my stray lambs that have wandered out of sight and am herding them under one roof, not so much for the reader's sake, but my own. Where are you, my little loves, and where have you gone? Who wrote these and why? I have a need to know, so that I can understand my life.

These stories from my life span from 1984 to 2014. Most were written for specific audiences, a university or high school lecture, a journal, an anthology, often at someone's request. In the beginning, I didn't have a lot of confidence to speak as myself. I used the scrim of poetry and fiction. The truth told slant, as Emily Dickinson instructed. To speak as me required learning to come out from behind the screen.

In an early autobiographical response compiled in a book of Chicano interviews, not only were the facts wrong (I was young enough to take the family at their word regarding story), but my own voice sounds stilted, as if I were wearing a big suit with suede patches and smoking a pipe. I disown that first essay and don't include it here for those reasons.

I've excluded almost all of the few reviews, critical essays, and interviews I wrote early on for Third Woman Press and/or when I was literature director at the Guadalupe Cultural Arts Center, in San Antonio, as they didn't seem to fit the theme or didn't age well. Some of the interviews I conducted with other writers remain untranscribed, and maybe it's best they stay that way. I've withheld as well introductions or epilogues to books when they couldn't stand alone—fenders without the car.

My memory knows more about me than I do. It doesn't
lose what deserves to be saved.

—EDUARDO GALEANO

The memories I present here are a way of claiming my real
life and differentiating it from my fiction, since there seems to be
so much out there assumed or invented about me. (There is no
truth to the rumor I died, for instance, as was once reported on
Wikipedia. And, as far as I can remember, I was never a prostitute
in Tijuana, as one Spanish-language newspaper claimed, though
it makes for a terrific story.) Rather than write an autobiography,
which I have no inclination to do at the moment, a form of weaving one's own death shroud, I offer my personal stories as a way
of documenting my own life.

Most of the selections included in this collection were tinkered
with for unity, to dodge repetition when possible, or just because
my standards have gotten higher with time. Some existed formerly only in spoken form until I figured out how to transcribe
them. Often I had to tell the story over and over till it felt complete.
When this happened, it's likely I couldn't remember the "true"
event anymore, but I could understand myself better. I think it's
like this for most people. We tell a story to survive a memory in
much the same way the oyster survives an invading grain of sand.
The pearl is the story of our lives, even if most wouldn't admit it.

In 1985 the literary critic Tey Diana Rebolledo invited me to
give what would be my first academic lecture, for the Modern
Language Association conference in Chicago. I was terrified and
broke down with laryngitis. I had to deliver the paper in a stage
whisper swallowing glass after glass of hot water till somehow

I managed to get to the end. It may have made no huge difference to the MLA and the world, but it was a great success to me all the same, and that success gave me courage to keep writing more nonfiction prose. I thank Tey now for her encouragement and faith all those years ago. (What happened to that first paper, *sólo Dios*—only God knows. This was BC.)

I thought at first to arrange the sequence of these stories as if they were rooms in a house, placing each selection in a different area as if the reader were entering a dwelling—the threshold for the introduction; the hall for a story about connections; the stairway for spiritual ascension; etc.

In the end, for clarity's sake, I was compelled to arrange the stories in the sequence I wrote them. Even if the story had been told before, each time I told it I hoped I was getting a more perfect truth, adding a layer of nacre, making the story more complete and whole. The further away a story, the more clearly you can see it, I've always said, because only then can you see yourself.

Flipping through a journal written in January of 1983, I found my younger self traveling on a National Endowment for the Arts fellowship through Europe and reporting, after meandering for a month in borrowed homes, how ecstatic I felt finally when I was lodged at an arts colony and lent a house of my own and a typewriter.

A house. A writing machine. These two go hand in hand for me. A home makes me feel like writing. I feel like writing when I'm at home. Nowadays, I would add that I need one more thing in order to write—my animals. When they are with me, I am at home.

––––––

In Mexico, feast days are celebrated with magnificent firework displays called castles. These *castillos,* set up in the street or public plaza, are not made of mortar and stone, but of *carrizo,* reeds. Fireworks are tied to a gigantic *carrizo* pyramid with the more complicated and stunning pyrotechnics on top, like the wedding couple crowning a cake. Part of the extraordinary pleasure in witnessing the show is that the viewers stand as close as they like to the falling fireworks like a foolhardy rock concert mob. There are no safety measures taken that I can see. At any moment madness and mayhem might spontaneously erupt. I think this is part of the allure.

The first tier is lit, three images rotating and whirling and setting off a tepid spray of sparks into the crowd—a star, a sunflower, a flag, blazing briefly till they fizzle in a tail of gauzy smoke. But it's the higher levels that terrify and delight, growing more elaborate as they rise, more dangerous, taking our breath away with their splendor, dusting us with ash and leaving us coughing and blinking.

Finally the crown of the castle is ignited. The crowd shifts its weight. Folks crane their necks. Abuelitas cover their heads with their black shawls and cross themselves. Babies are held aloft like the helium balloons sold in front of the cathedral. Kids cling from streetlamps, as resilient as spider monkeys. This is what we all came for. It's why we've put up with throbbing feet, shoving crowds, and air stinking of sulfur and fried meat. It's time.

What is it? Can you see yet? Who? The Archangel Michael? Zapata? The chalice and host? No, look! It's the Virgen de Guadalupe! *¡Ay, qué bonito!* La Lupe blazing to life in sizzling pinwheels of green, white, and red—*el verde, blanco, y colorado*—for the Mexican flag, but also, I believe, for the holy trinity of Mexican cuisine—chili, onion, tomato.

Guadalupe begins to turn, slowly at first, *a despedirse,* to say goodbye, as is only proper. Then the Holy Virgin gains speed, pirouetting like an Olympic ice skater, whirling into the night sky, disappearing for a second before exploding like a dandelion and plummeting back to earth in a magnificent blessing of fireflies. This is how I imagine Death.

I have no children to tell the following stories, and even if I did, they wouldn't want to hear them. And so I offer them to you, my readers. As I write this, I'm entering my sixties. A new cycle in my life is opening and an old one closing. I'm in between lives and in between houses, writing from the other side of the U.S.-Mexico border, from within Mexico instead of from beyond it. And with that, I wish to look backward and forward all at once, before I transform myself finally into a pinwheel of light.

November 30, 2014
Casa Itzcuinapan
San Miguel de los Chichimecas, Guanajuato

Hydra House

Street leading to my house in Greece

I had a house in Greece once, on an island off the Peloponnesus. It was my first, and as such, holds a dazzling place in my memory. It belonged to an English couple who lived there summers. The autumn of 1982 it was mine.

Hydra is both the name of the island, a paradise absent of automobiles, and of the town, a cascade of stone houses and stairways spilling down the mountain to the harbor. It's where I finished *The House on Mango Street*. My house was a primitive structure set above the village with a wide view of town, sea, and sky. It was close enough to civilization, yet far away. Solitary but social. Remote enough to keep people at bay, and yet I could, when I wanted, come down to the port for company at the end of the day. A perfect balance of retreat and society for a writer.

I f mine were a tale from Ovid, my metamorphoses as a cloud began the year I moved to Provincetown in the summer of 1982. I planned to finish *The House on Mango Street* there before leaving for Greece. That's what I told my publisher, and that's what I promised myself I would do. I was so sure I'd be done by summer's end, I bought a one-way ticket from New York to Athens for September and a Eurail pass so I could travel across Europe on the cheap.

In Provincetown I shared an apartment under the stairs at the Fine Arts Work Center with Dennis Mathis, friend and personal editor since our days together in Iowa. Dennis was working as a house painter that season and came home in a deep funk that lifted only with a nap. All the same, he made time to read my daily output and offer comments, careful not to destroy what he called my quirky voice.

It was a kooky summer flooded with enough characters to people a Marx Brothers movie. We danced at moon parties on the dunes at night and at tea dances in the gay bars during the day. It's no wonder I had trouble concentrating on that other world inside my head.

In September I stuffed my unfinished manuscript in my suitcase and kissed Provincetown goodbye. I didn't know when I was com-

At home in Provincetown just before
leaving for Greece

ing back, but I knew I wouldn't be the same on my return, thank
God. If there was anyone I needed to get away from, it was me.

I wanted my life to change. After grad school I taught high
school, then worked as a college recruiter and counselor. I orga-
nized community arts events. I gave away my time to everyone
except my writing. I wanted to be a writer, but I had no idea how
to go about this except to travel. Where did I get this idea? Well,
for one, the movies. And for another, the exciting place names
trotting behind the author's name at the end of a text—Majorca,
Trieste, Marrakech, Tenerife. And then there were the biogra-
phies of well-known (male) writers behaving badly. I knew so little
about how women writers lived, and nothing about working-class
writers, even though I'd been to a writers' workshop. I wasn't sure

how to go about this business of becoming a writer, but I knew what I didn't want. I didn't want to live in New York or teach at a university—the former because I hated big cities (as a poor person), the latter because universities intimidated me (as a poor person). I wanted to live like a writer, and I imagined writers did this with a typewriter *and* a house by the sea.

At twenty-eight I felt provincial and naive. Fortunately my first national writing fellowship arrived; this was my now-or-never moment. At first I thought I would move to San Francisco to be near the Latino literary scene. But that dream seemed one I could easily reach without a grant, and I shelved that plan for later. Instead, I aimed for a more exotic geography. I was trying to please my Chicago nemesis, a man I considered sophisticated. I wanted him to admire *me,* instead of the other way round. To gain his approval I would do as he had done. I would become a world traveler.

My destination of choice was Patagonia, the tip of South America, with a plan to work my way north to Buenos Aires, home of all things I loved—the tango, Borges, Storni, Puig, and Piazzolla. But how could I manage it? The idea of traveling through Latin America was too overwhelming for a woman who'd never traveled alone outside of the States. And to make things worse, I knew the local men would think I was inviting their company just by traveling solo. Overwhelmed, I convinced myself it would be easier if I deferred Patagonia till I was a more seasoned voyager.

Luckily, earlier in the year I'd met Ifigenia, a poet of Greek descent. Ifigenia was going to Athens to visit family that fall, and she said I could tag along. We made plans to meet in September in Athens. This was a relief to me since I had nightmares that combined my greatest fears. I dreamt of being locked in a dark room with a ghost mouse. With Ifigenia alongside me, I felt calmer.

I have a vague recollection of sending a "My dog ate my homework" letter to my small-press publisher who was waiting for the promised manuscript by summer's end. What else could I do? There was no refund on my ticket to Greece. I flew away and tried not to think about him too much. He had an infamous temper.

I went to Athens first, staying with Ifigenia at her parents' home, a pristine apartment that smelled deliciously of moussaka. We poked around town seeing the requisite antiquities, and then off we went to Piraeus to visit the islands—actually only one, in the end, though we arrived with the original agenda of seeing others.

Hydra was where we went, because it was said to be full of artists, and Hydra was where we stayed, because it was heaven. We rented rooms in funky pensions and did the things writers do on Greek islands—sit under the awnings of outdoor cafés scribbling in journals, eating calamari, and making friends with the town's outrageous citizens. When we were done attracting eccentrics, we returned to Athens, where an angry letter from my publisher was waiting for me. I can't remember what it said, but if it was a cartoon, I would draw smoke coming out of the envelope. It was enough for me to realize I wasn't going anywhere till I finished that book.

The delay of my book made it impossible for me to keep my promise to my Chicago nemesis; we had planned to rendezvous in Morocco. I wrote and said I wasn't coming, and the reply was a sirocco of rage. I was writing my book, I couldn't come, but it was useless to explain. I was miserable. I'd chosen my writing over a man. It wouldn't be the last time.

And so we went back, Ifigenia and I. To *live* on Hydra instead of just visit. An island only a few hours from Athens, close enough to the Peloponnesus you could see it across the horizon.

In the beginning we lived near the horseshoe port with its day divided by boat whistles. "Here we are!" Or, "We're off!" Each letting us know the time of day without looking at a watch. Day tourists tumbled off huge ocean liners and took the same pictures of tavernas, flowered archways, and donkeys before climbing back on board and dashing away.

On our first Hydra visit we'd met two Greek-Egyptian brothers who had a shop at the far end of the harbor next to the café that sold paninis. Konstantinos and Vasilis Embiricos. They owned an odd gift shop filled with fur coats and cheap plaster imitations of Greek antiquities, a strange combination of dusty merchandise, made all the more bizarre by the sweltering autumn heat.

I liked the brothers Embiricos, and they liked me. Vasilis, the pudgy elder, looked like the film noir actor Peter Lorre, the same wide forehead, oily hair, and huge froggy eyes clogged with sorrow, as if they'd seen too much for one lifetime. He was divorced, separated, widowed? I can't remember. He was alone and lonely. Konstantinos, on the other hand, was as lean as a Giacometti, a striking man with a lovely little boy who lived in Athens with his mother. They weren't millionaires, indebted as they were to their expired alliances and the children these had produced. They lived on an interior street in modest houses they most likely rented and did not own, bright on the outside but dark as caves on the inside. Their street, like most streets on the island, was meticulously neat, with the cobblestones in front of their house scrubbed daily by fanatic Greek housewives.

When I was searching for lodgings, Konstantinos offered me his home, which unfortunately came with Konstantinos. For the short time I lived there I enjoyed how the mornings entered, the pleasure of admiring the light on the ceiling with its luster of a polished dime.

Then Konstantinos grew too fond of me, and I searched for a house of my own. I took the first one shown, at the top of the mountain, practically where civilization ended and wilderness began. (Ifigenia joined me in the beginning, but the stairs eventually defeated her. I counted over three hundred and fifty steps from the port to my door. In the end she found writing in the cafés more to her liking and moved into lodgings near the port.) I signed a two-month lease for two hundred dollars a month, the same amount as the rent on my Chicago Bucktown flat, handing back the keys the morning I finished *The House on Mango Street,* November 30, 1982.

The Hydra house was a simple summer cottage. Like all Greek houses, it was whitewashed inside and out with lime each Easter. It had a high garden wall, thick walls, gentle lines, and rounded corners, as if carved from feta cheese.

From the upstairs bedroom window you felt you could leap and soar over the town, a geometry of sparkling sugar cubes that tumbled toward the sea. On the opposite shore lay a mirage of land called the Peloponnesus with its hazy mountain range, and above all this, a great indulgence of sky. The famous light of Provincetown had nothing on Greece. This was splendid, eternal, serene.

Our village was built like the amphitheaters of antiquity, entirely of stone. Every sound could be heard by every neighbor, whether it was a porcelain *filtzanaki* cup set back on its china saucer or a radio blasting Giorgos Salabasis's big hit of that season, *"S'agapao m'akous"* ("I Love You, Do You Hear Me?").

In the beginning, while the early October days were still warm, I set up my office in the garden under a canopy of grapevines dizzy with drunken bees. I borrowed Konstantinos's French typewriter, whose keys were set up differently than an English keyboard, and everything I typed that season—story, poem, letter—came out with the same consistent typing errors.

When I lifted my head from the page, the mountains across the mainland were a sun-faded lavender like vintage velvet ready to

dissolve into dust. Each day the sea a different shade of blue than the day before, and each shade of blue contrasting with those other strips of blue—sky and mountains.

One of the great delights of my Hydra house was pulling open the bedroom windows each morning, twin doors of three panes each, unlatching the shutters, a rattle and moan, a slight shove, and they would swing and open like arms spread out wide to belt out a song: sea, sky, garden pouring in. *S'agapao m'akous!*

The house, its windows and the joy of opening them: they found their way into my novel in the vignette "Sally" (or the vignette found its way into reality). Because my house was like the one the protagonist Esperanza dreams about, with windows that let in plenty of blue sky.

Once, at this same bedroom window I caught with my hands

what I thought was a huge moth, but between its fluttering I could see it was a velvety bird or bat or some other mythical creature halfway between insect and sprite. I let it go, too frightened to get a better look.

While living in the Hydra house, I had this dream. I dreamt I was swimming with the dolphins in the Aegean. We leapt in and out of the water joyously like a needle stitching the sea. This was all the more remarkable because in real life water terrifies me.

Living on Hydra was like this, somewhere between reality and the imagination. I lived a life enchanted and watched myself living this enchanted life tap-tap-tapping on a typewriter in a beautiful house with a view of the sea like the writers in movies.

I wanted to share my good luck and immediately invited all my friends and family to join me. But no one took me up on the offer. "Good lucky," as my mother might've said, or I would've never finished my book. I had two months to work.

I worked best at home and preferred to come down to the port only when I needed groceries, which was almost daily since I wasn't much of a cook. I woke at noon, strapped on the leather sandals I'd bought from the shoemaker at the port, and ran down to town two steps at a time, hurrying before the shops closed for lunch and their leisurely siesta.

At the harbor I'd buy cucumbers and yogurt and garlic to make tzatziki. I'd buy eggs for breakfast. I'd buy olives scooped out of a barrel with oil and wrapped in a twist of wax paper and a thick slice of sopping feta cheese. Then on the way back up the mountain I'd stop at a little shop crowded with patrons eating standing up like horses, and there I'd make my last purchase, a bit of grilled lamb for my dinner.

There was water all around us, but there were no fish. The waters had been fished clean, Konstantinos explained. I did venture out once with him to fish for calamari one night but never again. To witness the calamari gasping in our boat after we'd caught them was too much for me and made me cry. But it wasn't enough to stop me from enjoying them the next day with olive oil and lemon.

Near Konstantinos's house there was a bakery that sold delicious spinach-cheese pies that I bought hot from the oven along with fresh loaves of bread I'd slice and wedge with Swiss chocolate bars. I weighed 118 pounds then and must've burned the calories climbing the three hundred and fifty steps up to my house. How else to explain this miracle?

The cost of living on Hydra was high for the locals because practically everything was imported, including drinking water. Even though the island's name meant "water," this was just a memory from centuries before when Hydra once boasted several natural springs. Hydra had no water left, just like the sea had no more fish. It had to import its supply from the mainland, as it did just about everything else, including the meager produce. Sad oranges, bruised apples, a few cucumbers, maybe onions. Going to the market felt as if we were living in times of war, but now in retrospect it may have been that way only for me, the one who woke at noon and had to make do buying the dregs.

There was only one vehicle on Hydra, a huge truck that hauled off the garbage to some remote part of the island, a place that scared me when I thought about it. Our island existed only for the self-centered port and the nearby hippie village of Kaminia, with great bluffs between the two towns that looked down into water flooded with schools of dangerous jellyfish.

At night I worked on the kitchen counter because a hanging lamp above was the only proper lighting in the house. If I'd had a good workday, I'd go down into the port afterward to meet Ifigenia, or to dine with Konstantinos at a taverna, or at his brother Vasilis's house because Vasilis liked to cook, or to dance at a disco, or to have an ouzo at a bar after a day of channeling stories.

Though I enjoyed company, I was happiest when I stayed aboard my own landlocked ship, content to admire the world from that remote vessel called home. I would linger at my bedroom window like Penelope awaiting her Odysseus, the garden overflowing with grapes, plumbago, and jasmine on one side, and on the other the busy port bobbing with ocean liners, humble fishing boats, and millionaire yachts.

My house was just a cottage, yet it was the most beautiful place I'd ever lived, then or since. I mooned over it like a lovesick teenager, and the house absorbed my adoration. In the day I left the double doors and the windows open, the light as soft as a pearl, the house full of wind. Cement sinks and floors, exposed plumbing, banquettes built into the wall, a rudimentary kitchen with a camping cooktop fueled by a tank of propane. Nothing fancy. *Someday I will have a house just like this,* I told myself. Its simplicity gave me infinite pleasure, and this pleasure allowed me to write.

Hydra, Hydra, Hydra! A flag flapping in the wind. I loved its intimacy. I could walk everywhere. I loved the privacy of its high walls. I sat at my bedroom window with one leg indoors and one leg out, as if straddling a great white winged horse, admiring both the interior and exterior worlds at once.

I was at home. I considered even staying forever. But I couldn't reason how. I was not Greek. I would have to learn an entirely new culture. These were not my people, not my cause. And how would I earn my living? *Ah, if only . . . ,* I thought to myself.

Was it true there were as many chapels on the island as there were days of the year? I don't know. But there were enough miracles, or so it seemed to me. Once Konstantinos plucked a jasmine flower from a vine and gave it to me, and I was as astonished as if he'd pulled a rabbit from a hat. I had no idea jasmine grew on

walls. I'd never seen a jasmine flower till that night, white as the moon, milky and sweet.

The wondrous thing about the island was that there was no way for a criminal to get away. I could walk home alone at night without fear. Everybody knew who you were and where you were going, and could stop you before you left the island. Whether this sense of safety was true or not, it was a novel feeling for me as a woman and as a Chicagoan. I'd never felt like this before and seldom have since.

———

The greatest marvel of all, I wrote every day, or at least that's how I remember it. I wrote in longhand and then typed what I'd written, wrote corrections over my typed text until I couldn't understand the knotted string called my handwriting. Then I'd type the page clean again from the beginning, a process that repeated itself over and over, and which I enjoyed, because it allowed me to hear the text, like a composer listening to music inside his head.

Where are those sheets of paper now? I wonder. Probably in

the Hydra garbage pit, a place of horrors, I imagine, overrun with giant rats on the far side of the island, every bit as squalid as the other side was glamorous.

Was I reading during this time? I can't imagine otherwise. I know I had a paperback copy of *The Necessity of Art: A Marxist Approach* by Ernst Fischer, which I tried to finish to impress my Chicago nemesis, but there are passages underlined only in the early chapters, though I carried the book around with me through Greece, Italy, France, Spain, and Yugoslavia, trying to appear intelligent. I remember none of it.

The tavernas were democratic agoras where the rich and the not-so-rich crossed paths. I recognized the colossal head of Ted Kennedy in the taverna where I was having lunch one rainy afternoon with Konstantinos and Vasilis. Ted and company had stepped off a sparkling yacht and were busy chewing on the same greasy potatoes and overcooked chicken as we were.

The island boasted handsome stone mansions built by millionaires, old sea captains, and, rumor had it, pirates, ancient and mod-

ern. They certainly looked like they'd taken a treasure to build. Who these wealthy were, I never knew. Everyone sitting at the cafés looked as affluent or poor as everyone else. In that sense it appeared an egalitarian society, though we knew that wasn't true.

To live on an island with land in sight is calming. Huge liners slid into the port depositing their day tourists. Hydrofoils hovered above the water speeding to and from Piraeus like nervous dragonflies. Our harbor stank of cat urine, dead fish, seaweed, retsina. All the while the sound of water constantly sloshing against the mossy stone walls of the port. The Greek men tossing their *kompoloi,* worry beads, loafing all day long at the cafés, eyed the fresh crop of foreign women in scanty summer wear trotting off the boats, while the Greek women, Greek tragedies of their own making, were more industrious than worker ants, cleaning, always cleaning, their task, like that of Sisyphus, never ending.

We watched hoteliers hovering about the incoming tourists as soon as they stepped off the boat plank, hoping to lure them to their lodgings. And nobody intervened to warn the young girls in backpacks about the pension near the clock tower whose owner was a notorious peeping Tom. No matter. They'd find out soon enough.

The Greeks had a nonverbal language I had to learn to decipher. When they flicked their head and ticked with their tongue after you asked them a question, it didn't mean "What a stupid question!" but simply "no." And when they shouted when they spoke to you, you learned not to take it personally. This was the usual tone they used when talking to one another.

It was while living on Hydra that I realized the Greek women had the same sad hoarse voices as the seagulls. I imagined they had metamorphosed like in a tale by Ovid. They were the most beautiful women I saw in Europe, with agate eyes, lovely beings even with their harsh voices. But their beauty spoiled too quickly, while the men's charms endured.

Because ours was an island without vehicles, there was no way to lug things uphill except by hand or by donkey. The routes the animals took were littered with fresh dung. The men who herded these beasts spoke a donkey language made up of sounds like "brrrr," and tongue ticks like the one that meant "no," and shouts I hoped the donkeys learned not to take personally, but it seemed they did. They were sensitive creatures who cried with their heads thrown back to the sky. *Pobrecitos*.

Since there were no street names on Hydra when I lived there, to give an address you had to take someone by the hand, or give very specific directions: "Do you know the house with the wall with the double-headed eagle? Take a left there and go up and up following 'Donkey Shit Lane,' you can't miss it, follow their trail, and then when you get to an overpass covered with jasmine, the second house on the right, by the olive tree. That's where I live."

———

There was a woman from Germany on the island I'll call Liesel. She had worked with the famous directors from the New German Cinema—Fassbinder, Herzog, Wenders. Liesel lived in a beautiful house with several terraces where the mountain refused to budge. It made for a magical experience entering that house with its high whitewashed walls and olive and lemon trees and bougainvillea, its rooms sparsely but beautifully decorated with items dragged with great effort from Vienna or Cusco. Every object in Liesel's house looked like it was ready for its close-up—a wooden bucket sitting under a brass garden spigot, an antique bentwood bed in the center of an empty room, a kitchen basket dangling from a wooden ceiling beam with a hairy rope.

Liesel's job in her filmmaker days had to do with scouting locations, finding permission to shoot there, assisting in arranging the set, drumming up extras, making sure of continuity, and many other details that sounded glamorous to a non-filmmaker. While working in South America on Werner Herzog's *Aguirre, the Wrath of God,* she contracted a mysterious disease that came and went and left her doubled over in pain. As a result several filmmakers had pooled resources and bought the Hydra house Liesel occupied but did not own. I was not told the reason for their generosity. I was told it was because she was dying. Liesel was quite convinced of this and was often sick enough to convince others too. Perhaps she was dying now and then. Who knows? I only know it spooked the local Greeks to have such a pale woman with hair and skin the color of a ghost meandering in the cemetery at night and cursing at them during the day because their garbage blew into her garden.

I accompanied Liesel on one of her cemetery excursions. I was fascinated by the Greek graves with their lit oil lamps and unsmiling portraits of the dead imprinted on the headstones just like the Mexican cemeteries, and so long as I wasn't there alone, I didn't feel afraid. I was fond of Liesel. She told marvelous stories of a life lived with her foot on the accelerator. At the time she seemed old to me, though now I realize she was younger than I am as I write this.

When I was introduced to islanders, the big question on my mind was "Where did Leonard Cohen live?" I asked and asked, but no one knew or would tell me. I needn't have looked far. There were enough creative geniuses all about. I have in my journal from that time a postcard by the Juilliard-trained performance artist Charlotte Moorman, the cellist who played nude with a cello made of video screens in 1967 and was the muse of Nam June Paik, the founder of video art. I met her at one of the cafés, where she generously gave me her address and invited me to look her up when I went to New York, but I was too shy and never did.

I had a friendship during this time with a woman almost a decade younger than me. Her name was Willhemina. She was a southern belle who had been sent to live with an aunt in Paris. (In my imagination this aunt looked like the old lady who befriended Babar the elephant.) Somehow Will had managed to wash ashore alone on Hydra. Men ancient and nubile were gaga over Will. She had the wide square face of a farmer's daughter; pale, freckled skin; strawberry-blond hair; and eyes as sparkling as the Aegean. She was pretty, not beautiful, and there was a disproportion to her body that made me wonder what all the fuss was about. But she was young and had once been a cheerleader, and men like that, I guess.

Will told me about the mandatory diet pills dispensed to all the cheerleaders at the southern university she attended, and it made me want to cry out, "Aw, honey!" And one night when we shared Vasilis's apartment, she told the story about her abortion. She was an island Holly Golightly, surviving episodes that made me shiver. Where, I wondered, were her goofy parents?

Will said the only thing she missed about the United States was marshmallows. I sent six bags to her when I got home, but they went halfway around the world and boomeranged back to Texas with several postmarks on them stating "Return to sender." Whatever happened to Will, I'll never know. It wouldn't surprise me if she was married to a Greek tycoon.

My own personal life was a mess. I had multiple love affairs because I wanted to protect my heart from the Chicago nemesis. We were in an open relationship, he told me, which meant it suited his wishes, not mine. But it was useless. The less he needed me, the more I wanted him. Independence inspires admiration, and admiration is an aphrodisiac.

Will and me at the Hydra Port

I would try to win his admiration for decades without being aware he was mixed up in my head / heart as the father archetype, till finally one day I realized I would never gain his approval. But then I didn't need his approval anymore. He was a figment of my imagination.

Meanwhile, back on the island, Konstantinos and I shared a brief romance, but it sputtered out after a few days, leaving only a wisp of smoke.

Konstantinos at forty seemed old to me at twenty-eight. Sometimes when we were intimate, his face transformed into a skull, and I felt as if I were sleeping with Death, though I never told him this. He had large feline eyes, a thin face with extraordinary cheekbones, tousled gladiator hair, and a chin covered with a trim Odysseus beard. He looked precisely like those handsome Egyptian portraits found on the mummies of Fayum, with their eyes as dark and moist as Greek olives. I can see Konstantinos's charms clearly now, but at the time I knew him I was distracted by the novelty of the boys who hovered about, having dated an older man when I was their age.

When I moved out of Konstantinos's house, I went on my way with my life without giving him a second thought. He may have admired my independence, and this may have bound him tighter to me. As I write this I apologize for any pain I might have caused Konstantinos by my carelessness, and I forgive the nemesis who similarly caused me the same.

During my season on Hydra my skin was copper from having lived two seasons on two coasts—the Atlantic and the Aegean. I wore my hair long and curly like the Cretan priestesses who leapt over the backs of bulls and held snakes in their hands. I was creating. I had my own money. And, I had a house of my own. This to me was power.

Men came into my life often, and often I found them charming. It was easy to reason, "Why not?" But there was only one I held in my heart: Dimitri, a Greek sailor, who helped distract me from the Chicago nemesis. The others were simply *pasatiempos.*

My Greek sailor sailed away after a short, intense passion. When I first met him at the port, he told me his name in a gentle and sleepy voice. I liked him immediately. His eyes of *The Thousand and One Nights.* His prizefighter's body with a chest like the shield of Achilles. Come to think of it, he looked like a young Javier Bardem. No wonder I've been wild about Bardem all these years.

––––––––

The Hydra house and *The House on Mango Street* are united together in that voyage. An eternal moment, like being in love. I try from this distance to remember where I wrote each of the vignettes from *House,* but I can only place a few, and as I had no computer then and no place to store my drafts as a voyager, must rely on memory.

The night I began the book in Iowa, I wrote the first chapter, "The House on Mango Street," "Meme Ortiz," and a vignette that fell by the wayside.

When I was working as a high school teacher in Chicago, I wrote "Darius & the Clouds," "Chanclas," "Minerva Writes Poems," "Geraldo No Last Name," and "The Monkey Garden."

"The Family of Little Feet" was born during the year I was a counselor at Loyola University, my alma mater, after a comment a student made about my own small feet. "Alicia Who Sees Mice" and "What Sally Said" were also based on something spoken by one of my counselees. During this same time in my life I shared "The First Job" with the Chicago writer James McManus. Jim took my work seriously and reminded me to do the same, and this was just what I needed to hear at that time of wobbling faith in my own creative powers.

I finished several vignettes while in Provincetown. Which ones, I can't be sure. But I remember starting and finishing "Elenita, Cards, Palm, Water" on that round oak library table next to the window that caught the feet of the upstairs tenants stomping up and down the stairs.

One morning, in Athens just before waking, I dreamt the first line of "The Three Sisters." "They came with the wind that blows in August, thin as a spider web and barely noticed." Maybe being in Greece made me think in threes; I was a big fan of Robert Graves's *The White Goddess.* I tucked that sentence in my journal and ferried it to Hydra, where I wrote the vignette.

One night, with only my flashlight and the moon illuminating the way, I climbed the steps to my Hydra house. I was wrestling with whether to write a story of a violation. I felt protective of my protagonist. I didn't want any harm to come to her. There was also the difficulty of how to write a story the character didn't want to tell. And how would I write it if I had no firsthand experience either as victim or witness?

But then I remembered something that had happened to me in the eighth grade. How a wild boy had grabbed my face against my will and kissed me one night when I was walking home on North Avenue with a girlfriend. How my friend, wiser to the world, had walked off the curb to the street and left me behind alone when this boy and his buddy approached.

The two were possibly no older than we were, but there was something about their swagger that warned her, *"Uh-oh, trouble."* I was the one there for the taking. He lunged. I moved my face, but not fast enough, and his mouth landed awkwardly on one eye. It was my first kiss.

He said, "I love you, Spanish girl." Then they galumphed off roaring, mightily pleased with themselves.

"Did he hurt you?"

"I'm okay I'm okay I'm okay," pretending it was nothing. But I wasn't okay. I couldn't talk about it in words, not even to myself. How my body spoke about it for years. How I told no one and tried to forget it, but trying to forget only made it bob up to the surface like a drowned lady in that swampland called dreams.

On the island I was on the same writing schedule as I am today. Midday till sunset. Then I would slip on my leather sandals and fly with the winged feet of Hermes down the three hundred and fifty stone steps to civilization. It was in a way an ideal life. A cloistered convent in the day and The Pirate Bar at night. The eccentric population of the island within reach when I needed their company.

Was I sharing what I was writing with anyone during those two months? Did I show anything to Ifigenia, who was also a writer? I don't remember any feedback. I typed in the afternoon and sometimes typed through the night. Although I didn't write the vignettes in linear order or arrange them in a fixed order as I wrote them, and though I told my publisher to suggest an arrangement, I knew intuitively how they were supposed to line up. Two months later when I was lodged in the South of France, I would send instructions to my publisher and make that specific sequence clear.

Toward the end of November, terrible storms with their wild Medusa hair of lightning arrived, sometimes canceling the boats that came and went. I moved my office indoors, but eventually was forced to finish my last week on Hydra down at the port at Vasilis's house because my house had no heat and, as it was made entirely of stone, was as damp and cold as a mausoleum.

Vasilis liked for me and Will to stay at his place when he was away. I think he thought it enhanced his reputation to have two young girls, one dark, one fair, coming in and out. I'm reminded here of something Carlos Fuentes said, how Don Juan doesn't realize when he's turned into Don Quixote.

As I write this, a memory I'd forgotten bubbles to the surface. Vasilis and I are seated on his couch one evening. He lunges forward, his face of a sad prisoner hovering toward me; he's pushing me on my back, trying to kiss me. But I spring up like a punching clown and laugh so hard, he never tries it again.

The night I finished *House,* I was staying at Vasilis's second-floor apartment. It was on a narrow alley beyond the bakery, with no view of the sea but a lovely view of the town and the night sky. I seem to remember the apartment was heated with steam, but this might just be my memory. It was snug and cozy, decorated in the Eastern way with carpets everywhere. Vasilis had gone to Athens, and I had with me that night a tall Greek boy, whom I did not love, with dark raccoon rings under his eyes. I spent my last days on the island with him; I can't remember why. Men were nuisances when I was writing. They demanded you come to bed at once. They had urgent hungers. But once you fed them, like children they fell asleep. Then I'd get back to my writing.

I was saving a record from Vasilis's collection for the moment when I finished the book. Strauss's "Blue Danube." How quiet the world was that night. There was just the circle of light above my page. It was near four in the morning when I came to the end. I was relieved that the boy in the next room was snoring. This joy was mine, and I wanted to savor it alone.

I opened the windows and pushed the heavy wooden shutters apart even though it was crisp outdoors. They parted with a creak, and the moon stepped in. It was a clear evening filled with stars. The full moon wasn't expected until the next night, but that evening the night was ablaze, the moonlight washing the white town blue.

The first notes of "The Blue Danube" began, gently, timidly at first. The sky was overwhelmed with strange clouds that night, I remember. I watched them stretch and yawn with the opening notes, and as the music gradually gained momentum, they grew more animated. In the end, they finished hurtling past as swift as a school of fish darting through that sea called the sky.

When the waltz ended I got my Walkman and ran through the blue town to the sea, with Astor Piazzolla and Gerry Mulligan in my ears. When I got to the walkway between Hydra and Kaminia, I climbed up on the wall and began to dance, feeling every bit the sorceress. "I finished!" I shouted, and could see the fishing boats going out for calamari, because calamari is fished only at night. "It's bad luck to see a woman when one is fishing," Konstantinos told me. And I wondered if the sailors could see me dancing on the wall like a witch, cursing because they wouldn't catch any calamari that night.

Then I remembered Liesel, and I went to say goodbye. Liesel was always awake at night, so I wasn't afraid to call on her at that hour. Years later Liesel would tell me we danced under the moon that night, though I don't remember. It was all brief and hurried. I had to pack and catch the first morning hydrofoil, and it was almost dawn when I knocked on Liesel's door.

At daybreak I kissed the raccoon boy goodbye, deposited the house keys, and got on the hydrofoil to Athens, where I mailed the manuscript off from the Syntagma Square post office without making a copy. This seems incredibly reckless to me now in this age of computers, but that's what my life was like BC.

A decade later when I returned to Hydra, I thought I'd remembered the island perfectly, but when I stepped off the boat, I was aware there was one thing I'd forgotten. The cool breath that rises from the damp stone even in the summer.

Every now and then the sound of a rooster crowing or the mournful cry of a donkey takes me back to my island. Why do I

On the rooftops, Hydra

call it "my"? I wonder. Some part of it was given to me for keeps, I believe. Writing today from this distance, it's as if I'd always lived in that house with windows looking out to the garden and sea.

I thought I was Penelope during my Greek days, but now I realize I was Odysseus. "As you set out for Ithaka / hope your road is a long one, / full of adventure, full of discovery." As in Cavafy's poem, I am grateful for the marvelous journey.

No Place Like Home

This was one of two pieces written for the Thomas Wolfe Lecture, the University of North Carolina, Chapel Hill, October 21, 2014. The second, "A Borrowed House," is included near the end of this collection.

When Thomas Wolfe was already a successful author someone asked him if he would consider moving back to North Carolina. He said, "My writing is my home, now."

So it was in the 1930s—when the writer Betty Smith moved to Chapel Hill she found herself at home here in more ways than one. First, she found a place that was calm and safe and affordable for a single mom raising two kids, and calm and safe and affordable are essentials for a writer. While living in Chapel Hill, Smith found another home. She came home to a book that would give her permission to write her own best seller, *A Tree Grows in Brooklyn*. Wolfe's *Of Time and the River* guided her back home. It was while living in Chapel Hill that Smith was able to see her childhood more clearly, see her Brooklyn, admit what set her memories apart from others in Chapel Hill, from her own Brooklyn family. So often you have to run away from home and visit other homes first before you can clearly see your own.

The same thing happened to me when I went off to live in the foreign terrain of Iowa for graduate school. It held up a mirror to myself and allowed me to see what made me different from my workshop classmates, to go home to my Chicago childhood, to the neighborhood and people only I knew, the stories that were mine alone and not those of my brothers or cousins or friends. While at Iowa I began a book that wasn't part of my thesis, but which served to shelter me during my time there. I needed shelter. Maybe I was never more homeless than during those two years in graduate school. I found my home in the country-folk monologues of Mexican writer Juan Rulfo, the anti-poetics of Chilean poet Nicanor Parra, the rage of Malcolm X.

We find ourselves at home, or homing, in books that allow us to become more ourselves. Home "is not just the place where you were born," as the travel writer Pico Iyer once noted. "It's the place where you become yourself."

When I was a young student in Chicago, big-shouldered Carl Sandburg's lyrics showed me the way to sing with syllables. I was directed to Mango Street by way of Gwendolyn Brooks, who wrote about the bean eaters in the Bronzeville kitchenettes of South Chicago, of folks who live in cramped apartments with shared bathrooms and not enough hot water. I knew plenty of bean eaters too, but they lived in the Mexican communities of Pilsen, Humboldt Park, Little Village, or Logan Square. Hot water was also a commodity in my home even though we didn't have to share it with neighbors; we were neighborhood enough in a family of nine. Sandburg and Brooks—their books said, "Come on in!"

The golden pen of Nelson Algren gave Studs Terkel a lift home for keeps and a day, and Studs in turn revolutionized radio by recording the oral histories of the little guy, the never heard, the brave and exhausted from Kentucky to Guanajuato working in factories and steel mills, too busy to get downtown for a little culture. It was Studs who introduced Pablo Neruda's poetry to my mother from the radio on top of the refrigerator next to the slouched loaf of Wonder Bread. The kitchen was my mother's classroom, and she was promoted from the ninth grade to the

My mother, Studs Terkel, and me

University of Life with a PhD. Studs schooled her. Studs showed her the way home.

I was lucky enough to tell Studs this before he departed for the great big radio station in the sky, and he was lucky enough to meet his star pupil, Elvira Cordero. I have a photo of my mom and me and Studs in the WGN studio, all of us looking surprised Divine Providence could bring us together, but that's Divine Providence for you.

In the Mexican writer Elena Poniatowska's novel *La Flor de Lis,* this dialogue occurs more than once between the protagonist and others:

> —But you're not from Mexico, right?
> —I am.
> —It's that you don't look Mexican.
> —Oh, yeah, well, what do I look like?
> —A gringa.
> —Well, I'm not a gringa. I'm Mexican.
> —*A poco.* You gotta be kidding.

Some artists belong very much. Perhaps not so much to their home country, but their adopted one. Elena Poniatowska was born in Paris, but came to Mexico to live with her grandma as a young girl during World War II. She spoke French at home, English at school, and learned Spanish from the poorest members of Mexican society, the indigenous domestic workers—the cook, the nanny. This Mexican Spanish embraced Elenita, and she embraced it back to such a degree that she won the highest literary honor for a Spanish-language writer—the Cervantes Prize—for writing so essentially Mexican, it's made her writing almost untranslatable. She has become an ambassador for the voiceless, a courageous voice in a country where speaking up can cost you your life.

I remember seeing Carlos Fuentes speak at the University of Illinois, Chicago, when I was *una jovencita,* a young thing. What command! What presence! The public adored him. Adored! Well, that one was the ambassador of everything, so handsome and dapper, like a Mexican Cary Grant. Who wasn't going to pay attention to him?

I remember Fuentes sprang to his feet, ran down the aisle, and gamboled onto the stage like a kid goat. He read something . . . I don't remember what, except I remember I didn't understand a word. But what is engraved in my memory was the little leap onto the stage, a Mexican hat dance of sorts that only someone with the utmost self-confidence could give before uttering a syllable. *En esos tiempos, en ese país.* In those times, in that country.

I'm reminded too of the many occasions I was in the audience for the lectures of Jorge Luis Borges. Every time he came to Chicago, we thought it would be the last since he was so old. There would always be a huge wave of disciples, and *un silencio enorme,* a great silence, even before he opened his mouth and spoke. The master Borges was already an elderly man, and blind besides, which, as he himself admitted, inspired kindness.

En esos tiempos, in those times, *el maestro* Borges sat on a chair and leaned, it seemed to me, on a cane. At least he is leaning on a cane in my memory. He spoke of marvels, things that cause astonishment, labyrinths, mirrors, stories that leave you with your mouth open, because he liked to tell those kinds of stories.

And like a blind Tiresias, Borges spoke as a prophet to those of us who were writers. His work appealed to young writers. He was experimental and avant-garde. The form of his fable stories, the ones that later would be published in the U.S. in a collection called *Dream Tigers,* especially impacted me, a new genre between poetry and fiction, even though Borges's poetry seemed to me then, as it does now, old-fashioned. But it was his stories, many less than a page, that inspired me to invent a new form of writing, a novel like a pearl necklace, without being aware of Elena Ponia-towska's diminutive story cycle, *Lilus Kikus.*

I don't want to appear pretentious and say I write like *el maes-tro* Borges. I only want to say that it was his *Dream Tigers* that gave me permission to dream in the same way that Kafka gave Gabriel García Márquez permission to dream, that Thomas Wolfe gave permission to Betty Smith. Sometimes we need permission, encouragement, someone to fill our heart with desire, because without desire you can't invent anything.

I don't know how I wound up writing a book of fiction while in a poetry workshop, but I know that the International Writing Workshop at Iowa and books from the Latin American Boom allowed me to find my way home at a time when I felt I didn't belong.

I don't know anything, but I know this: whatever is done with love, in the name of others, without self-gain, whatever is done with the heart on behalf of someone or something, be it a child, animal, vegetable, rock, person, cloud, whatever work we make with complete humility, will always come out beautifully, and something more valuable than fame or money will come. This I know.

The House on Mango Street was written in a period of complete impotency. As a high school teacher, I had no idea how to save my students from their own lives except to include them in my writing, not for their sake, but for my own. I couldn't undo myself from their stories any other way. How do you get any sleep at night if you witness stories that don't let you go?

During the 1968 Olympics in Mexico City, a student demonstration took place in a plaza called Tlatelolco. Thousands of students were massacred by the police, including Elena Poniatowska's brother. She said she didn't want to be an accomplice to impotency, and so she wrote *Massacre in Mexico,* a book that gave Elena a home in Mexican letters by inventing a new genre, a book made of oral testimonies. I think the great opportunities in life arrive when we are in this state of grace.

And so, I find myself coming home when I read Thomas Wolfe. The Gants are my family, their crowded rooms shared intimately with strangers called family. They take me in and happen to lead me to my own crowded rooms in a house on Mango Street, or a falling-apart fixer-upper on El Dorado Street in San Antonio, Texas, in a novel called *Caramelo,* with a mom who also has big real estate dreams.

Wolfe guided Betty Smith all the way home to Brooklyn in his own writing about the same terrain. And Betty Smith writing about growing up poor, growing up ashamed because she was poor, sheltered my mother when she was a young woman trying to find her way from poverty and shame out to her true home. I am kin of Betty Smith, and Betty Smith is kin of Thomas Wolfe, and so we are branches of the same tree. Your people are my people, whither thou goest, me too.

The paradox for a working-class writer is that we are never

more exiled from our real homes, from the blood kin we have honored in our pages, than when we have drifted away from them on that little white raft called the page.

I had dinner recently with two other Latina writers, and I asked them if their families had spoken to them yet about their new books, and we paused and looked around and blinked. None of us could admit our books had brought us closer to our families. Not once in the recent or faraway past. Maybe it's as the writer Cherríe Moraga says: they don't need to read our books; they have us.

I know for myself I can't go back home to that place where I was raised except through stories, spoken or on paper. Once when I tried to invite a relative to a reading I was giving in Chicago, she looked at me, exasperated, and said, "Sandra, I'm your family, I'm not your fan."

I should've said, "But I'm *your* fan." Of course, I didn't think to say this then, but I'm a writer, and I'm saying it here now.

Instead, I look for my kin in my fellow writers. Those I know in person and those I know on the page. I feel fortunate at least to open books and be invited to step in. If that book shelters me and keeps me warm, I know I've come home.

Luis Omar Salinas

Luis Omar Salinas was one of the Fresno School of poets who influenced a younger generation of poets like myself. His work reminded me of the Spanish poets because of its lyricism and flights of the imagination, but now in hindsight he reminds me of the self-taught artist Martín Ramírez, who wrestled his demons into art. I would meander into my own darkness three years after meeting him. I wish we could have a conversation now. I'd ask him how he managed to become a poet coming from a working-class home, how he dealt with living at home as an adult with his father, was it true he was once with the marine reserve, did the madness arrive before or after, and did he ever talk to *un curandero* or a therapist? I would've mentioned that I too was bullied by hard-core Chicano activists who thought my writing not Chicano enough. Rereading this article I realize I was too young a writer to understand everything Salinas was telling me. I had to live a life first and then ask myself the hard questions later.

This article appeared in the June/July 1984 issue of *Tonantzin,* the magazine of the Guadalupe Cultural Arts Center, where I was literature director at the time. Salinas visited in April and May of that same year as part of a series of readings that included Norma Alarcón, Cherríe Moraga, Helena María Viramontes, Ana Castillo, Pat Mora, Rolando Hinojosa, Evangelina Vigil, Alberto Ríos, and Ricardo Sánchez, among others. With the exception of the poetry cited, the Salinas quotes are drawn from a conversation we had just before his performance at the Guadalupe Theater.

A version of this selection was reprinted in the 2014 anthology *Messenger to the Stars: A Luis Omar Salinas New Selected Poems and Reader,* edited by Christopher Buckley and Jon Veinberg.

I Salute the Dead

In this drunken town
bitten by the whores
of Texas, I pause with
a beer to salute the dead.

Someone's in my house
—the dead child of Texas
haunts the woodwork

and the child is everywhere
tonight waiting for the dawn,
tomorrow maybe playing
in the mud.

My nephew asks if the black
children he sees on TV
are the poor, and I reply,
"We are the poor."
He cannot understand,
and I know this house
is as poor as this drunken
town
and I drink my beer and
hiccup into song.

Darkness Under the Trees / Walking Behind the Spanish: Poems
by Luis Omar Salinas, Chicano Studies Library Publications,
University of California, Berkeley, 1982

I t was Salinas all right, his hand extended out to greet us. Salinas the poet came to town to read his poems. Salinas the man approaching us at the San Antonio airport. Salinas the creator of "her lips have the softness / of olives crushed by rain." Salinas arriving with a smaller version of himself in a brown suit—Salinas and Salinas's father. The elder Salinas speaking the gentle Spanish of grandmothers and children. An exchange of formalities. Yes, their flight had been fine. No, this was not their first visit to San Antonio, recalling a relative's death and a funeral that had brought them here three years before.

Salinas seemed timid, tired, sad like an uncle who has never married. A man who used language sparingly, yet the Salinas I knew of the poems seems intoxicated with language, leaping from one scintillating image to the next, "words coming as confused larks . . . play[ing] games."

Had I not been familiar with the Salinas photograph on the cover of *Prelude to Darkness,* had I not known Salinas's face with its quixotic pucker at times turned into an enigmatic wince as if a bee had stung him, Salinas drawing a cigarette to his lips, Salinas young, frozen forever in that black-and-white photo in the *Entrance: 4 Chicano Poets* anthology, had I not known the face that approached us, the same, slightly fuller, slightly sadder, I wondered if I would have recognized him from his poems alone. Salinas the romantic, Salinas the lyrical, the somber Salinas of the poetry.

Here he was all right. *El mero chingón de poesía,* as the poet *chingón* José Montoya had crowned him. A poet with five books to his credit, winner of the Stanley Kunitz Award, the recent recipient of a GE Foundation Award. Shy. Pauses. Reluctant answers to our inquiries.

We took him for a brief tour of San Antonio, the usual tourist attractions, pointed out the Alamo, the River Walk, took him to El Mercado. A trolley car passed by. "If we had time we'd get on one of those," I said. Salinas just smiled. It was hard to tell what he was enjoying as we drove around and pointed to things one must point to. It was hard to tell what he was thinking in his silences. When we stopped at the Instituto Cultural de México, where he sat beside the Olmec stone head, patiently allowing himself to be photographed and rephotographed, I couldn't help but draw a connection between the face Salinas wore and the other ancient face of stone.

Salinas, after all, was coming "home" to Texas. He had been born here, in Robstown, but had moved away at the age of eight to California, a move crucial, Salinas states, to his becoming a poet.

"Actually the phenomenon of becoming a poet was rather an accident, just mere knowledge of people and also my willingness to get involved. It's strange, you know. It's fate. I could've been somebody else, a bricklayer, a carpenter, or a shoe salesman. If there hadn't been *la revolución* [referring to the Chicano movement of the 1960s] and all this interest in Chicano literature, I probably wouldn't have become involved in it, or if I hadn't gone to college, or had I gotten married as I planned at twenty-six."

Salinas admits he "fell in" with the writers on the West Coast, writers like Jon Veinberg, Peter Everwine, Philip Levine. Does this perhaps explain his popularity in non-Chicano circuits? How is it, then, that the poetry of Luis Omar Salinas is embraced beyond the Chicano literary community?

"I don't know why," Salinas admitted sincerely. "I really don't know how to explain it. I've always considered myself a Chicano poet, even though the writers who influenced me were not Chicano. I feel a personal kinship with the Spanish poets. Hernández, Jiménez, Lorca. But definitely I'm a Chicano poet," Salinas responded defensively during an open mike the night prior when asked about his political direction. "Every Chicano writing is a Chicano writer. Chicano poetry is human poetry—that's where the heart of the matter lies—human compassion."

Salinas seemed less comfortable with questions on the political theory of his work. "There has to be some kind of tension, some kind of conflict," Salinas confessed. "Most writers are at odds with their environment or at odds with themselves. For the poetry to be of any consequence, the poet must have a fight on his hands.

"In my life," Salinas continued, "there has always been a battle with madness, bad friends, lack of money, romances that didn't work. All played a part in my alienation. Most poets are on the *triste* side." He chuckled. "I guess there's been a lot of sadness in my life."

As to whether these hard times helped his writing, Salinas disagreed. "No, but they did ask for courage. How can a person write under bad circumstances? But I'm a poet that deals with all facets of experience. I don't hold anything back. And poetry, of course, is like magic. It helps to balance my life. That balance is very important. When I'm not writing, I tend to lose balance."

Curiously Salinas seems at home in his odd role as poet. The poems attest to this. Salinas addresses Salinas, creates a persona of himself, divides himself into two in much the same way Jorge Luis Borges speaks of a Borges and a Borges in "Borges and I."

"Yes, I have always felt comfortable as poet, even more so in my early years in college. Lately I find it more difficult to write. When I don't travel as much as I used to, the same kind of poems come up, and you don't want that. I have periods like this when I don't write for months."

How does he explain, then, the ten-year gap between *Crazy Gypsy,* his first book, and the rapid succession of the four others that followed?

"After *Crazy Gypsy* I came back from a strange purgatory," Salinas explained. "I was dying, in a sense, spiritually, and the poems seemed to get better as I wrote them. *Crazy Gypsy* was written at the height of my youth. Basically it's a struggle to survive and to write and not go crazy, not commit suicide. Books were a way of saving myself. My friends were encouraging, my family.

"My grandfather was a poet and an orator too, but none of his work survived. He wrote a lot of things in fixed verse, rhymed lines and all that. I don't remember him very well, but I do have a poem I wrote for him.

"And, of course, my family has been very supportive of my

being a poet. My mother has an eighth-grade education, my father a fourth-grade, but they're very sharp and perceptive. I always show my poems to my father, and he makes comments. He can tell me where a bad line is. He's always been a help. My mother, she says 'That's good' every time I bring a paycheck home from doing a reading. Only she says I should stay out of bars. She's afraid I'll escape into Cervantes's world of fantasy at times."

––––––––

Tuesday, May 1st. The day of the poetry reading. Salinas arrives at the Guadalupe Theater, where he is to share the stage with the San Antonio poet Art Muñoz. Salinas is handsome in his suit and tie, spick-and-span, like an altar boy. He blushes a little when I compliment him.

"You know," Salinas confided before the reading, "coming here to San Antonio and meeting you and the Guadalupe staff and everyone is one of the real highlights in my life. Everyone has been very kind. Chicanos have been very supportive of me, and I'm pleased about that. And very grateful."

"Does that surprise you?" I asked.

"In a way," he said, and smiled. "In a way, I *am* surprised."

And then the reading began. Forget his nervousness the night before, his lack of eloquent answers regarding theory or politics. He reads his poems, suddenly, simply. Because all at once one understands Salinas is not a poet of rhetoric and theory. He is a poet of the heart, of that "human compassion" that is Chicano poetry. Salinas the poet and Salinas the man merge into one, vulnerable and lovely.

"We all strive for the muse," Salinas had said earlier to me in regard to poetry. "We all strive to achieve some things. In my life if anything at all has happened or hasn't happened, it's a little bit of fame, recognition. Bread, dreams, and poetry. That's all I'm after."

I thought of this as he read his poems in that strange, lyrical voice that is only his, bright and buoyant as any poet in the world.

Applause and the reception awaiting Salinas the poet. Salinas slipping back into the other, the less eloquent, the shy one. But before we step out into the lobby and the many visitors anxious to speak to the poet, Salinas the man draws me aside next to the thick velvet curtains and confesses, beaming, "You know, this is a big deal for me."

And you could tell, it was.

Falling in Love with *Enamoramiento*

The San Antonio Museum of Art invited me to be part of a visitor's guide that would highlight favorite works in their collection. This was back in 2006. I don't know what became of that project; I never saw my words in print. Maybe they thought what I wrote too scandalous. I never asked. I was just glad to have thrown a few rose petals at an artist whose work I've long admired, the sculptor José Luis Rivera-Barrera, a San Antonian originally from Kingsville, Texas. Although he worked in various materials, Rivera preferred working with wood, especially native mesquite.

When I first came to San Antonio in 1984, I remember being invited to José's show at a gallery on Broadway about three or four miles from my garage apartment. It was a special feat for me to attend back then, because I had to take a bus, and it was Sunday, a day when they arrived only once an hour. Coming from Chicago, I had no idea it would've been faster if I'd walked. After what felt like a long, long trek, I was rewarded by the splendor of José's work. I admired a giant cockroach out of Kafka, which the painter César Martínez would trade for later and display in his home for many years until he was foolish enough to sell it. I wanted more than anything to take home a torso of a pregnant woman whose belly begged to be rubbed. The sculptures seemed as alive as when they were trees fighting against the Texas heat to survive. I couldn't afford to buy José Luis Rivera-Barrera's work back then, and possibly can't now either, but to this master craftsman, in gratitude for inspiration and excellence, I bow.

They're nudes of a man and woman leaping to meet each other in a kiss. José Luis Rivera-Barrera carved them from a single block of mesquite, and it's my favorite art piece in all the San Antonio Museum of Art. It's called *Enamoramiento*—falling in love.

I wait till the guard wanders away, then crawl beneath the torso of the mesquite man. My friend Dr. Ellen Riojas Clark told me to do this. I don't know why, and I don't know why I do it.

"It's anatomically correct," a male voice says.

I turn my head and see a pair of polished black shoes, climb out sheepishly, and show the guard my authorization papers.

"The museum invited me to write about this piece," I say, but the guard just smirks and walks away.

How do I explain? I came to admire at all angles a sculpture that speaks of the sacred, not of the mundane. Of that moment when two beings kiss and are infinite.

It's as if the sculptor José made this with his eyes closed from the memory of the body of his beloved, from the memory of that native land, his own body. It's as if he is remembering the force of love.

It's a sculpture that draws us to it and draws us away, the way one might feel both fascinated and embarrassed to intrude on such a private moment. The dimples and hollows, *las tetas* with their wide Mexican areolas, the *mexi/indio* feet, square and fat as tamales. *Tanto amor.* The hollow of the belly button, *el hueco del ombligo* of the tree, so full of magic you want to leave your prayers here.

Something of the power and holiness of the mesquite is pres-

ent still. The wood remembers the hardscrabble seasons strug-
gling for life. A dynamic thrust, a thirst, a need, a push against all
odds.

I know the artist only to say hello. But when I look at this work,
I see in that tree, hoarded like rain, all the love a man could feel for
a woman in one brief life.

Marguerite Duras

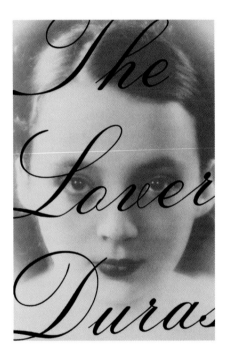

I remember the face of the young girl on the cover of Duras's *The Lover,* and I remember liking that girl with Greta Garbo eyebrows. I didn't know then it was the author in her youth. I was in the Librería Gandhi in Chimalistac, Elena Poniatowska's neighborhood in Mexico City, before an appointment with Elena. To be more exact, it was Norma Alarcón who had an appointment with Elena; I was tagging along. So this was when I first met the great Elena and this was also when I first met Marguerite. I would later read Duras's other books that retell the same story as in *The Lover,* books written before and after. And like Christopher Isherwood's *Christopher and His Kind,* it would aim to tell again a story from youth, but with revisions, as if with age we come closer to the bull's-eye of being admitted the truth. The science writer Jonah Lehrer claims we never revisit a memory without altering it. If this is true, then perhaps all memory is a chance at storytelling, and every story brings us closer to revealing ourselves to ourselves. I promise to revisit what goes unsaid here in my next collection. The critic and *Washington Post Book World* editor Marie Arana prompted my writing this for a February 2005 publication. I felt like I'd been waiting forever to tell this story; it leapt like a dolphin from my heart to the page.

I was thirty the summer I met Marguerite Duras's *The Lover.* This was in Mexico City, 1985. I was supposed to be finishing my book of poetry. The truth, I was fleeing the man who had created and then destroyed me. In a few months Mexico City would be destroyed too, by earthquake. In a few years, Emiliano Zapata* would rise from the dead in Chiapas. But this was before. Without knowing what lay ahead I boarded a bus south to San Cristóbal and disappeared into the fury of jungle and fury of story that is Duras's novel.

The story begins in a second-class bus just like the one I was riding that day, but in colonial French Vietnam. A young girl

---

* On New Year's Eve, 1993, in the Mexican state of Chiapas, the Mayan Indians rose up under the name of Mexican revolutionary leader Emiliano Zapata in defense of their land and rights.

crosses a river, and then crosses color and class lines in love. I'd done much the same in my disastrous affair.

I read through several landscapes, and finally on the perilous mountain road beyond Tuxtla Gutiérrez I found myself at the book's finale, when the lover, unlike my lover, declares his love for her. After all and everything. After their lives were almost over. He still loved her, he would always love her, he said.

Then it was as if I'd been poured back into the shell of my body. And I became aware of the heat of the bus seat sticking to my back and thighs, and the hoarse grinding of the bus gears as it lurched us forward, and the snoring of my bus companions, and the drowsy jungle scent.

To say I was overwhelmed at that moment wouldn't be precise. At that moment with events quivering before and after me, and me in that nowhere and everywhere called my life, I was, as one would say in Spanish, "emotioned." I had read the novel in Spanish, the language of my lover, the language of my father. And now the last sentence, in Spanish, reverberated inside me like a live thing. I wanted to slide the dusty bus windows down and shout in that language to all the savage beauty of the world—"He said he would love her until death, did you hear? *¡Hasta la muerte!*"

Huipiles

When the San Antonio Smithsonian Museum in 2007 proposed featuring local collections of *huipiles,* indigenous tunics, I was invited to participate as well as write something for the catalog. It allowed me to think about a trip I took to Chiapas to finish my first collection of poetry. Any trip south to Mexico always brought me great surges of creativity. I thought I was going to rent a house and work alone while there, but instead my time in San Cristóbal was filled with anxiety and sadness.

Norma Alarcón and I were in a local tourist coffeehouse when we ran into a young Japanese tourist we'd recently met. She had a scratch on her face, but I didn't think much of it until she told us her story. She said she had been visiting a church in the middle of the afternoon, and a man had raped her there. And just now in the crowded plaza, she had seen her attacker again, but by the time she found a policeman, he was long gone. This is what had happened, and this is what she told us under the shade of a lamp over a coffeehouse table.

Her testimony filled me with dread. I can't remove that anguish from my memory of San Cristóbal. It flooded me with a thread of despair I felt while there and which I still feel almost thirty years later, as if it had just happened. As if she were still telling and telling her story.

I started wearing *huipiles* the summer before the big earthquake hit Mexico City. 1985. I was traveling with Norma Alarcón, first to the Mexican capital, then on a bus ride to Oaxaca, and finally to Chiapas on mountain roads so reckless and wicked, they made you instantly devout.

Before this trip, I don't think I'd ever traveled to Mexico without my *familia*. Usually I was accompanied by my mother and my father, even as an adult. This isn't as strange as it sounds. Mexicans are clannish and accustomed to traveling with family until the day they die.

To tell you the truth, I've always been terrified of traveling

One of my first *huipiles*

alone in Mexico the way only *pochas* (American *mexicanas*) can be terrified. Not because we know too little about this country we are visiting, but because as Mexicans from the U.S. side, we know too much. But that's another story.

Norma was researching the feminist writer Rosario Castellanos, who was from Chiapas, and that was why we traveled so far south, almost to the Guatemalan border. Me, I had a small grant from the Illinois Arts Council and a book to finish. There was money in my jeans pockets, purpose in my heart, and my buddy Norma to travel with.

I was homesick for a house of my own. I'd rented one in Greece a few years before, and that was where I'd finished my first book. Now I had to finish a book of poetry, and Norma's press, Third Woman, was impatient to publish it. So it was with this idea of renting a house and borrowing a typewriter that I tagged along with her.

But Chiapas isn't Greece. It's mountain cold and damp, even in the summer, and one of the poorest regions of Mexico. We entered not only another country, but another time. Founded in 1528, well before Plymouth Rock, San Cristóbal de las Casas is a town of stout churches, cobbled streets, and markets filled with the most humble members of humanity—the barefooted, the cross-eyed, the harelipped: citizens from another century.

When we got there the summer of 1985, I didn't know about the community lands stolen in the previous centuries, nor that the people would rise up soon to reclaim those lands under Subcomandante Marcos. Or about the villages flooded after dams were built to power Mexico City. Or the destruction of the rain forest.

I only knew darkness imposed a curfew. That everyone watched the latest episode of a telenovela from the few televisions available at cafés or shops. That the town was divided among the Ladinos (the non-Indian Mexicans, or Indians who had forgotten their traditional dress and language and spoke only Spanish), the tourists, and the Mayan people themselves, who were at the bottom of the social ladder (Chontales, Tzotziles, Tzeltales, Tojolabales, Mames, and Lacandones). And that, except for a small portion of midday, the weather was foggy and cold.

After a lot of asking, I did find a house for rent, a stone cottage with thick walls and windows shuttered with wood, instead of glass, that opened to a misty garden. It was charming to my eyes, but Norma asked, "How are you going to heat this place?" In Chiapas, homes are heated with wood, and their inhabitants smell of *leña,* fire and smoke. I lost courage and returned to my cell at the *zócalo,* a hotel with doors like a medieval prison and the austerity of a nunnery with none of the charm.

Back then I wore my hair short like a boy. I dressed in the same clothes I'd worn in Europe—a denim jacket and jeans, or a denim mini; a long Greek scarf wrapped twice around my neck and knotted at the throat; and, because of the cold, a beret. It was on this trip, deep in Mexico, deep in Mayan country, that I realized I was *una gringa.*

In the village of Chamula I visited a Mayan Catholic church smoky with copal, the earthen floor carpeted with pine needles. Women wrapped in dark shawls swayed on their knees, kids huddled quietly beside them. The devout offered eggs and bottles of Coca-Cola, and lit thin tapers, the air buzzing with their murmured prayers. Community guards watched over us to make sure we didn't take pictures. This was a church that seemed more pagan than Christian, without pews or kneelers, with statues of saints dressed in miniature *huipiles,* the tunics native women have worn since before Columbus, layers and layers, one atop the other, and each wearing over all this a necklace of mirrors.

To make myself less conspicuous, less an intruder, and to be more respectful, I pulled my Greek scarf over my head and knelt too. Something holy was shimmering in the smoky air. Of this I was sure. It was one of the most sacred places I've ever visited, then or since.

I typed my poetry manuscript on the only typewriter-for-hire I could find—at the typing school, a storefront like any other local business with a corrugated metal curtain for a door and nothing separating the outdoors from the indoors but a high stone step. Dogs and flies wandered in freely. Lechers and *enamorados* lingered past and made *ojitos.* All the world was welcome to watch the *jovencitas,* girls practically, type-type-typing to earn a certificate, a ticket out of their *miseria.*

I typed, too. In my jean jacket and mini. I typed love poems, poems about being dumped, poems about sex and passion. If anyone knew what I was writing, I thought, they would drag me to the authorities, put me in stocks, and stone me to death. I sniffed, wiped away my tears with my Greek scarf, and typed my dirty poems among the chaste virgins, wondering under the bare lightbulbs how Destiny had brought me here to a town called San Cristóbal de las Casas, to a room noisy with typewriters, full of women, all of us young, dreaming our foolish escape.

This was when I first started buying *huipiles,* my first from the women's collective of Mayan weavers, who created work of fine craftsmanship, not the cheesy stuff for sale on the U.S.-Mexico border.

I still own this first *huipil,* a simple cotton tunic with multicolored weavings on the neckline and red bands along the center, as beautiful as the day I bought it. Its price was the equivalent of forty U.S. dollars, and I waited a day before buying it. Forty dollars was a big bite from my arts council grant.

While in San Cristóbal, I met a Mayan woman whose name I never knew, but in my notes I called her Madame Butterfly. She sold butterflies in front of the one café where all the tourists hung out. She and her children caught the butterflies I sent home to my brother Lolo.

She was dressed in the traditional Tzotzil *huipil,* a heavy blouse embroidered with red, yellow, and black wool, over a wraparound skirt of indigo. And though I was wearing woolen socks and thick shoes, she was barefoot, her feet caked with mud.

Up on the mountain is where she said she lived. She pointed behind a gauzy cloud. "Up there," she said, the fog already descending for the night. She said she had to walk and walk, tugging her little ones who were standing before me, and lugging on her back the sleeping baby.

She said they often left home in the dark and often got home in the dark. She told me all these things, and I felt sad I couldn't invite her inside to have dinner. They wouldn't have served her. So I bought all her butterflies, stiff and fragile as dried flowers, even the mangled ones with broken wings.

Then I found the used *huipiles* in shops all along the typing school street. As the daughter of an upholsterer, I know how to look at the seams and at the reverse to measure quality. By pulling the garments inside out, I could read their history.

Here was a little patch of polka-dot fabric; here a collar of embroidered flowers salvaged from some older garment; here the neckhole so narrow, I wondered how a woman ever managed to pull it over her head.

Some were finely woven with birds and flowers and animals in tight, perfect stitches. Some stitches did not look handmade, but, as the Mexicans like to say when a job is badly done, as if she had made it with her feet; no doubt a young girl in a hurry to be doing something else. Some still gave off a scent of *leña.* Who wore this, and why did she have to give it up? How much was she paid? And where was she now? Would a woman give up her most prized possessions unless she was desperate?

Did she have to work like Madame Butterfly because of a husband who left her with little ones? Did the civil wars of Central America force her to sell her clothes? Where did a woman like this pee when she had to relieve herself in the city? Who looked after her and her kids when she was sick? I thought all these things as I bought my first *huipiles,* guilty that I could afford a dozen, even with my small arts grant, and sad and sorry for the women who had to let them go.

When I got back to the hotel and showed Norma my splendors, she asked gruffly, "What are you going to do with all those?"

"I thought I could wear them," I said without conviction. "Or maybe hang them on the walls."

Once I got back I *did* hang some on walls. Then, *poco a poco,* little by little, I started to take them down and wear them. Only in the United States at first. Not in Mexico. Because I didn't wish to appear disrespectful to the women who made them.

Since that trip, I've added to my textile collection over time, and included items from across Mexico. I've met other women who collect and wear these "poor women's clothes," because that's what they are, clothes of the most humble segment of society.

I know it astonishes my Mexico City relatives that I dress like their servants, *indígenas* who come in from their villages and who wear their Indian clothes at first until they're shamed into dressing like city folk. But on the U.S. side of the border, we take up these garments without the class and cultural restrictions of Mexico. I like to mix the Mexican garments in nontraditional ways, maybe a Tehuana *huipil* with a Tahitian sarong, or a Oaxacan skirt with a man's Chiapaneco vest, to create something new, something no one in Mexico would do.*

Nowadays, because I live in Texas, I prefer the *huipiles* from *tierra caliente,* the hot lands, especially from Oaxaca. They're the ones I most often reach for to go to work—to write, that is. The fancy ones I save for being the Author.

For work, on the days I go barefoot, when I sometimes forget to comb my hair, when I'm anxious to forget my body and need to be comfortable, without any underclothes binding or biting me, I like my everyday *huipiles de manta,* of sackcloth. The ones I can stain with coffee or a taco and I won't grieve. The ones I can throw in the wash. My Mexican muumuus, my prison clothes, my housedresses.

My spiritual mother and *maestra* is la Señora María Luísa Camacho de López, a walking Smithsonian of stories and information regarding Mexican folklore. I learned what I know about textiles thanks to this *hija de rebocero,* shawl-maker's daughter. Several of my prize pieces once belonged to her.†

I haven't inherited any textiles from any of my real *antepasados,* ancestors, I'm sorry to say.‡ I didn't know them. All I've got is a

---

* And here my *comadre* writer Liliana Valenzuela, who translates my books into Spanish, interrupts me for one moment: "Some women in Mexico City (and maybe other parts of the *república*) have been wearing indigenous clothing, perhaps since Frida Kahlo and other artists after the Mexican Revolution, and more recently during the '60s, '70s, '80s, and probably even now, mostly in universities. I remember when wearing *huipiles* and *blusas de manta* and *huaraches de cuero y suela de llanta* was de rigueur when I was an anthro student in Mexico City in 1980. We were a bit unusual, but by no means the only ones doing so. We perhaps would not mix and match the items with modern or items from other countries like you do, but in all fairness, some anti-imperialist *mexicanas y mexicanos* have been wearing these clothes for some time, mostly with jeans. I guess it was a statement of going against the grain of current commercial fashion, solidarity with indigenous communities, coolness factor, and who knows what else."

† They recently were donated to the National Museum of Mexican Art.

‡ Since writing this, I now have in my possession a shawl—*rebozo de bolita*—I found among my mother's things when she died. My aunt Margaret recently gave me a Virgen de Guadalupe souvenir scarf from the 1940s that once belonged to Felipa Anguiano, my

La Señora María Luísa Camacho
de López

framed baby's pillowcase my great-grandmother Victoria Rizo de Anguiano embroidered for the infant Elvira Cordero, my mother. A donkey in silk threads and the initials "E.C."

In my antique Mexican trunks, I preserve my collection of *huipiles*. I like to think the *huipiles* I own were made by women like my grandmothers, and were, in a sense, their library.

Maybe the women of my family wove on a backstrap loom hooked to a tree in the courtyard, or maybe they embroidered in the shade, after their housework was done. And instead of writ-

grandmother. I added these textiles to my installation "A Room of Her Own," an altar for my mother exhibited at the National Museum of Mexican Art, Chicago; the National Hispanic Cultural Center, Albuquerque (a photo of this installation is on page 289); the Smithsonian American History Museum, Washington, D.C.; and the Museum of Latin American Art, Long Beach, California.

ing books, which they could not do, they created a universe with designs as intricate and complex as any novel. These things I think because I can't imagine my literary antecedents writing any other way than with needle and thread, weft and warp.

I consider the irony of being able to purchase *huipiles* made by women who go barefoot. Now only the most privileged North American ladies can afford to buy the museum-quality *huipiles*. Ladies like me.

In San Antonio there's a group of women called "las Huipilistas," a new class of Latinas. They're professors, lawyers, artists, and activists who can afford to snatch up with the fervor of game hunters the very fine *huipiles* that cross our paths, because they're getting harder and harder to find. In a time when 75 percent of the manufacturing industry is owned by American corporations operating in Mexico, when indigenous communities can no longer afford to stay in their villages and are forced to migrate north, the craft of these textiles may be lost altogether, and this clothing gone forever.

It's been more than two decades since Norma and I made that trip south to San Cristóbal. Norma, the retired university professor, who favors T-shirts and sweats, hot-pink streaks in her hair, and high-top tennis shoes, recently asked me this favor: "Hey, Sandra, next time you go to Mexico, see if you can't find me a *huipil*. I'd like to hang one on my wall." *That's how it begins,* I think.

Each time I wear a *huipil*, I'm saying, "Look, I know I can afford Neiman Marcus, but I'd rather wear an indigenous designer from Mexico, something no one else in the room will be wearing."

I wear this textile as a way for me to resist the mexiphobia going on under the guise of Homeland Security. To acknowledge I'm not in agreement with the border vigilantes. To say I'm of las Americas, both North and South. This cloth is the flag of who I am.

Vivan los Muertos

Elle magazine approached me to write a travel feature for their October 1991 issue, but since I'd just come home from being on the road, I offered to write about an earlier trip I'd taken in 1985 to Mexico, in the wake of the worst earthquake of the century. I wish I'd written about what I'd seen in Mexico City that autumn when the destruction created a citywide Day of the Dead installation on every block. Or of the guerrilla artists who camped out in Tepito, one of the city's poorest and most vice-ridden neighborhoods, and taught art under plastic tents set up in the streets. Or about the San Antonio Abad seamstresses who rose up from the wreckage of their sweatshops and created a labor union after witnessing bosses hauling out machinery from the factories instead of searching for coworkers. Or of the two seamstresses invited to Austin for a fund-raiser to benefit their union. They stayed with me at the Dobie Paisano Ranch during my residency in the fall of 1995. On the night of their event, flash floods locked us in, but not even roiling waters could stop these determined women. Austin buddies drove up to the opposite shore of the creek and tossed a rope. I watched as the two *mexicanas* waded safely across the raging stream as bravely as St. Christopher and the infant Jesus. The fund-raiser turned out to be a great success, raising a lot of money for the garment workers' cause. But by the time I gathered my thoughts for the following piece, the quake (at least in the U.S.) was yesterday's news.

My family doesn't celebrate Day of the Dead. Nobody in our neighborhood sets up an *ofrenda* altar in memory of deceased ancestors.* I was north-of-the-border born and bred, an American Mexican from "Chicano, Illinois," street tough and city smart, wise to the ways of trick or treat. I looked at the dead as American kids do, through the filter of too many Boris Karloff movies and Halloween.

I wish I'd grown up closer to the border like my friend María Limón of El Paso. There, as in Mexico, Day of the Dead can be an occasion for whole families to trek out to the *camposanto,* the holy ground, with brooms, buckets, and lunch basket, a day to feast with the ancestors who once a year return *del mas allá,* from the beyond, November lst for the *angelitos,* the dead children, November 2nd for deceased adults. Gravesites are weeded, tombstones washed, fresh flowers arranged, and an offering of favorite food set out for the deceased—an on-the-spot picnic for the dead and the living.

I once asked my Mexican father, "Didn't you ever have an altar for Day of the Dead when you were little?"

"I think your *abuela* lit candles on her dresser and prayed," he said.

"But no *ofrenda* in the living room, no dishes of *mole,* and *xempoaxóchitl,* marigold flowers, no midnight vigils in the cemetery, no shot glasses of tequila set out for the departed, no sugar skulls or loaves of *pan de muerto,* or *calavera* poems, or copal incense, or paper-cutout decorations, or framed photos of family members, or anything?"

---

* At the time I wrote this I was spiritually innocent. I've learned a lot since and install *ofrendas* regularly as a ritual of memory and respect, and for personal transformation.

My father's mother, Trinidad del Moral

"No, no, no, no, no," my father said. "We're from the city. That custom belongs to the Indians." In other words, my father's Mexico City family was too middle class, too "Spanish" for that pagan phenomenon whose roots go back to a pre-Columbian America.

The year María Limón and I went to Mexico in search of Day of the Dead I was thirty. As the naive American children of immigrants, we were filled with nostalgia for an imaginary country—one that exists only in images borrowed from art galleries and old Mexican movies. We wanted to know Death with her Mexican nicknames: La Flaca, La Calaca, La Catrina, La Huesuda, La Pelona, La Apestosa, La Llorona. Skinny, Skeleton, She-Dandy, Boney, Baldy, Stinky, Weeping One.

That same year, Death herself swept through the streets of Mexico City. The earthquake of 1985 claimed at least ten thousand lives. We went to investigate personally who needed our financial assistance the most, since we didn't trust handing our relief funds to the government agencies. On any given block in the capital spontaneous curbside *ofrendas* appeared before the rubble of a building—votive candles and marigolds scattered next to a heap of family photographs, a child's toy, a dusty stray shoe.

Our *ganas de conocer,* our longing to know, eventually led us to the state of Michoacán, west of Mexico City. It was a short trip to Morelia, the state capital, a quick bus ride to Pátzcuaro, and then a ferry across the lake to the island village Janitzio, famous for its fishermen who still fish with those beautiful butterfly nets and for its Day of the Dead festivities.

Like the returning deceased, we were returning from the beyond too, from *el más allá.* From *el norte,* where the tradition of Day of the Dead would be all but forgotten except for a generation of artists who have reintroduced it to the community in an attempt to reclaim a part of our indigenous past. We were making our way south the way our ancestors had made their way north.

"*¿De dónde vienen?*" the Pátzcuaro vendors asked us, our clothes and accents giving us away. "From Chicago, El Paso, Austin, San Antonio." Ah, *pochas,* they thought—that awful word meaning north-of-the-border Mexicans.

We spent the day at the Pátzcuaro market watching the town prepare for the night's celebration: women carrying bundles of marigolds, red cockscomb, and airy bunches of Mexican baby's breath called *nubes,* clouds; market stalls throbbing with oranges displayed in radiant pyramids, dizzying palettes of spices, towers of chocolate for *mole,* and huge stalks of sugarcane.

In the main plaza under the arcades, the candy lady let us take pictures if we'd buy something. *¡Muy bonito!* Her candy pretty with pastel icing, glitter, and foil. Marzipan hearts decorated with roses, sugar ladies and sugar dogs, sugar ducks and sugar angels, sugar corpses in their sugar coffins, all arranged neatly on freshly ironed embroidered cloth. I picked a sugar skull and had my name added with blue icing, a personalized service at no extra charge.

The toy vendor sold the Mexican version of the chattering teeth—a chattering skull, pull-string skeleton puppets, skeleton miniatures with Death doing everything from driving a taxicab to playing in a mariachi band. Shelves of the traditional Day of the Dead bread were on display as well, round loaves with bone designs on top, or corpses with their hands folded on their breasts. Everywhere the living busied themselves with this business of welcoming the recent and the long-ago dead.

That night, as we rode the ferry across Lake Pátzcuaro and the fog began to rise from the lake, the village of Janitzio spiraled from the water, lit as bright as a birthday cake. All the shops open, strings of lights decorating everything. Vendors welcomed our arrival hawking fish cakes from big baskets. Doorways were framed with arcs of marigolds.

The doors were left open to allow passersby to peer in and admire the altars. In one house with heavy wooden doors, an old woman sat alone in a room aflame with a thousand candles illuminating a sea of photographs, the dead in her life outnumbering the living.

We wound our way past a huge public altar in the main plaza, dedicated to the victims of the Mexico City disaster, toward the church graveyard. The *camposanto* was just a bald square of dust, a walled dirt yard lumpy with haphazard headstones, nothing at all like the cemeteries we know in the United States where everything is neat order and disciplined grass.

The villagers busied themselves finding their relatives. "Are you there? How are you?" Candles were set up on the grave slab. A symmetry of flowers. A bowl with clean, starched linen and Day of the Dead bread. Some yellow and orange squash for color. Dishes and candleholders all saved for this once-a-year occasion.

María Limón and I had brought our own *ofrenda.* We sat down on a tombstone no one had remembered and set out our offering to her father and to my grandfather. I had brought a cigar and a Kraft caramel for my *abuelito,* and María had her father's passport with his last photo. Would the little dead one sleeping here mind if we borrowed his grave? We'd come from so far away. A villager at the next tombstone nudged her family and pointed to us with her chin, but no one said anything. Compared to everyone else busy arranging flowers and food, our portable *ofrenda* looked pretty sad. "It's the thought that counts," I said to María.

"And do you stay here with the food all night?" we asked our neighbors.

"Oh, no, we just keep a vigil for a while and then take the food home after the spirits have visited and savored it all."

But how late, I don't know. We were so cold sitting on that slab of rock, as if Death herself were piercing us, that we left before the vigil was over.

Because we weren't able to find a room in Pátzcuaro, we had to flag down a bus to take us to Uruapan, an hour away. We found two seats next to a window that wouldn't close. We stuffed the night dampness out with wadded newspaper and tried to sleep. The night wind of Michoacán smelled of sweet grass.

Was it right, do you think, to do what we'd done and place our little makeshift altar there? We'd meant well. Two *pochas* dressed in blue jeans and berets. Maybe we hadn't seen the spirits. Maybe the spirits could be seen only by the villagers. I wasn't sure. All the ride back I'm thinking. That fine split between my Mexican self and my 'Merican self, those two halves that don't fit.

"María, I'm afraid of ghosts, aren't you? Sometimes I get terrible nightmares."

"Those are just bad spirits trying to mess with you when you're asleep," María said. "Don't you know any good spirits?"

"Spirits?"

"Like someone you were close to when they were alive; your grandfather maybe."

"My *abuelito*?"

"He's a spirit. Next time you have a bad dream call your *abuelito*. Whenever you're afraid, just call him. He'll protect you."

I hadn't thought about my grandfather being someone whose strength I could summon the way I called my family when I needed a loan. The idea of a ghost being *familia*, someone who loved you and would never hurt you, was new to me.

María Limón fell asleep before I could ask her any more questions. I watched the landscape rise and fall, thick leafy silhouettes across the green, green land and sky a deep thing, the moon following and following us, whole and round and perfect.

Straw into Gold

In the spring of 1987, I was living in Austin, Texas, in a garage apartment too small even for two people furiously in love. To add further sorrow to the situation, I was unemployed most of the eight months there.

This lecture was written before hope ran out. Dr. Harriett Romo, then a professor at the University of Texas, invited me to speak to her class. This was before Austin gave me the boot to Chico, California, and my first university job.

I was still optimistic when I wrote this and had the ambitious idea to create a lecture that included slides thanks to the assistance of my then paramour, a photographer.

If some of the sentences sound overly dramatic and smug, it's because they were undercut by a funny visual, or because I was genuinely amazed at my life at the time. I repeated the lecture many times after until, in one of my many moves across the country, the slide carousel was stolen from a San Antonio storage unit. (Luckily, I have most of the original photos.) In retrospect, it's an ironically upbeat portrait of my life given that by the end of 1987 I'd blaze into a meteoric depression I'd later dub Hell's Basement.

When I was living in an artists' colony in the south of France, some fellow Latin Americans who taught at the university in Aix-en-Provence invited me to share a home-cooked meal with them. I had been living abroad almost a year then on

Self-portrait on my front porch, Vence, 1983

my writing grant, subsisting mainly on French bread and lentils so that my money would last longer. So when the invitation to dinner arrived, I accepted without hesitation. Especially because they promised Mexican food.

What I didn't realize when they made this invitation was that I was supposed to be involved in preparing the meal. I guess they assumed I knew how to cook Mexican food because I'm Mexican. They wanted specifically tortillas, though I'd never made a tortilla in my life.

It's true I'd witnessed my mother rolling the little armies of dough into perfect circles, but my mother's family is from Guanajuato—*provincianos,* country folk. They knew only how to make flour tortillas.* My father's family, on the other hand, is *chi-*

---

* When I wrote this, I was naive enough to believe flour tortillas were from Guanajuato, the land of the black, blue, gray, and yellow tortilla, but, no, not flour. My mother made flour tortillas, which she no doubt learned from her mother. But flour tortillas are from

lango, from Mexico City. We ate corn tortillas, but we didn't make them. Someone* was sent to the corner *tortillería* to buy them. I'd never seen anybody make corn tortillas. Ever.

Somehow my Latino hosts had gotten ahold of a packet of corn flour, and this is what they tossed my way with orders to produce tortillas. *"Así como sea."* Any ol' way, they said, and went back to their cooking.

Why did I feel like the woman in the fairy tale who was locked in a room and ordered to spin straw into gold? I had the same sick feeling when I was required to write my critical essay for the MFA exam—the only piece of noncreative writing necessary in order

the northern Mexican region and the Southwest U.S. My mother's parents lived in El Paso; Flagstaff; Rocky Ford, Colorado; Kansas City; and finally Chicago when they emigrated from central Mexico. Somewhere in their meanderings, flour replaced corn.

* Invariably that someone was a servant, an indigenous woman, usually from the country. My father's family was middle class. But these were themes I didn't think about back then.

to get my graduate degree.* How was I to start? There were rules involved here, unlike writing a poem or a story, which I did intuitively. There was a step-by-step process needed, and I had better know it. I felt as if making a tortilla—or writing a critical paper, for that matter—was a task so impossible I wanted to break down into tears.

Somehow, though, I managed to make tortillas—crooked and burned, but edible nonetheless. My hosts were absolutely ignorant when it came to Mexican food; they thought my tortillas were delicious. (I'm glad my mama wasn't there.) Thinking back and looking at an old photograph documenting the three of us consuming those lopsided circles, I'm amazed. Just as I'm amazed I could finish my MFA exam.

I've managed to do a lot of things in my life I didn't think I was capable of and that many others didn't think I was capable of either. Especially because I'm a woman, Latina, and an only daughter in a family of six sons. My father would've liked to have seen me married long ago. In our culture men and women don't leave their father's house except by way of marriage. I crossed my father's threshold with nothing carrying me but my own two feet. A woman whom no one came for and no one chased away.

To make matters worse, I left before any of my six brothers had ventured away from home. I broke a terrible taboo. Somehow, looking back at photos of myself as a child, I wonder if I was aware of having begun already my own quiet war.

I like to think that somehow my family, my Mexicanness, my poverty,† all had something to do with shaping me into a writer.

---

* That terrible essay was written with neither conviction nor truth. It was a hoop I had to jump through, and jump I did. I had no clue how to write such an essay and disavow it now.

† I'd never use the word "poverty" now; "poor," maybe. My cousin Anita said, "I thought your family was rich compared to us." Wealth is relative (forgive the pun).

Kiki (Keeks) and me

I like to think my parents were preparing me all along for my life as an artist even though they didn't know it. From my father I inherited a love of wandering. He was born in Mexico City, but as a young man he traveled into the United States vagabonding. He eventually was drafted and thus became a citizen. Some of the stories he has told me about his first months in the United States with little or no English, surface in my stories in *The House on Mango Street,* as well as others I have in mind to write in the future.* I inherited from him a sappy heart. He always cries when he watches Mexican soaps—especially if they deal with children who have forsaken their parents.

My mother was born like me—in Chicago of Mexican descent. It's her tough, streetwise voice that haunts all my stories and poems. An amazing woman who loves to draw and read books and can sing an opera. A smart cookie.

When I was a girl we traveled to Mexico City so much I thought my grandparents' house on Fortuna, number 12, was home. It was the only constant in our nomadic ramblings from one Chicago flat to another. The house on "Destiny Street," number 12, in the Colonia Tepeyac would be perhaps the only home I knew, and that nostalgia for a home would be a theme that would obsess me.

My brothers also figured in my art. Especially the older two. Henry,† the second oldest and my favorite, appears often in poems I've written and in stories, which at times only borrow his nickname, Kiki. He played a major role in my childhood. We were bunk-bed mates. We were co-conspirators. We were pals. Until my oldest brother came back from studying in Mexico and left me odd woman out.

---

* I'd write my father's stories in *Caramelo.*

† My brother Henry "Kiki" or "Keeks" Cisneros is not the Henry Cisneros who served as mayor of San Antonio and secretary of housing during the Clinton administration. My Henry is an artist and musician.

Cisneros grandparents' house, Fortuna #12, Colonia Tepeyac, Mexico City

What would my teachers say if they knew I was a writer now? Who would've guessed it? I wasn't a very bright student. I didn't much like school, because we moved so much and I was always new and funny looking. In my fifth-grade report card I have nothing but an avalanche of Cs and Ds, but I don't remember being that stupid. I was good at art, and I read plenty of books, and Kiki laughed at all my jokes. At home I was fine, but at school I never opened my mouth except when the teacher called on me.

When I think of how I see myself, it would have to be at age eleven. I know I'm thirty-two on the outside, but inside I'm eleven. I'm the girl in the picture with skinny arms and a crumpled skirt and crooked hair. I didn't like school because all they saw was the outside me. School was lots of rules and sitting with your hands folded and being afraid all the time. I liked looking out the window and thinking. I liked staring at the girl across the way writing her name over and over again in red ink, or the boy in front of me who wore the same dim shirt every day. I imagined their lives and the houses they went home to each evening, wondering if their world was happy or sad.

I think my mother and father did the best they could to keep us warm and clean and never hungry. We had birthday and graduation parties and things like that, but there was another hunger that had to be fed. There was a hunger I didn't even have a name for. Was this when I began writing?

In 1966 we moved into a house, a real one, our first real home. This meant we didn't have to change schools and be the new kids on the block every couple of years. We could make friends and not be afraid we'd have to say goodbye to them and start all over. My brothers and the herd of boys they brought home would become important characters eventually for my stories—Louie and his cousins, Meme Ortiz and his dog with two names, one in English and one in Spanish.

My mother flourished in her own home. She took books out of

My eighth-grade graduation photo
from St. Aloysius

My mother in front of the garage of our
Campbell Street house

the library and taught herself to garden, to grow roses so envied we had to put a lock on the gate to keep out the midnight flower thieves. My mother has never quit gardening.

This was the period in my life, that slippery age when you're both child and woman and neither, I was to record in *The House on Mango Street*. How was I to know I'd document the women who sat their sadness on an elbow and stared out a window?

I've done all kinds of things I didn't think I could do since then. I've gone to a prestigious university, studied with famous writers, and taken an MFA degree. I've taught poetry in schools in Illinois and Texas. Writing awards arrived, and with them I ran away as far as my courage would take me. I've seen the bleached and bitter mountains of the Peloponnesus. I've lived on an island. Admired

At the Woolworth's counter
in San Antonio

the Venice moon in winter. Lived in Yugoslavia. Visited the Nice flower market. Witnessed the daily parade of promenaders in a village in the pre-Alps.

Texas is another chapter in my life, land of Polaroid-blue skies and big bugs. I met Chicano artists and *políticos,* including a mayor with my last name. Texas generously granted me the Dobie Paisano fellowship, a six-month residency on a 254-acre ranch. Texas also brought Mexico back to me: in the sky, the food, the feast days, and, most important, the language.

Back in the days when I would sit at my favorite people-watching spot, the snaky Woolworth's counter[*] across from

---

[*] Which has since been torn down to make way for a Ripley's Believe It or Not Museum. My friend the artist Rolando Briseño thinks this is hilarious and totally appropriate given that the Alamo is a believe-it-or-not story too.

the Alamo, I couldn't think of anything else I'd rather be than a writer.* I've traveled and lectured from Cape Cod to San Francisco, to Spain, Yugoslavia, Greece, Mexico, France, Italy, and now today to Texas. Along the way there has always been straw for the taking. With a little imagination, it can be spun into gold.

---

* At fifty-nine I can think of plenty of things I'd rather be than a writer: a *curandera;* a cartoon voice-over actor; a flamenco dancer; a bandoneon player; an opera singer; a comedienne; a shoe designer; a medium; a milliner; a popcorn vendor; a florist; a mattress tester; a dog sitter; a window dresser; a textile curator; a henna hand painter; a judge on *RuPaul's Drag Race.* Anything more social.

A Tango for Astor

I've been delirious about the music of Astor Piazzolla since I first heard it in the mid-1970s, a combination of tango, jazz, symphony, and chamber music. I've always felt his music tells my story.

Piazzolla was as extraordinary a musician as he was a composer. His principal instrument was the bandoneon, a devil of a device perched on the knee like an accordion but as mighty as an organ. Near the end of his life he said his greatest wish was that his music would continue to be heard in the year 2020. Given that his compositions are now a staple in the repertoire of many musicians from Yo-Yo Ma to Al Di Meola, it seems likely his wish will be granted.

Thanks to Piazzolla I had a longtime dream of running off to Buenos Aires and learning to dance the tango. But when I finally got there and watched the protocol of the tango halls, it took me back to the passive high school sock hops I hated as a teenager. If you were female you had to sit on the sidelines and wait for a man to pick you, and then you had to simper and smile and make him feel great-full. That's not for me. So I gave up on that dream and just bought the shoes.

Still, I'd love to imagine I can play the bandoneon myself, make it twist and squeal and whine and howl like a fabulous orgasm. It must be wondrous to do that with an instrument, though I'm told the bandoneon takes a lifetime to conquer. Oh well, *ni modo,* nothing to be done about it in this life.

I think Piazzolla's music demands you dance alone, preferably under the stars. After I've written and there's no one about to make me feel silly, I like a glass of wine as plush as the menstrual wall, a cigar like the kind my grandfather *el coronel* smoked, and Piazzolla. This induces me to write poetry for reasons I don't want to understand.

I delivered the following for a 2005 dinner lecture at St. Mary's University in San Antonio. It was a story I'd told enough times out loud. But telling a story on paper is a whole other matter. Out loud you can rely on gesture and voice, facial expressions and pauses to help create a picture. When you write a story down you have no props but the words, the punctuation, and the white spaces in between. The white spaces for me are as important as the black print. They're like the sheet music the musicians follow when they perform a composition. Everything should already be there for the reader to follow.

I met the Argentine tango composer and musician Astor Piazzolla in 1988, on a Sunday, April 24th, at the Great American Music Hall on O'Farrell Street, San Francisco. I'm sure of the date because I have a signed flyer to prove it. I needn't have bothered. The date is engraved in my *corazón*. The year before I'd barely survived the thirty-third year of my life, a time when you die and, hopefully, are resurrected.

So 1988 was the year of my resurrection. I remember driving the five hours from Chico, California, where I was a guest professor, convinced Astor Piazzolla, the man who had revolutionized tango, had come to California to meet *me*. The year of my near death I'd lost my purpose for living. I know it sounds overly dramatic, but that's the truth. I was tired of the nuisance of staying alive. I couldn't understand why I was put on the planet if I couldn't seem to do anything that would earn me my keep. I was weepy and nervous and skittish as a cat. In Texas I'd been without a job for almost a year. A friend teaching at Cal State, Chico, was taking a temporary leave, and he had recommended me for his position.

The last thing I wanted was to teach at a university. I'd never felt at home there. The truth was I didn't feel smart enough as a student, let alone as a professor. Yet here was a job at a university being offered to me. I was so broke, I was forced to overlook my terror and take it.

I borrowed money from my family for the umpteenth time, dragged my thrift-store furniture in a trailer, and soon discovered what I had feared all along: I was a failure. The lethargy of my freshman composition students compared to the adults I'd taught at community centers convinced me I was no good, I was worthless, I was a dud. At least, that was the way I saw it then.

And if I wasn't any good at teaching . . . and if I was thirty-three years old and still borrowing to get by . . . and so what if I'd written a book that earned me hardly enough to cover a few months' rent . . . and I hated being in academia, feeling like I had to know everything when I hardly knew anything . . . and what if I was discovered for being the fraud I was . . . and if I had to borrow money from my family one more time, well . . . I'd lost my will to go on.

But a national writing award arrived in the nick and reminded me why I was put on the planet, and now here I was, and here *he* was, Astor Piazzolla, one of the greatest musicians and composers of the new tango, the greatest, in my opinion, coming to play. For me!

I'd been introduced to the music of Piazzolla in my mid-twenties by my nemesis, the Zapata of my heart, who inspired several poems and stories and my travels through Europe so that I might become exactly like him, worldly and sophisticated, instead of the naive fraidycat that I was.

Piazzolla's music, a tempest of notes, came by way of this man, my lover, who in a sense was the same as the music. A yelp caught somewhere between pain and pleasure. A howl filled with longing and despair. The little burn a mouth leaves on the flesh. Intense, tender, comical, ferocious, faithless, and, ultimately—doomed. All of this haunts me when I listen to Piazzolla's compositions, merging the traditional Buenos Aires tango with New York avant-garde jazz. Piazzolla taught me how to become the artist I wanted to become.

"It's like this, you fool," I imagined Piazzolla saying. "Listen." And the yowl of his bandoneon, a collision of beauty and tragedy bloodied together, became my teacher. I was hungry to serve my apprenticeship.

When I was lost, sad, defeated, frustrated with my writing,

with my life, I had only to listen to Piazzolla's music, and it would shine a light beam into the night, an arrow piercing a target, a guide as pure and steady as the North Star.

This explains my supreme arrogance and naïveté in the darkness of the Great American Music Hall that day in 1988. *El maestro* emerged onstage all in black, as black as his bandoneon, dignified, divine. Then he began. A music that rose up terrible like a knife held at one's own heart, weepy, melodramatic, corny, wonderful all at once. Violin, bandoneon, cello, piano like rain. I had to stand up and lean against a pillar, blow my nose with a cocktail napkin. When the lights blinked on for intermission, I took off backstage.

I wasn't drunk. How to explain the absolute confidence of my mission? I shoved the swinging doors that separated the gods from the rabble and marched right in. Surprisingly, there were no security guards, no bouncers or police. No one. Just a sad, empty corridor too shabby to shelter greatness.

Outside an open doorway I heard voices, and suddenly lost my courage. Then the outrageousness of my actions caught up with me. Astor and his musicians were probably exhausted and taking a well-deserved break. I was at a loss for what to do next.

Luckily somebody appeared to solve the problem, a young guy with the same idea of meeting his idol as me, but with more bravado. We started jabbering, loud enough so that eventually Piazzolla popped out to see why we were there.

The fan knew exactly what he wanted; he asked for an autograph and handed Piazzolla a cheap yellow flyer announcing the evening's event. What else could I do, but get ready to do the same. But what would I say to him?

First I had to tell him. I had to tell him what I'd been holding in my heart all these years. I wanted to say, *Astor, your music has buoyed me through so many disappointments, through the exploding cigars of love, through near deaths, through my own death and resurrec-*

tion. *I traveled to find myself when I listened to your music. It was your music I listened to for courage when I first arrived on the Greek islands in the Aegean, and on the boat that pulled me away from Greece where I finally finished my first novel, and on the cold nights in Paris, when I didn't have any money and was sleeping on the floor of the Argentines. Astor, you don't know. It's been so hard to invent myself and become the writer I've wanted to become. I had to run away from home. I had to buy a one-way ticket to Athens because I'd never been anywhere alone before even though I was almost thirty. And when I was washing my socks in the sink on a cold winter morning in Chicago or in Tuscany, in the pre-Alps of southern France, or in South Texas, riding across town on a bicycle, or driving across country, Astor, you taught me with your music the kind of passion I wanted to reach in my work. I'm aware, Astor, you struggled to find your own voice, how your teacher Nadia Boulanger advised you to take up the instrument you had abandoned because you were embarrassed by the bandoneon. She was reminding you to remember who you are, and making you feel less ashamed and praising you for being no one but you, and sent you back to that despised part of yourself, because it was you you had abandoned, and in that monster of a box you'd been able to leap from the sentimental to sentiment, which is a fine line, and how the traditionalists wanted to murder you for what you did to their tango, and how it had been so hard for me to become a writer, but your music, Astor, your music had shown me, when I was cold and afraid, to be fearless. You made the tango yours, Astor, and it became mine the years of my twenties, and now in my early thirties, having just barely escaped the maw of death, that terror was in your music, Astor, everything was in your music, the nemesis I loved who abandoned me, and how from that open wound, I had transformed the yelp into a howl, and that howl was my work, inspired by you, Astor, do you understand?*

All this I thought while the guy in front of me was getting his flyer signed. And now it was my turn, and Astor Piazzolla in his black trousers with their sharp creases, in his silky black shirt and polished black boots, Astor with only his hands and face illuminating the moment, was reaching out and taking my flyer from my hand. I stood there with my mouth open a little.

Now as he signed I needed to tell him. It was my chance, yes. I could say it now. I could tell him. Now!

"Señor Piazzolla," I said breathlessly. "Your work. Is. My life!"

He nodded, passed my flyer on down the line to his fellow musicians to sign, and then . . .

My moment was gone.

I clenched that autographed flyer in one fist and wobbled back to my seat feeling foolish and weepy. *Your work is my life!* What was I thinking?

Then I put my head down to write. "Thing in my shoe, / dandelion, thorn, thumbprint, / one grain of grief that has me undone once more, / oh my father, heartily sorry I am for this right-side of the brain / who has alarmed and maimed and laid me many a day now invalid low." And when I raised my head, I had a new book of poetry. Just as if I'd gone through childbirth, my body changed, startling me with flesh where I'd once had bone. I put my head down again, and again when I raised it, another book, and again my body altered, so that I was no longer myself, but a woman staring at a woman from the other side of water. Books and more books, and more changes to the house one calls the self.

Young people get in line to meet the author and have their book autographed. I am the author they've come to meet. Some of them barely able to talk, their eyes like ships lost at sea.

"You don't know what this means to me," they say, fumbling with the page they want me to sign. "You just. You just don't know."

Only Daughter

In the year of my near death, 1987, I was sick over a ten-month period. Had I been ill with something physically visible, I might've known to run and see a doctor. But when we are sick in the soul, it takes a long time to realize a spirit wound that won't heal is equally as dangerous as a flesh wound that can't.

The following was written in 1989 as I was rising from that dark night. It overwhelmed me then and overwhelms me now to realize the timing of these accolades; they could've arrived posthumously. I've learned since then that despair is part of the process, not the destination.

Once, several years ago, when I was just starting out my writing career, I was asked to write my own contributor's note for a literary anthology. I wrote, "I am the only daughter in a family of six sons. *That* explains everything."

Well, I've thought about that ever since, and yes, it explains a lot to me, but for the reader's sake I should have written, "I am the only daughter in a Mexican family of six sons." Or even: "I am the only daughter of a Mexican father and a Mexican American mother." Or: "I am the only daughter of a working-class family of nine." All of these had everything to do with who I am today.

I was / am the only daughter and *only* a daughter. Being an only daughter in a family of six sons forced me by circumstance to spend a lot of time by myself because my brothers felt it beneath them to play with a *girl* in public. But that aloneness, that loneliness, was good for a would-be writer—it allowed me time to think and think, to imagine, to read and prepare myself for my writer's profession.

Being only a daughter for my father meant my destiny would lead me to become someone's wife. That's what he believed. But when I was in the fifth grade and shared my plans for college with him, I was sure he understood. I remember my father saying, *"Qué bueno, mi'ja"*—that's good. That meant a lot to me, especially since my brothers thought the idea hilarious. What I didn't realize was that my father thought college was good for girls—good for finding a husband. After I finished four years of college and two more in graduate school, and still no husband, my father shakes his head even now and says I wasted all that education.

In retrospect, I'm lucky my father believed daughters were meant for husbands. It meant it didn't matter if I majored in something silly like English. After all, I'd find a nice professional eventually who might marry me, right? This allowed me the liberty to putter about embroidering my little poems and stories without my father interrupting with so much as a "What's that you're writing?"

But the truth is I *wanted* him to interrupt. I wanted my father to understand what I was scribbling, to introduce me as "My only daughter, the writer." Not as "This is my only daughter. She teaches." *"Es maestra"* were his exact words. Not even *"profesora."*

In a sense, everything I have ever written has been for him, to win his approval even though I know my father can't read English words. My father's only reading includes Mexican comic books—*La Familia Burrón,* his chocolate-ink *Esto,* a Mexican sports magazine, or *fotonovelas,* little picture paperbacks with tragedy and trauma erupting from the characters' mouths in bubbles. My father represents, then, the public majority. A public who is uninterested in reading, and yet one whom I'm writing about and for, and privately trying to woo.

When we were growing up in Chicago, we moved a lot because of my father. He suffered bouts of nostalgia. Then we'd have to let go our flat, store the furniture with Mother's relatives, load the station wagon with baggage and bologna sandwiches, and head south. To Mexico City.

We came back, of course. To yet another Chicago flat, another Chicago neighborhood, another Catholic school. Each time, my father would seek out the parish priest in order to get a tuition break, and complain or boast, "I have seven sons."

He meant *siete hijos,* seven children, but he translated it as "sons." "I have seven sons," he would say to anyone who would listen. The Sears employee who sold us the washing machine. The short-order cook where my father ate his ham-and-eggs

Our family en route to Mexico City, c. 1964;
I am seated on my mother's right.

breakfasts. "I have seven sons." As if he deserved a medal from the state.

My papa. He didn't mean anything by that mistranslation, I'm sure. But somehow I could feel myself being erased. I'd tug my father's sleeve and whisper, "Not seven sons. Six! And one daughter."

When my oldest brother graduated from medical school, he fulfilled my father's dream that we study hard and use this, our head, instead of these, our hands. Even now my father's hands are thick and yellow, stubbed by a history of hammer and nails and twine and coils and springs. "Use this," my father said, tapping his head, "and not this," showing us those hands. He always looked tired when he said it.

Wasn't college an investment? And hadn't I spent all those years in college? And if I didn't marry, what was it all for? Why would anyone go to college and then choose to be poor?

Last year, after ten years of writing professionally, the financial rewards started to trickle in—my second National Endowment for the Arts fellowship; a guest professorship at the University of California, Berkeley; my book sold to a major New York publishing house.

At Christmas, I flew home to Chicago. The house was throbbing, same as always: hot tamales and sweet tamales hissing in my mother's pressure cooker, and everybody—my mother, six brothers, wives, babies, aunts, cousins—talking too loud and at the same time, because that's just how we are.

I went upstairs to my father's room. One of my stories had just been translated into Spanish and published in an anthology of Chicano writing, and I wanted to show it to him. Ever since he recovered from a stroke two years ago, my father likes to spend his leisure hours horizontally. And that's how I found him, watching a Pedro Infante movie on television and eating rice pudding.

There was a glass filmed with milk on the bedside table. There were several vials of pills and balled Kleenex. And on the floor, one black sock and a plastic urinal that I didn't want to look at, but looked at anyway. Pedro Infante was about to burst into song, and my father was laughing.

I'm not sure if it was because my story was translated into Spanish, or because it was published in Mexico, or perhaps because the story dealt with Tepeyac, the *colonia* my father was raised in and the house he grew up in, but at any rate, my father punched the Mute button on his remote control and read my story.

I sat on the bed next to my father and waited. He read it very slowly. As if he were reading each line over and over. He laughed at all the right places and read lines he liked out loud.

He pointed and asked questions, "Is this so-and-so?"

"Yes," I said. He kept reading.

When he was finally finished, after what seemed like hours, my father looked up and asked, "Where can we get more copies of this for the relatives?"

Of all the wonderful things that happened to me last year, that was the most wonderful.

Letter to Gwendolyn Brooks

I once ran into Gwendolyn Brooks in the basement of the Stop & Shop in downtown Chicago. This was when she knew me as a high school teacher and not as a writer. She was standing in line at the bakery counter looking like a mother coming home from work.

"Miss Brooks, what are you doing here?"

"I'm buying a cake," Miss Brooks said matter-of-factly.

Of course she was buying a cake. Still, it didn't seem possible then that poets of her stature went downtown on the subway and bought themselves cakes. Gwendolyn Brooks was famous, maybe the most famous person I knew then, and I admired her greatly. I'd been reading her work since high school. To meet her at a university or bookstore was one thing. But here she was waiting to buy a cake! She didn't look like a Pulitzer Prize–winning author. She looked like a sparrow or a nun in the modest brown and navy she always wore.

Like Elena Poniatowska, she taught me what it is to be generous to others, to speak to every member of your public as if *they* were the guest writer, and not the other way round.

This generosity and way of honoring her readers has made me see her not only as a great poet but as a great human being, and this, in my book, is the greatest kind of writer of all.

This letter was written while I was guest professor at the University of New Mexico, Albuquerque.

Dear Ms. Brooks,

It is what Winnie-the-Pooh would call a blustery day here. Or what Miss Emily would designate a wind like a bugle. From over and over the mesas, snapping dust and terrifying trees.

I am in my pajamas though it's past midday but I like my leisure to dream a little longer when I am asleep, and continue dreaming on paper when I am awake. I am rereading your wonderful MAUD MARTHA again, a copy you gave me, and which I am very grateful to have. I remember when I first discovered that book, in the American library in Sarajevo, across from the famous river where the archduke was shot that started a world war. And it was there too that I read T. S. Eliot's collected poems. If you go to Sarajevo and look at the chapter on PRACTICAL CATS you'll see a cherry stain on one of the pages—because I was reading the book on the opposite bank of the river, under a row of cherry trees in front of my American friend Ana's apartment house, and at the moment I was reading about one of Eliot's cats—the Rum Tum Tugger?—a wind shook a cherry loose that landed with a startled plop on the page. And my heart gave a little jump too because the book wasn't mine. A wine-colored stain against the thick creamy pages.

I mean to teach it one day along with other books that use a series of short interrelated stories. Perhaps with Ermilo Abreu Gómez's CANEK and Nellie Campobello's CARTUCHO albeit the translations of both are crooked. The form fascinates. And I'd done as much with MANGO STREET, though I hadn't met your MAUD yet. Perhaps I was "recollecting the things to come."

Ms. Brooks, please know I haven't quite disappeared altogether from the land. I've been migrant professor these past years, guest writer in residence at UC Berkeley, UC Irvine, the Univ. of Michigan at Ann Arbor, and now here for one semester. All for the sake of protecting my writer self. Some years dipped low and some reeled to high heaven. But now the days are good to me. I have a new book due out from Random (see enclosed reviews), and I have sold my little house on Mango to the big house of Vintage. Both books slated for this April. And it seems my life is a whirl like the wind outside my window today. Everything is shook and snapped and wind-washed and fresh, and, yes, that is how it should be.

I only wanted to say this to you today. That your book gives me much pleasure. That I admire it terribly. I think of you often, Ms. Brooks, and your spirit is with me always.

un abrazo fuerte, fuerte,
Sandra

My Wicked Wicked Ways

The reissue of my first book of poems by Knopf in 1992 demanded commentary. After publishing them with a small press the first time, I'd felt a strange postpartum depression. We'd never talked about pro-choice regarding publishing poetry when I was a student in the graduate poetry workshop; it was assumed if you wrote poems you had to publish them, or you weren't a real poet. A given. Like being a woman meant you had to have a child to make you a real woman. Or did you?

It seems to me the act of writing poetry is the opposite of publishing. So I made a vow to myself after that first book to choose to *not* publish poetry from then on. I'd say what I had to say publicly in fiction, but poems were to be written as if they could not be published in my lifetime. They came from such a personal place. It was the only way I could free myself to write/think with absolute freedom, without censorship. From then on, I'd toss them under the bed like Emily Dickinson. And for a time, that's what I did.

When I finally moved from a little publishing house to a big one a decade later, I was reluctant to have the early book of poems reissued, but I felt that a hardback from a big New York press would help Norma Alarcón's small press, Third Woman, which had taken a chance on me.

I was asked to write a new introduction and agreed to do so. But then, of course, writer's block stepped in. The only way to get around my fear was to trick myself. After many false starts, I found the way to do this was by writing my introduction in verse. It was finished in June of 1992, in Greece, on the island of Hydra, the same place I'd finished *The House on Mango Street* ten years before. The *Los Angeles Times Book Review* published the poem on September 6, 1992, as "Poem as Preface." I want to add as I relook at this poem now as a woman at the end of my fifties, I *can* and *do* enjoy living alone. And, yes, despite all my whining, I love to work.

I can live alone and I love to work.
—MARY CASSATT

Allí está el detalle. (There's the rub.)
—CANTINFLAS

Gentlemen, ladies. If you please—these
are my wicked poems from when.
The girl grief decade. My wicked nun
years, so to speak. I sinned.

Not in the white woman way.
Not as Simone voyeuring the pretty
slum city on a golden arm. And no,

not wicked like the captain of the bad
boy blood, that Hollywood hood-
lum who boozed and floozed it up,
hell bent on self-destruction. Not me.
Well. Not much. Tell me,

how does a woman who?
A woman like me. Daughter of
a daddy with a hammer and blistered feet
he'd dip into a washtub while he ate his dinner.
A woman with no birthright in the matter.

What does a woman inherit
that tells her how
to go?

My first felony—I took up with poetry.
For this penalty, the rice burned.
Mother warned I'd never wife.

Wife? A woman like me
whose choice was rolling pin or factory.
An absurd vice, this wicked wanton
writer's life.

I chucked the life
my father'd plucked for me.
Leapt into the salamander fire.
A girl who'd never roamed
beyond her father's rooster eye.
Winched the door with poetry and fled.
For good. And grieved I'd gone
when I was so alone.

In my kitchen, in the thin hour,
a calendar Cassatt chanted:
Repeat after me—
I can live alone and I love to . . .
What a crock. Each week, the ritual grief.
That decade of the knuckled knocks.

I took the crooked route and liked my badness.
Played at mistress.

Tattooed an ass.
Lapped up my happiness from a glass.
It was something, at least.

I hadn't a clue.

What does a woman
willing to invent herself
at twenty-two or twenty-nine
do? A woman with no who nor how.
And how was I to know what was unwise.
I wanted to be writer. I wanted to be happy.
What's that? At twenty. Or twenty-nine.
Love. Baby. Husband.
The works. The big palookas of life.
Wanting and not wanting.
Take your hands off me.

I left my father's house
before the brothers,
vagabonded the globe
like a rich white girl.
Got a flat.
I paid for it. I kept it clean.
Sometimes the silence frightened me.
Sometimes the silence blessed me.

It would come get me.
Late at night.
Open like a window,
hungry for my life.

I wrote when I was sad.
The flat cold.
When there was no love—
new, old—
to distract me.
No six brothers
with their Fellini racket.
No mother, father,
with their wise *I told you.*

I tell you,
these are the pearls
from that ten-year itch,
my jewels, my colicky kids
who fussed and kept
me up the wicked nights
when all I wanted was . . .
With nothing in the texts to tell me.

But that was then.
The who-I-was who would become the who-I-am.
These poems are from that hobbled when.

Who Wants Stories Now

I delivered this speech about my friend Jasna the same day I wrote it, March 7, 1993, for an International Women's Day rally in a park in downtown San Antonio, Texas. I'd lived in Sarajevo before the 1984 Winter Olympics, and the topic in the news that season was the Yugoslav war and the rape of Bosnian women. I hadn't talked about my time there or my friend still living in Sarajevo, because I felt guilty I couldn't do anything. But when I was invited to speak at the rally, I accepted, even though I was clueless what I could possibly say. The night before I remember fumbling about my library looking for inspiration when a book Jasna had given me fell off the bookshelf. It was a book by the Vietnamese Buddhist monk Thich Nhat Hanh, *Being Peace*.

I remember reading my speech at the rally and being surprised midway by my own tears. Because I didn't want to be defeated by my emotions, I started shouting the text like a crazy lady, and my words bounced and reverberated across the Texas buildings. Afterward, I just wanted to dart off and hide, but several women came up to me and offered to sit with me at a weekly peace vigil. This was something I could do. In the next few days, I learned that *The New York Times* would reprint my article in their op-ed pages on March 14, 1993, and finally National Public Radio in the spring of 1994 performed my story and a letter Jasna subsequently wrote to me from war-torn Sarajevo ("Two Letters"). I moved from a place of powerlessness to action. Doing something, however small, is what Thich Nhat Hanh taught me then and continues to teach me whenever I feel I can't possibly make a difference.

N*ema.* There isn't any. *Nema.* It was the first word I learned when I crossed the border into Yugoslavia in 1983. *Nema.* Toothpaste?—*Nema.* Toilet paper?—*Nema.* Coffee?—*Nema.* Chocolate?—*Nema.* But yes, plenty of roses when I was there, plenty of war memorials to fallen partisans and mountains screaming "TITO" in stone.

It's true. I lived there on ulica Gorica, with that man Salem, the printer, in the house that used to be the grocery. There, behind the garden wall of wooden doors nailed together. That was the summer I spent being a wife. I washed Turkish rugs till my knees were raw. I washed shirts by hand. With a broom and a bucket of

Jasna at her house in Sarajevo, 1983

Jasna and me, Austin, Texas, 1984

suds I scrubbed the tiles of the garden each morning from all the pigeon droppings that fell from the flock that lived on the roof of the garden shed. It was summer. Everything was blossoming. Our dog Leah had fourteen puppies. The children in the neighborhood came in and out the garden gate. The garden was filled with walnuts and fruit and roses so heavy they drooped.

And you lived across the street, Jasna Karaula. In the house that was once your mother's, and before her, her mother's.

I have your recipes for fry bread, for your famous fruit bread, "It always turns out good," you said, your rose bread, "Sometimes it turns out good." You were filled with potted begonias and recipes and sewing and did all the amazing domestic chores I couldn't/can't do. You're difficult. You smoke too much and are terribly moody. I knew you that summer before your divorce, that summer before the Winter Olympics. That afternoon I met you on the wooden bench outside the summer kitchen of our garden, and in that instant when I looked at you, when you looked at me, it was as if you'd always known me, as if I'd always known you. Of that we were convinced.

After I meet you, I'm always to be found across the street at your house, helping you fold the wash, or talking with you while you iron, or keeping you company when you lay out a dress pattern, or helping you whitewash the walls of your house that was once your grandmother's, and then your mother's, and then yours. You would come to the United States to visit me, to Austin, Chicago, Berkeley, San Antonio, and begin translating my stories into Serbo-Croatian. We were just getting the stories published in Sarajevo when that damn war ruined everything. Who wants stories now? There's no shortage of stories when there's no heat, or bread, or water, or electricity. *Nema, nema, nema.*

The little watercolors I painted for you, the photos of us hiking the Sarajevo mountains, the letters about the divorce, the abortion, the lace embroidered curtains, the flowered tablecloth you made by hand, your grandmother's house on ulica Gorica, number 26, with its thick stone walls and deep-set windows, its dust, its forever need of repair, the one your father helped you fix, the one where you wedded and divorced a husband, the house where I made you a piñata and we celebrated your birthday and joked it was the only piñata to be had in all of Yugoslavia. Remember the afternoons of *kaffa,* roasted in the garden, served in thimble-sized cups, the Turkish way. The minarets and the sad call to prayer like a flag of black silk fluttering in the air.

Jasna. It's ten years since that summer I lived on ulica Gorica with Salem's family. I haven't heard from you since last summer. When I was in Milano, you called my hotel, left a number for me to call you, but it was too late already. The lines were impossible by then, the war already begun in Sarajevo. The war you said would never reach Sarajevo.

When there was still time, you didn't leave. Now I hear you

won't leave. Your mother sick, too frail no doubt to travel, your sister Zdenka never strong enough to even make a decision. I imagine it's you who is taking care of them both. I'm certain of this.

In a letter that reached me by way of London, you write, "Ask your government to stop sending us 'humilitarian' aid. We need water, electricity, birds and trees, we need this horrible killing to stop, now, immediately, because long time ago it has been too late."

Is it too late already, Jasna? I'm told your house has been damaged. What does that mean? Are you living in the first floor because the second floor is gone? Is the roof open to the sky? Is there still a roof? Can you sleep there in that darkness, in this winter cold ringed by mountains as tall, as icy as the Alps? A town famous for its snow and mountains. I was there the summer before the Winter Olympics. And you said the houses of Sarajevo were cold in winter, even then when there was no war, when there was fuel. How must it be now, in March, when spring is still so far away, when there is no fuel to be had, how must you be managing?

I've talked to your sister Veronika in Slovenia. I've talked to your brother Davor in Germany. We light our candles and are sick with worry. I dreamt you, Jasna Karaula. You're not dead. Not yet. I can say this with certainty, because I know you too well, and if you died, you'd come and tell me. That's how it is between us. That's how it's always been.

And you haven't visited me in a dream except to have coffee. In the last dream, we drank *kaffa* together in broken cups, broken because of the war I understood. I remember I held you and hugged you before waking as if we were saying goodbye until the next dream. Jasna, I'm afraid.

I'm afraid I'm not capable of saving you. I know those streets of Sarajevo. This war is not far away. This war is happening on ulica Gorica where I lived, where you live, in the house on the top of the hill, number 26. I can walk there in my mind, I know the way. I've been inside the minarets, the churches, the cafés. I know this town. I know your house. I've heard the evening prayer call and watched the devout kneel on their prayer rugs all facing Mecca, the single star and crescent moon of the Muslim graves, the Cyrillic script of the Orthodox church with its golden domes, the candles of the Catholic church of the Croatians, I've been there. I've sat at your table, raised a glass of *slivovitz,* toasted to your country and mine, drunk *kaffa* in toy-sized cups.

This is real. I'm not making this story up for anyone's amusement. A woman is there. She's my friend, take my word for it. That city, those streets, those houses. Where I washed rugs and scrubbed floors and gave away puppies and had coffee in the open cafés on Titograd Street. Look, what I'm trying to say is my friend is missing. This is a city where cherry trees blossomed the summer I was there, if you go to the American library on the banks of the Miljacka River, there is a copy of T. S. Eliot's poems with one page stained with a cherry that fell from a tree while I was reading it, I'll show you the page. I picked walnuts for the cake you made in a summer that was ripe and abundant with fruit and peace and hope, the upcoming Olympics on the horizon.

A woman is there. In the old part of the town, up the hill, up too many steps, in the neighborhood nearest the Gypsy borough, on ulica Gorica, number 26. It's the second house from the corner, on the right, after ascending the steps. That house was once her grandmother's, and then her mother's, and then hers.

Mr. President of the United States, leaders of every country across the globe, all you politicians, all you deciding the fates of nations, your excellencies of power, the United Nations, dear Mr. Prime Minister, *querido* Señor Presidente, Mr. Radovan Karadžić, Mr. Alija Izetbegović, Mr. Cyrus Vance, Lord David Owen, fellow citizens, human beings of all races, I mean you listening to me and not listening, Dear To Whom It May Concern, God, Milošević, Pope John Paul, Clinton, Mitterrand, Kohl, all the nations of the planet Earth, my friends, my enemies, my known and unknown ancestors, my fellow human beings, I've had it with all of you.

She's in there. Get her out, I tell you! Get her out! Get them out! They're in that city, that country, that region Bosnia Herzegovina, there in that oven, that mouth of hell, that Calvary, that Dachau, that gas chamber, that Chernobyl, that holocaust, that house on fire, get her out of there, I demand you.

I demand you march, take a plane, better take a tank. Take some of these blankets I have, my beautiful new home, my lovely silk suits, my warm stockings, my full belly, my refrigerator with things to eat, my supermarket, my spring weather, my electricity, my clean water, my pickup truck, my U.S. dollars, my trees and flowers and nights soundless and whole.

I demand you go right in there. I demand you give me a sword mightier than this useless pen of mine. I demand you arrive in Sarajevo. I'll take you to ulica Gorica, I'm afraid, but I'll take you. Spirits of all you deceased relatives and friends, my ancestors, my compatriots, fellow human beings, I demand, I ask, I beg you.

In the name of civilization. In the name of humanity. In the name of compassion. In the name of respectability. In the name of mankind. Bring that woman out of there. That woman, *hermana de mi corazón*, sister of my heart. I know this woman. I know her mother, I know her sister as well. They're in that city. In that awful place that was once so peaceful a woman could walk alone at night unafraid.

About words. I know what my demands mean. I know about words. I'm in the business of words. There's no shortage of words in Sarajevo. I'm a writer. I'm a woman. I'm a human being. In other wars I remember watching Buddhist priests set themselves on fire for begging for no less than what I ask for, and what good did it come to?

A woman I know is in there. In that country. A woman I love as any woman would love a woman. And I am in San Antonio, Texas, and the days and the hours and the months pass and the newspapers cry, "Something must be done!" Somebody, someone, help this somebody.

And I hear that somebody. And I know that somebody. And I love that somebody. And I don't know what to do. I don't know what to do.

La Casa Que Canta

When I met the photographer Mariana Yampolsky, I was look-ing for a way to be an artist and to love someone. Now at fifty-nine I feel quite content and whole just as I am. I love writing, I live alone—if one can call five dogs alone—and I am perfectly at ease as a pond of water. I desire nothing. Except a house. And, on a regular basis, a box of salted French caramels.

I need to mention that I began this piece well before Mari-ana's death in 2002, but was prompted to resurrect and fin-ish it on April 1, 2003, for a San Francisco exhibit in Mariana's honor.

During the New Year of 1985, a snowstorm arrived in South Texas that fell so hard all of San Antonio shut down and pipes burst. I was away for the holidays and came back to the city and my apartment to find my books had been soaked with water. At that time I couldn't afford bookshelves, and my books sat on the floor. To add grief to sorrow, I remember finding my finest treasure, a Mariana Yampolsky book, destroyed by the flood. It was *La Casa Que Canta,* the house that sings, its pages as wavy as if someone had cried a thousand tears upon them.

I spent the rest of the night ironing my books, the apartment steamy as a dry cleaners, as determined to save my treasures as any art historian saving Florence. It wasn't the best restoration job, but it would have to do. *La Casa Que Canta* had been published in a limited edition and was already out of print.

I have often returned to that book, to draw inspiration, to remind myself what it is that captivates me about Mariana, about Mariana's houses, about Mexican houses in particular. To Mariana, the more humble the house, the more splendid, something to be looked at with respect and awe. She documented the homes that would never be featured in the glossy pages of *House & Garden.* These were houses where floors were pounded silky by bare feet, architecture where everything had the unmistakable air of being made by hand, homes forgotten in the countryside and dusty towns, full of *duende.* The arabesque of a hinge. A door made of dried organ cacti. Deep-set windows like eyes. A porch with two flowered chairs snoozing in the half-sun. A kitchen wall splendid with enamel pots and dishes. A hammock, a hat, a crib hanging from a house beam. A tortilla toasting on a *comal.*

Mariana and Arjen, at my house

Several years later, I finally replaced that ripply *La Casa Que Canta* with a clean copy found in a rare bookstore in downtown Mexico City. By then I had acquired a house of my own finally, and, at long last, bookshelves.

Mariana Yampolsky and her husband, Arjen van de Sluis, came to San Antonio just at this point in my life. I immediately invited them to my house, seated them on my couch for a photo portrait, and admired them shamelessly. I entertained Mariana with the story of my original *La Casa Que Canta* and made her sign my new copy. She wrote—*"¡tu casa es muy muy bonita! ¡tú eres bonita! ¡y lo que escribes más!"*

Whenever Mariana spoke, Arjen looked at her with the sincere adoration of a man made foolish by love. For her part, Mariana treated him with the diffidence and annoyance of an only child or a pampered Pekingese.

The photo I took of them is somewhere, who knows where,

but I remember it looked like this: two leaning into each other like houses slouched with time, and, like it or not, in love, after everything and always.

It occurred to me that this couple had the secret to what I was looking for. I asked how was it they had remained together so successfully for so many years when all my own loves had never lasted as long as my toaster. What was the secret of being an artist—I meant, of course, a woman artist—and keeping a man?

"Respect," Arjen replied. "For what you each do."

"Ah, is that it?"

"Yes," he said, and I seem to remember Mariana nodding.

They rose to leave, and Mariana invited me to their house in Tlalpan, on the southern edge of Mexico City. "Soon," I said, without knowing that the book I was writing would delay that "soon" to "*nunca.*"

"*Hasta pronto,*" Mariana said, which translates literally as "until soon," but means "until later."

"Goodbye," we each said. "Goodbye, goodbye." As lazily and luxuriously as if we were in control of our own destinies.

Mercè Rodoreda

I often remember where I was when meeting a book that sweeps me off my feet. I remember the moment and the intimate sensation of devouring a beloved text as distinctly as I recall the most sensual encounters of my life. Is it like this for everyone, or is it like this only for those who work with words?

I want to believe that everyone falls in love with a book in much the same way one falls in love with a person, that one has an intimate, personal exchange, a mystical exchange, as spiritual and charged as the figure eight meaning infinity.

I remember the bus ride from Oaxaca City to San Cristóbal de las Casas, and how somewhere after Tuxtla Gutiérrez, in the dizzy road between that city and San Cristóbal, I finished Marguerite Duras's *The Lover*.

And I recall an especially unforgettable rainy night in a London garret forfeiting dinner for Jeanette Winterson's *The Passion,* as if it were an indulgence of expensive chocolate creams.

So I first read Mercè Rodoreda's novel *The Time of the Doves* under the sun in a courtyard in Berkeley, California, on the hottest day of autumn, 1988, and only when I finished the book did I raise my head and realize I was sitting in the hydrangea blue of twilight.

I have borrowed, I have learned from this borrowing.

The following first appeared as an introduction to the Graywolf Press edition of *Camellia Street,* September 1993. It was written before Internet search engines were ubiquitous.

There are no camellias on Camellia Street. Maybe once, recent or long ago, but not when I was there last spring. *"Las calles han sido siempre para mí motivo de inspiración . . ."* Rodoreda wrote in a prologue to one of her novels, "The streets have always motivated me to write." So it's on the streets of Barcelona I go in search of her.

Of Rodoreda one French critic said, "One feels that this little working woman in Barcelona has spoken on behalf of all the hope, all the freedom, and all the courage in the world. And that she has just uttered forth one of the books of most universal relevance that love—let us finally say the word—could have written." He was talking of *The Time of the Doves,* a novel introduced to me by a Texas parking lot attendant—"Don't you know Mercè Rodoreda?" he asked. "García Márquez considers her one of the greatest writers of this century." A recommendation by García Márquez *and* a parking lot attendant. They couldn't both be wrong. I asked the attendant to scribble Rodoreda's name on a check deposit slip, and a year later, I bought the book and read it cover to cover all in one afternoon. When I was finished, I felt as foolish as Balboa discovering the powerful Pacific.

Who is this writer, this "little working woman" who arrived too many years too late in my life, but just in time. What I know of Rodoreda I've gathered from introductions, prologues, blurbs, book jackets—bits and pieces from here and there that tell me facts, that tell me nothing. I know she was born on the 10th of October (1909 according to one source, 1908 according to another), an only daughter—like me—of overprotective parents, but unlike me, she is an only child. At twenty-five she publishes her first novel. At thirty, she receives a prestigious literary prize for her book *Aloma*. She is a prolific writer in the years before the Spanish Civil War, writing novels, publishing short stories in several important literary journals. Was she married? Did she have children? Did her husband want her to follow her life of letters or did he say, "Mercè, enough of that, come to bed already"? And when she went to bed, did she wish he wasn't there so she could go to bed with a book? I don't know for certain, but I wonder.

I know with the war she takes refuge for a time in Paris, and, later, Geneva. Some of her books—*The Time of the Doves,* for example—are finished in Geneva, where David Rosenthal, her English translator, says she eked out a survivor's existence, but what exactly does he mean? Did she mop bathrooms and tug bed linens taut, type doctoral dissertations, wipe the milk moustache from the mouth of a small child, embroider blue stars on sheets and pillowcases? Or work in a bakery like Colometa, the protagonist of *The Time of the Doves,* her fingers tired from tying ribbons into bows all day? I can't know.

For two decades when she lives exiled from her language, Rodoreda does not write. At least, she does not publish. I know she has said that during this time she couldn't bear the thought of literature, that literature made her feel like vomiting, that she was never as lucid as during this period when she was starving. I imagine myself the months I lived without English in Sarajevo, or the year I lived without Spanish in Northern California—both times not writing because I could not brave repeating my life on paper. I slept for hours hoping the days would roll by, my life dried and hollow like a seedpod. What would a writer do not writing for a year? For twenty?

She is in her early fifties when she begins to write again, her masterpiece—*La plaça del Diamant* (*The Time of the Doves*)—the story of an ordinary woman who happens to survive the extraordinary years of a war. A few years later Rodoreda finishes *El carrer de les Camèlies* (*Camellia Street*). 1966. Rodoreda is fifty-eight years old.

When I first arrive in Barcelona in the spring of 1983, Rodoreda is dying, but I don't know she exists. It will be years till I meet the Texas parking lot attendant who first pronounces her name for me. I'm wandering the streets of Barcelona without enough money to eat. I spend the day looking for Gaudí buildings, walking instead of riding the bus to save money. When I have seen all the Gaudí I can manage, I buy the train ticket back to the French-Italian border where I live. I have enough pesetas left to buy a roasted chicken. On the train ride back, I devour that bird like a crazy lady.

May of 1992, the spring before the Olympics. It's Sunday. I'm in Barcelona again, this time to promote one of my books. I'm staying at a hotel on las Ramblas. This time I don't have to go without eating. My meals arrive on a shiny tray with linen folded into stiff triangles and bright silverware and a waiter who opens his arm like a magician.

"I want to go here," I say, pointing on the map to la Plaça de la Font Castellana where Camellia Street begins or ends.

"There?" the taxicab driver says. "But there's nothing there."

"It doesn't matter, that's where I want to go."

We drive past shop windows and leafy boulevards, apartment buildings sprouting graceful iron balconies and into Gràcia, the neighborhood of Rodoreda's stories. But when we arrive finally at la Plaça de la Font Castellana, I realize the taxicab driver is right. There's nothing here but a noisy rotary, a swirl of automobiles and chain-link fence, the park below under construction.

Is this la calle de las Camelias? The buildings boxlike and ugly, walls a nubby gray like a dirty wool sweater. On one corner a plaque verifies "Carrer de les Camèlies." There aren't many gardens left anymore. Hardly one. Did they destroy them all in the war?

Pinched between two ugly buildings, a small one-family house from the time of before, something like the house of my grandmother in Tepeyac—several potted plants, a stubborn rosebush, but no camellias. I stand outside the gate peering in like someone trying to remember something. I've arrived too late.

When I can't bear the noise of Camellia Street anymore, the stink of cars and buses and trucks, I duck down a side street, zigzagging my way the several blocks to la Plaça del Diamant.

It's nothing like I'd imagined. Bald as a knuckle, funny looking as the Mexico City *zócalo*. Tall apartment buildings hold up the little handkerchief of sky. Light—milky as an air shaft. Were there once trees here, do you suppose? Air throbbing with children and motorbikes, goofy teenagers hitting and then hugging each other, schoolgirls on the brink of brilliant catastrophes.

In one corner of the plaza, almost unnoticeable, as dark and discolored as the sad bronze-colored buildings, a bronze sculpture of a woman with doves taking flight—Rodoreda or Colometa, perhaps? Somebody has drawn a penis on her lower torso. Whose kid did this? A dog has left three small turds at the pedestal. Two children race round and round the sculpture giddy and growling like tigers, and I remember the joy of being chased around the statue of some green somebody—Christopher Columbus?—in Chicago's Grant Park when I was little.

I've brought my camera, but I'm too shy to take a picture. I choose a park bench next to a grandmother singing and rocking a baby in a stroller. When I don't want people to notice that I'm looking at them, I start writing and it makes me invisible.

Querido agridulce amargura de mis amores,

I've walked from el carrer de les Camèlies looking for Rodoreda. Here I am in the famous Plaça del Diamant filled with kids and motorbikes and teenagers and abuelitas singing in a language I don't understand.

And now the boys' soccer game has just begun. A fleet of mothers with babies on their wide hips sail past. A girl with long pony limbs and a camera is shouting "Uriel" to Uriel, who won't turn around to have his picture taken. Somebody's little one in a stroller stares at me like the wise guy he is until out of view. A tanned mother, plump as a peach, is being a good sport and playing Chinese jump rope with her girls. The soccer ball thuds on my notebook, knocking the pen from my hand. The one with a crooked grin and teeth too big for his mouth arrives with my pen and a shy "perdón."

Everyone little and big is outdoors, exiled or escaped from the cramped apartments of I-can't-take-it-anymore. All of Barcelona here at some age or another to hide or think or pull the plastic caterpillar with the striped whirligig, to kiss or be kissed where the mother won't see them. I think of the park near my mother's house in Chicago, how she can't go there, afraid of the drug dealers. I think of the Los Angeles riots of a few weeks ago. How the citizens of Barcelona own their streets. How they wander fearless in their neighborhoods, their plaza, their city.

I've come looking for Rodoreda, and some part of her is here and some part isn't . . .

"What is it about Rodoreda that attracts you to her?" a Catalan journalist will ask. I fumble about like one of Rodoreda's characters, as clumsy with words as a carpenter threading a needle.

Rodoreda writes about feelings, about characters so numbed or overwhelmed by events they have only their emotions as a language. I think it's because one has no words that one writes, not because one is gifted with language. Perhaps because one recognizes wisely enough the shortcomings of language.

It is this precision at naming the unnameable that attracts me to Rodoreda, this woman, this writer, hardly little, adept at listening to those who do not speak, who are filled with great emotions, albeit mute to name them.

The House on Mango Street's Tenth Birthday

Where was I in November 1993 when I wrote this? I hardly remember. I'd bought my first house the year prior. The porch roof needed fixing, and my desk chair needed a replacement cushion. I was writing *Caramelo* full-time like a woman adrift at sea with only the stars for guidance. Foremost in my mind causing my compass to flounder was the deadline.

I never work well with anything that requires time management: cooking, for example, and least of all book projects. How can one predict how long a book will take to be born? And what a big breech baby *Caramelo* was turning out to be.

When I put my novel aside to write this introduction, I thought I could answer the most frequently asked questions from my young readers once and for all, and that would be that. But maybe young readers don't read introductions. The questions come back again and again.

I hope the following selection will allow readers to understand I'm all my characters. And I'm none of my characters. I can write a truth only if I get out of the way and disappear. And from this Houdini trick, amazingly enough, I reappear. Without intention.

The twenty-fifth-anniversary introduction to *Mango Street* is also included in this collection. See page 270.

It's ten years since *The House on Mango Street* was first published. I began it in graduate school, the spring of 1977, Iowa City. I was twenty-two years old.

I'm thirty-eight now, far from that time and place, but the questions from readers remain: "Are these stories true?" "Are you Esperanza?"

When I started *The House on Mango Street,* I thought I was writing a memoir. By the time I finished, my memoir was no longer memoir, no longer autobiographical, and had evolved into a collective story peopled with several lives, from my past and present, placed in one fictional time and neighborhood—Mango Street.

For me, a story is like a Giacometti sculpture. The farther away it is, the clearer I can see it. In Iowa City, I was going through too many changes. For the first time I was living alone, in a community different in class and culture from the one where I was raised. This caused me so much distress, I could barely speak, let alone write about it. The story I was living in my early twenties would have to wait, but I could tell the story of an earlier place, an earlier voice in my life, and record this on paper.

I found my voice the moment I realized I was different. This sounds pretty simple, but until Iowa City, I assumed the world was like Chicago, made up of people of many cultures and classes all living together—not happily all the time, but still coexisting. In graduate school, I was aware of feeling like a foreigner each time I spoke. But this was my land too. This isn't to say I'd never felt this "otherness" before in Chicago, but I hadn't felt it as deeply. I couldn't articulate what was happening then, except I knew when I spoke in class I felt ashamed, so I chose not to speak.

My political consciousness began the moment I could name this shame. I was in a graduate seminar on memory and the imagination. The books assigned were Vladimir Nabokov's *Speak, Memory,* Isak Dinesen's *Out of Africa,* and Gaston Bachelard's *The Poetics of Space.* I enjoyed the first two but, as usual, said nothing, just listened to my classmates, too afraid to speak. The third book, though, left me baffled. I didn't get it. Maybe I wasn't as smart as everyone else, I thought, and if I didn't say anything, maybe no one else would notice.

The conversation, I remember, was about the house of memory, the attic, the stairwells, the cellar. Attic? Were we talking

1525 North Campbell Street, Humboldt Park neighborhood, in Chicago, the model for *The House on Mango Street;* my room was the one above the door.

about the same house? My family lived upstairs for the most part, because noise traveled down. Stairwells reeked of Pine-Sol from the Saturday scrubbing. We shared them with the tenants downstairs: public zones no one thought to clean except us. We mopped them, all right, but not without resentment for cleaning other people's filth. And as for cellars, we had a basement, but who'd want to hide in there? Basements were filled with rats. Everyone was scared to go in there, including the meter reader *and* the landlord. What was this guy Bachelard talking about when he mentioned the familiar and comforting house of memory? It was obvious he'd never had to clean one or had to pay the landlord rent for one like ours.

Then it occurred to me that none of the books in this class, in any of my classes, in all the years of my education had ever discussed a house like mine. Not in books or magazines or film. My classmates had come from real houses, real neighborhoods, ones they could point to, but what did I know?

I went home that night and realized my education had been a lie—had made presumptions about what was "normal," what was American, what was of value. I wanted to quit school right then and there, but didn't. Instead, I got mad, and anger when it's used to act, when used nonviolently, has power. I asked myself what I could write about that my classmates couldn't. I didn't know what I wanted exactly, but I did have enough sense to know what I didn't. I didn't want to sound like my classmates; I didn't want to keep imitating the writers I'd been reading. Their voices were right for them but not for me.

Instead, I searched for the ugliest subjects I could find, the most unpoetic, slang, monologues where waitresses or kids talked their own lives. I was trying as best I could to write the kind of book I'd never seen in a library or in a school, the kind of book not even my professors could write. Each week I ingested the class readings, and then went off and did the opposite. It was a quiet revolution, a reaction taken to extremes maybe, but it was out of this negative experience that I found something positive: my own voice.

Mango Street is based on the speech of the Chicago streets where I grew up. It's an anti-academic voice—a child's voice, a girl's voice, a poor girl's voice, a spoken voice, the voice of an American Mexican. It's in this rebellious realm of anti-poetics that I tried to create a poetic text, with the most unofficial language I could find. I did it neither ingenuously nor naturally. It was as deliberate to me as if I were tossing a Molotov.

At one time or another, we've all been made to feel the other. When I teach writing, I tell the story of the moment of discovering and naming my otherness. It's not enough to simply sense it; it has to be named, and then written about from there. Once I could name it, I wasn't ashamed or silent. I could speak up and celebrate my otherness as a woman, a working-class person, an American of Mexican descent. When I recognized the places where I departed from my neighbors, my classmates, my family, my town, my brothers, when I discovered what I knew that no one else in the room knew, and spoke it in a voice that was my voice, the voice I used when I was sitting in the kitchen, dressed in my pajamas, talking over a table littered with cups and dishes, when I could give myself permission to speak from that intimate space, then I could talk and sound like myself, not like me trying to sound like someone I wasn't. Then I could speak, shout, laugh from a place that was uniquely mine, that was no one else's in the history of the universe, that would never be anyone else's, ever.

I wrote these stories that way, guided by my heart and by my ear. I was writing a novel and didn't know I was writing a novel; if I had, I probably couldn't have done it. I knew I wanted to tell a story made up of a series of stories that would each make sense if read alone, or that could be read all together to tell one big story, each story contributing to the whole—like beads in a necklace. I hadn't seen a book like this before. After finishing my book, I would discover story-cycle novels later.

While I was writing *Mango Street,* I remember reading Nicanor Parra's *Anti-Poems* and loving their rebellion toward "Poetry," just as I'd been delighted by Carl Sandburg's wise-guy, working-class voice and Gwendolyn Brooks's *Bronzeville* poems. I remember I was trying to write something that was a cross between fiction and poetry—like Jorge Luis Borges's *Dream Tigers,* a book whose stories read like fables, but with the lyricism and succinctness of poetry.

I finished writing my book in November 1982, in Greece, miles from the Iowa cornfields. I traveled a great distance from the book's inception, both physically and mentally. And in the meantime, lots of things had happened to me. I'd taught Latino high school dropouts and counseled Latina students. Because I often felt helpless as a teacher and counselor to alter their lives, their stories began to surface in my "memoir"; then *Mango Street* no longer was my story, but became all our stories. I arranged and diminished events on *Mango Street* as I came into my feminism. I gathered different parts of other people's lives to create a story like a collage. I merged characters from my twenties with characters from my teens and childhood. I edited, changed, shifted the past to fit the present. I asked questions I didn't know to ask when I was a teenager. But best of all, writing in a younger voice allowed me to speak, to name that thing without a name, that shame of being poor, of being female, of being not quite good enough, and examine where it had come from and why, so I could exchange shame for celebration.

In grad school, I'd never been trained to think of poems or

stories as something that could change anyone's life but the writer's. I'd been trained to think about where a line ended or how best to work a metaphor. It was always the "how" and not the "what" we talked about in class. Even while I was teaching in the Chicano community, the two halves of my life were at odds with each other—the half that wanted to roll up my sleeves and do something for the community, and the half that wanted to retreat to my kitchen and write. I still believed my writing couldn't save anyone's life but my own.

In the ten years since *Mango Street* was first published those two halves of my life have met and merged. I believe this because I've witnessed families buying my book for themselves and for family members, families for whom spending money on a book can be a sacrifice. They bring a mother, father, sibling, cousin along to my readings, or I'm introduced to someone who says their son or daughter read my book in a class and brought it home for them. And there are the letters from readers of all ages and colors who write to say I've written their story. The raggedy state of my books that some readers and educators hand me to sign is the best compliment of all.

Am I Esperanza? Yes. And no. And then again, maybe. One thing I know for sure: you, the reader, are Esperanza. So I should ask, What happened to you? Did you stay in school? Did you go to college? Did you have that baby? Were you a victim? Did you tell anyone about it or did you keep it inside? Did you let it overpower and eat you? Did you wind up in jail? Did someone harm you? Did you hurt someone? What happened to Margarita, Fatboy, Gizmo, Angélica, Leticia, María, Rubén, Silvia, José, Dagoberto, Refugia, Bobby? Will you go back to school, find somebody to take care of the baby while you're finishing your diploma, go to college, work two jobs so you can do it, get help from the substance-abuse people, walk out of a bad marriage, send paychecks to the woman who bore your child, learn to be a human being you're not ashamed of? Did you run away from home? Did you join a gang? Did you get fired? Did you give up? Did you get angry?

You are Esperanza. You can't forget who you are.

I Can Live *Sola* and
I Love to Work

I wrote the following as a keynote speech for the national conference of the Women's Caucus for the Arts, January 24, 1995, San Antonio, Texas. I often wove my creative writing into my speeches. As I've said before, the idea of delivering a speech scared me then; I didn't feel I was an authority on anything, least of all me. But performing finished poetry or fiction made it easier for me to bridge my thoughts in between.

It's interesting for me to reread this and remember how much Texas felt like home once. This was especially so when I found my tribe, a group of artists and art lovers whose careers intersected with my own, making my evenings effervescently social. But San Antonio is all about tribes, and once your tribe breaks up or migrates, you're on your own.

I'm forty years old. I'm a writer earning her keep by her pen. I can live alone and I love to work. And since we're in San Antonio, Texas, I feel it important to add I'm not related to Henry Cisneros, the ex-mayor and current secretary of housing, although I do have one brother, a cousin, two uncles, had a grandfather and a great-grandfather by that name. I mention this because I want to make it clear I didn't grow up with family or political connections that might have opened doors for me. The truth is, I'm an uphol-

My aunt Lily (Eulalia Cordero) holding
me in her arms on my baptism day, and
my maternal grandmother, Felipa (María
Romualda Felipa Anguiano de Cordero)

sterer's daughter, and there were a hell of a lot of doors I had to
wedge open, not to mention kick down.*

My mother is a housewife, her mother was a housewife,
and her mother, and before her, who remembers? In my family, women are so anonymous their grandchildren don't know

---

* Rereading this at fifty-nine years of age, almost twenty years later, I want to add there
were and are a lot of women I have to thank who opened doors for me and continue to
shove me forward. Their names are in the acknowledgments as well as scattered throughout these pages.

their names, and if they're remarked upon at all, it's only to note who they married, who they gave birth to. These women, the so-and-sos, my ancestors. Who wanted to be like them? Not me, I thought—I wanted to be a who, as in the *Who's Who* directory. I wanted something other than somebody's mother, someone's wife.

During my twenties, I wrote my first book of poetry and my first book of fiction. I was just out of graduate school, teaching high school because I was too afraid to apply for a teaching job at an institution of higher learning even though I had an MFA from the Iowa Writers' Workshop. Applying for a job at a college or university might confirm my worst fears—that I didn't belong in the world of letters, that I wasn't smart enough, good enough. In graduate school, I often felt like an intruder, intimidated by the wealth and sophistication of my classmates. So how could I possibly feel I had anything to offer as an instructor? I took a job teaching high school dropouts in the barrio, and on weekends, when I wasn't too exhausted, I tried to write.

I remember someone gave me a women's calendar, and I cut out a Mary Cassatt quote, "I can live alone and I love to work," which I taped to the refrigerator and repeated daily like a mantra. Every month, when the apartment was empty, when there wasn't enough heat, when there was no new love or old to distract me, I would fall into a terrible grief and cry for hours. I couldn't explain where all this sadness came from. Was *this* the writer's life? The truth was, I didn't like living alone and to hell with work. I wanted to be happy.

The twenties are a difficult decade for any woman, but I'd felt they were especially so for me. I was living alone; not unusual for a white woman, but a rare thing for a Mexican American daughter who had left her father's house with neither husband nor child. Rather, I'd fled the racket of my parents' home with poetry as my excuse. Solitude, I claimed, was the necessity of every artist.

My eldest brother hissed, "We know why you *really* want to be alone." Fueled by my brother, Father suspected the worst—I had a sexuality. Like all Mexican fathers, Father wanted me to remain neuter until a man came to ask him for my hand, and if no one came to ask, neuter I was to remain, destined until death to the old maid's task of "dressing saints." I can joke about all this now, but back then it was terrible to receive my father and elder brother's condemnation. I was no better than la Malinche, Hernán Cortés's Mexican mistress, who aided the Spaniards in conquering Mexico. I had betrayed my culture, they said, and I was young enough to half-believe them.

Father blamed my college education for ruining me. After all, I was behaving just like those white women with loose morals, loose drawers, and loose ideas—like living alone without the support and protection of *la familia. ¿Vas a vivir sola?*

Sola. No one in my family lived solo, not even the men. They stayed home until marriage and sometimes did not leave even then.

Back then, crying was so much a part of my life, I assumed everyone cried as regularly as I did. At night in my drafty Chicago apartment, I prayed burglars wouldn't break in and mice wouldn't gnaw through the walls. Maybe Father was right. Where was the writer I imagined I'd be—happily tap-tapping on a typewriter in a house by the sea?

THE POET REFLECTS ON HER SOLITARY FATE

> She lives alone now.
> Has abandoned the brothers,
> the rooms of fathers
> and many mothers.

They have left her
to her own device.
Her nightmares and pianos.
She owns a lead pipe.

The stray lovers
have gone home.
The house is cold.
There is nothing on TV.
She must write poems.

I was writing a book called *My Wicked Wicked Ways,* which one male friend found disappointingly unwicked, but he was looking for wicked as defined by a man, or perhaps a white woman. And neither men nor white women could help me in my route to be an artist. I wouldn't discover the Latina feminists until later. Because I knew no Latinas who could guide me, I had to invent myself, or reinvent myself, as Mexican feminist Rosario Castellanos so aptly put it. Until I met Norma Alarcón, then just a graduate student at Indiana University, I didn't realize how difficult it had been for me to break out of that Bastille, my father's house. My Chicana feminism began with Norma, by sharing our stories, comparing our escape routes out of our fathers' houses, and claiming the right to a life of letters.

The poems from the *My Wicked Wicked Ways* manuscript earned me a national writing fellowship. My escape from the Midwest—at last!—first to Europe, and later to Texas—yes, *sola.* I have to admit moving to Texas was one of my years of terror, worse than traveling to a foreign country where I didn't speak the language. After Europe, Texas was a foreign country to me; when I arrived in 1984, I thought I'd landed in Macondo, that sleepy jungle village from Gabriel García Márquez's *One Hundred Years of Solitude.* This couldn't be the United States. It was as magically unreal as Latin America. How, for example, could a city so undeniably Mexican hail itself on taxi placards as "San Antonio, All American City"? Or where else would a parrot find its picture on the front page of the newspaper beneath the headline "Called to the Witness Stand"? It was wonderful or scary, depending on your point of view.

I'd expected the women's community to take me in, for it to be there for me as it had been in the Midwest, but the community of women I found in San Antonio was fractured, divided by color and class, and isolated from itself, let alone from communities beyond its own region. Like the citizens of Macondo, I found it a community locked in its provinciality, still discovering ice, still discovering that the world is round. I was surprised it was the gay community that sheltered and nurtured me, specifically the Latino visual artists, and they are still, for the most part, the crowd I run with. I reason this is because they too understand about having to reinvent oneself, about taking from tradition that which nurtures and abandoning the elements that would mean self-destruction.

I have a theory—one's most charming trait is also one's fatal flaw; the one thing you like about somebody is usually their worst defect as well. So too with communities. The *comadre-ismo,* as I've witnessed it, has kept other women out. On the other hand, the opposite extreme of this xenophobia is the over-nurturing among the women that creates the "That's nice, *mi'ja"* syndrome, which doesn't help anybody in the long run and fosters mediocrity.

As a Latina, I don't want to inherit certain legacies. I don't want to inherit mothers laying down their lives like a Sir Raleigh cloak and asking everyone to step all over them. I don't want to inherit my mother's fear of doing anything alone or her self-destructive anger. I don't want to inherit my paternal grandmother's petty jealousies and possessiveness. I don't want to inherit my maternal grandmother's silence and passivity.* I don't want to *quedar bien,* be nice, with the men around me at the expense of my own dreams and happiness. I don't want to be the mother of twelve children, seven, five, even one, but I do want to write stories for one child, five, seven, twelve, a million children.

I do want to inherit the witch in my women ancestors—the willfullness, the passion, *ay,* the passion where all good art comes from as women, the perseverance, the survivor skills, the courage, the strength of *las mujeres bravas, peleoneras, necias, berrinchudas.* I want to be *una brava, peleonera, necia, berrinchuda.* I want to be bad if bad means I must go against society—el Papá, el Pápa, the boyfriend, lover, husband, girlfriends, *comadres*—and listen to my own heart, that incredible witch's broom that will take me where I need to go.

I do want to create art beyond rage. Rage is a place to begin, but not end. I'm not as wise as my work, but I know if I take the writing deep enough, something larger and greater than myself will flash forth and illuminate me, heal me. I do want to devour my demons—despair, grief, shame, fear—and use them to nourish my art. Otherwise they'll devour me.

There are nights like a Gethsemane when I'm overwhelmed,

---

* When I originally wrote this essay, I took my mother's version of her mother for granted. Now that I'm older I realize my mother didn't like or know her own mother very well and dismissed her by claiming she was weak and passive, and implied she didn't want to be like her. What she saw as her mother's weak, passive behavior, I now recognize as strength and resilience. My maternal grandmother, Felipa Anguiano de Cordero, had to endure a great deal of physical and mental duress in order to survive. As a young girl, she was hidden under clay pots when the government or rebels descended on her village, in order to save her from rape. She was "abducted" by her husband-to-be, and had to make do and accept him as her husband because she had no other choice. In her lifetime, she endured the death of several children, both as babies and as adults. She emigrated with toddlers in hand and was possibly pregnant during her voyage north from Mexico to the States, all this during the violence of the Mexican Revolution. She had to make a new home for herself and her family in several U.S. towns, sometimes living in tents, before finally relocating to Chicago just before the Great Depression. At the end of her life she learned how to read. And—she had second sight, she could see with more than her eyes. This to me doesn't appear to be a weak woman. I look up to her now as a woman of great mental strength, fortitude, and courage.

by the work, the loneliness of my life as a writer, and wonder why I didn't take up something more sociable, like becoming a flamenco dancer or an opera diva, but I'm sure flamenco dancers and opera divas have the same complaints.

I'm convinced if we're to be artists of any worth we must lock ourselves in a room and work. There are no two ways around this one, no shortcut, no magic word to save the day. Take it as a given, you'll cry, despair, think you'll die, that you can't possibly do it, that it's a lonely task, you'll lose faith in yourself, especially at night. But when you finish crying and despairing, you can wipe your eyes and . . . the work is still there waiting. So you better roll up your sleeves and get moving, girl! Nobody's going to do the work for you. If you're serving others other than your art, then it just takes longer. In the words of Tillie Olsen, "Evil is whatever distracts."

And please don't come out of that workroom until the work is finished, otherwise you're liable to enter into "The Emperor's New Clothes." Your friends are likely to say, "Isn't it beautiful, isn't it lovely," because no one has the nerve to tell you the truth. Again the "That's nice, *mi'ja*" syndrome. We can't afford as women to be mediocre, or even good, especially not now. We don't have that luxury. Our best weapon in adverse times—excellence.

What grieves me after ten years of living here in Texas is that there are still women spinning straw into straw, or into brass, or into lesser metals, women doing the same art they were doing ten years ago or very little beyond it, which means they haven't given their art the time it deserves. At first I listened sympathetically to their tales of woe, but after ten years the victims are still victims, women carrying their little gray cloud on a stick—the husband who left, or the one they won't leave. And frankly I don't want to hear about your kids. We make choices. I'm not going to blame you because I'm childless; true, there is no one to get in my way, but there is also no one there to hug me when I need to be hugged.

We must spin our own straw, not our neighbor's. "Tell the truth. Your truth," the writer Dorothy Allison has written. There is power in your work if you come at it from that place uniquely yours, not your sister's, but yours. Otherwise we risk creating stereotypes. If I see another work of art that glorifies *la abuelita,* I'm going to throw a *berrinche.* Aren't our grandmothers worth portraying with all of their sins, and, frankly, women with sins are more interesting than *santas.*

After ten years of wandering I've found the house in the heart, the place where I belong. Ten years have passed since circumstances first brought me here, and though I'm self-employed now and could live anywhere, I've chosen San Antonio as my home. I've found finally a place that is all about self-invention. For me these borderlands match my interior landscape of being both Mexican and 'Merican at the same time.

I'm forty. I can live *sola* and, as much as I complain, the truth is, I really do love to work. In fact, I'm at my healthiest, happiest when I'm working. I didn't know my grandmothers, the so-and-sos, but I know my task is to invent their lives, or reinvent them, as the case may be, to give them names, to name their fears, sins, pettiness, dreams, secrets, shames, lies, pride, and power. Perhaps I'm lucky not knowing them. I'm not, after all, constricted by the truth and can give my imagination full rein. I like to think I'm inventing the truth. I'm listening to voices nobody listened to, setting their lives down on paper how many years later? And that writing is a resistance, an act against forgetting, a war against oblivion, against not counting, as women.

Tapicero's Daughter

I was commissioned to give this lecture by the Isabella Stewart Gardner Museum in Boston, and I delivered it in a hall fit for a king's coronation on September 19, 1995, as part of their "Eye of the Beholder" series. The house was packed, which only added to my nerves. I was also trying to finish *Caramelo,* a novel exploring my father's life, and thought writing the lecture would help give me clarity. Both my parents were still alive then. The original lecture included excerpts from my novel, which I've removed, but I've incorporated some of the ad-libbed comments from the performance and edited them here in a final written form.

The series concept was to invite contemporary artists to give an original lecture about an object within the collection. Because the ISG Museum was the personal collection of its namesake, an art collector/philanthropist/heiress, with a definitive request in her will that nothing be removed or altered, the lectures were an attempt to puncture insularity and let in fresh air.

And so, when I walked through the museum on my previsit, I paused among many fine and marvelous items, and with only an inkling of what I was doing, decided I would focus on upholstery. Jill Medvedow, the series curator, said, "We've never had anyone write about upholstery. Wonderful!" And that "wonderful" gave me permission to move forward. Loretta Lynn's *Coal Miner's Daughter* inspired the title.

It was the pre-digital era, and my lecture included two carousels of slides. The talk was the single most nerve-racking I've ever given in my life, bar none. I was still shifting slides around at the last minute. I felt sick and dizzy. Had I made this simple lecture too complicated? After all, unlike other artists in the series, I hadn't selected one single item from the ISG collection, but several. To make sure I was even more frazzled, I included the work of six contemporary San Antonio artists, several autobiographical photos from family albums, and slides of my mother's and my aunt's possessions I had to ask my brother to document without arousing their ire. It was a lot of stress and terror, until I heard the public laugh, and from then on, loads of fun.

I. *Cuando me muera, entonces te darás cuenta de cuánto te quiere tu padre.* (When I die, then you'll realize how much your father loves you.)

—MY FATHER

O nce there was a girl who was me.
        I hope you don't mind; this first image has a bit of nudity. And if you do mind, you can close your eyes. It's a topless photo of me. This is my first photo ever; I give photographers that same squint even now.

Every week when I was still a girl, my family and I would spend Sunday afternoons at a museum. We were nine in all—two adults, seven children—and this has a lot to do with why we went to museums, because Sunday was the day museums were free.

Mother was our social director. Father was our chauffeur, but his feet hurt all the time. Sometimes he came home from work so tired he couldn't untie his own shoes. He was by trade *un tapicero,* an upholsterer. On Sundays all he wanted was to lie down. But Mother

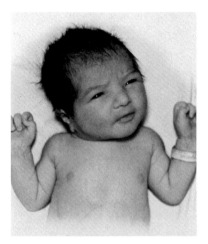

First portrait

couldn't drive and refused to take public transportation (she preferred to walk when possible ever since childhood, and when she couldn't, she reasoned that's what Father's car was for). So every weekend Father delivered us to the Chicago Field Museum of Natural History, the Museum of Science and Industry, the Art Institute, the Shedd Aquarium, and the Adler Planetarium, where he would dutifully wait for us on a bench or outside under a tree.

I was especially fond of the Field Museum, a lovely Greek temple of a building with giant mastodons in the foyer. In my head I pretended the Field Museum was my house and that Grant Park was my private garden. I pretended I was disguised as an ordinary citizen, and that all the visitors to my home walked right past me without recognizing me as me. And when it was time to leave and return to my real neighborhood of crowded buildings and crowded lives, to the little red bungalow on North Campbell Street that would later become the model for the house in *The House on Mango Street,* I pretended I was a girl in a fairy tale, disguised since birth as a *tapicero*'s daughter.

My museum house was just a fantasy, a tale I told myself before sleep to keep me quiet. It was a story I never told my parents or my six brothers. To tell, after all, would break the spell. How could I explain what it was I was hungry for?

At night Father soaked his blistered feet in a plastic tub while he watched TV and ate his dinner. What story, I wondered then, did Father tell himself to keep from crying? Once, when he was still a young man in Mexico City, Father had been *un fanfarrón,* a dandy. But then he ran away from home. It was the early '40s. He was headed to his uncle Parrot's house in Philadelphia. Somewhere in Memphis, Tennessee, the police picked Father up because, as he put it, there were no young men on the streets during those years of the war. Father was escorted to the nearest enlistment center. And by the time he got to the City of Brotherly Love, his draft papers were waiting for him.

Father in his *fanfarrón* days, posing in front of a
stranger's house, Mexico City

Father in the U.S. Army while stationed in Korea

That's the story Father tells about how he became a U.S. citizen, even though he couldn't speak English. That's how he wound up in occupied Japan and Korea, with other non-English-speaking infantrymen fleeing their own histories. And that's how Father got to be an upholsterer for the U.S. Army, practicing what little skills he'd learned from Uncle Parrot, the real upholsterer of the family, and making furniture for the officers' club.

After he was discharged, Father remained in the United States and married Mother. Unlike his fellow Chicanos, Mexicans born in the United States, Father thought he was better than everybody. I think this was because he was *un chilango*—that is, a citizen from Mexico City. People from Mexico City always think they're better than everybody else, because in their eyes Mexico City is the center of the universe. To him Mexico was civilized compared to the United States, where some of his fellow soldiers didn't even know how to hold a pencil and write their own name. Because Father couldn't speak English, he'd been put in a class with the illiterates, and this was an indelible experience for him since he'd studied to be an accountant, as he liked to remind us, at the Universidad de México. (Father dropped out after one semester because he was too busy socializing instead of studying, and his poor grades made him afraid to face his strict father. Instead, he ran away from home and wandered north. He would regret not finishing his studies the rest of his life.)

"¡Qué país tan bárbaro!" Father would say. What a barbarous country!

It was this overdose of pride that saved Father from the daily blows life dealt him. Father was proud even as *un tapicero.* He didn't work with a staple gun and strips of cardboard. No, sir. He was a craftsman. Eventually Father would work for an interior decorating firm on the North Shore, where the houses of Lake Forest, Winnetka, Kenilworth were as big as museums.

I grew up listening to Father muttering nervously each night about the leather wing chair he needed to finish for la Señora Carson's party. The chaise for la Señora Lassiter. The davenport he had promised la Señora Hudson in time for Thanksgiving. His *señoras* were fussy. But, thankfully, so was Father.

What Mother and I looked forward to was the expensive upholstery remnants Father brought home; leftovers from some inexperienced interior decorator might mean we could cover a flea-market footstool or a cushion for a love seat, if we were lucky, from the same bolt of fabric of a Senator Percy or even a Señora Stewart Gardner. It didn't stop there. Mother transformed fabric scraps into an elegant wardrobe for my Barbie dolls. An ivory brocade stole with matching turban. A silver metallic miniskirt. A sumptuous velvet opera cape.

By the time I stopped playing with dolls, Father's work was of such high quality he'd even been selected to upholster a White House antique. We bragged about that the way our ancestors bragged about the grandfather who played the piano for the president/dictator Porfirio Díaz.

I am thinking all this as I step into Isabella Stewart Gardner's house. I know I should be impressed by the Botticellis and Vermeers, but I'm looking at the furniture the same rude way my father checks out a chair before sitting down. Scrutinizing the seams, examining the fabric to see if the upholsterer knew enough to match the patterns, paying attention to the details that mean custom, quality work, work done with pride. Not something that looked *"como si lo hicieran con los pies,"* as if someone made it with their feet.

I remember Father bringing home things he found in between the couch cushions—foreign coins among the dog hairs, a beautiful gray pearl he made into a tiepin. (Don't ask why he didn't give it back. Would you?) And I can't help but wonder what was found in between Isabella Stewart Gardner's couch cushions after a lifetime of dinner parties.

I'm also hauling all of my life with me as I go through these rooms. All my relatives and friends. What strikes me is the similarities between the house of the wealthy art collector Isabella Stewart Gardner and my mother's, that supreme collector of anything found in thrift stores, garage sales, and liquidations, who planted the collector's seed in me. These cabinets filled with precious items remind me of my mother's china cabinets filled with *tiliches,* trinkets, the precious next to the not-so-precious.

I mean no disrespect to Isabella Stewart Gardner's exceptional collection, but considering her means, my mother too traveled far and wide ransacking flea markets and antique fairs, Goodwills and Salvation Armies, alleys and attics, and Chicago's Maxwell Street for her treasures. And they are no less dear to her, and she is no less adamant about anybody touching or altering their arrangement.

My mother's first-floor kitchen,
Keeler Street house

Three plaster Graces stand above my mother's kitchen sink and
are a family joke. They're not exactly a precise reproduction of
Antonio Canova's original. If you turn them around you'll notice
the forger took liberties: they all have droopy butts. My father
bought them outside the Vatican on my parents' first and only
trip to Europe. And they weigh a ton! Father dragged these three
around six countries like a personal penance. Someday I'll have to
put them in a story to make his labor worthwhile.

I'm also struck by another similarity between Isabella Stewart
Gardner's taste in furnishings and that of the community where I
was raised. Which leads me to my next point.

II. *No es desgracia ser pobre, pero es muy inconveniente.*
(It's no disgrace to be poor, but it's very inconvenient.)
—A Mexican saying attributed to my uncle Fat-face,
but no doubt picked up from some other clever *mexicano,*
who remains, like most clever *mexicanos,* anonymous

The poor don't want to be poor. In Brazil they work all year just so that at carnival they can dress like kings. In my neighborhood, the ideal was to live like a king, preferably in a palace like Versailles. Or like Empress Carlota's castle in Chapultepec. When you don't have access to Venetian antique dealers, where do you

Rossi's Furniture showroom

Furniture from the collection at the Isabella Stewart Gardner Museum

| Aunt Margaret's painting | *La Gitana,* Louis Kronberg, |
| | Isabella Stewart Gardner Museum |

shop to live like a king? Rossi's, West 26th Street in Chicago. This is what I thought when I saw Isabella Stewart Gardner's home.

(We were able to get these photos thanks to my brother Keeks, who told them we were shopping for a gift for our parents' upcoming anniversary. Not true, but it was a good story.)

I also thought about the artwork I grew up with as I wandered the museum. I paused in front of a portrait of a Gypsy lady, *La Gitana,* by Louis Kronberg; I didn't realize why until later when I got home. It reminded me of my aunt Margaret's house and the kind of paintings I grew up with. Aunt Margaret, by the way, did not buy this painting. It came with her second husband. She has two daughters, and she did not want that woman with her big *chichis* in their living room. But Uncle Richard refused to give her up. I remember as a child the painting spooked us, because no matter where you walked, the woman kept following you with her eyes. Later on, Aunt Margaret told me she found out some rich people who live in Water Tower Place had this very same painting, and that made her feel better about keeping it.

iii. We live like millionaires.

—FRANCO MONDINI-RUIZ after Danny López Lozano,
folk art seller and mentor

My friend Franco Mondini-Ruiz is an artist who sees elegance in the *rascuache,* the gaudy, kitsch, funky. Franco's shop, Infinito Botánica, is a place filled with the extraordinary and the divine, as he puts it. He is a painter, art curator, sculptor, businessman, and lots of fun at parties.

For my fortieth birthday he gave me a plate of chocolate-chip cookies wrapped in plastic wrap. But the chips were fourth-century Etruscan coins.

Once he removed all his furnishings from his house, borrowed interesting items from his friends, and created an installation in every room of objects lined up on the floor in a grid pattern, including the bathroom. It was beautiful, even though some of our things were never returned.

When Franco went to Mexico City, he was inspired to do the same grid design in a public space. He was staying in the old colonial center of downtown, in an apartment that looked out into a plaza. One night he got the idea to collect the garbage in the square and rearrange it like a chessboard. *"Ay, qué bonito,"* people on the street said, how beautiful. They didn't want anyone to touch it, not even the street sweepers the next morning.

Shortly after this installation, Franco was taken ill and hospitalized. Friends said it was from picking up corncobs from Mexico

Naturaleza Muerta, by Franco Mondini-Ruiz, Plaza Santa Catarina,
Mexico City

City streets. But knowing Franco, I think it was from picking up
worse things than corncobs, if you know what I mean.

When I was looking at the ironwork in the museum, I thought
of my friend Rolando Briseño. Rolando was commissioned by the
City of San Antonio to create a memorial on the San Antonio
River commemorating the 300th anniversary of the conception
of the city, on the site where a Spanish expedition celebrated their
first Mass in 1691.

Rolando also paints canvases that usually involve food and
fighting. Sometimes his paintings are painted on tablecloths. He's
a food purist, a man who doesn't even like to mix his rice with his
beans. The last time I had dinner with him, there was a big fight
over *mole,* Mexican chocolate sauce, but that's another story.

The artist Anne Wallace is originally from Galveston, but
now makes her home in San Antonio. Influenced by classical
Greek sculpture, Anne likes fragmentation in her sculptures and

Lunch tablescape, by Rolando Briseño

Amando en tiempo de guerra, by Anne Wallace

the gestures they might suggest. She works with regional Texas wood, like mesquite, and many of her pieces reflect her political involvement with Amnesty International and a refugee-assistance council on the U.S.-Mexico border. I include sculptures of Anne's influenced by fragments of classical statues, like ones found in the Isabella Stewart Gardner collection.

When I first visited the museum, I paused at a display of religious vestments, the kind Catholic priests wear when they celebrate Mass. And I couldn't help but think of my friend David

David Zamora Casas dressed to be noticed

Zamora Casas, a San Antonio painter, sculptor, and performance artist. Some of the outfits he wears are actual priest's vestments. It often gets confusing when people mistake him for a priest and ask for his blessing. This wouldn't be so scandalous, except he goes right ahead and blesses them. I thought if David were here he might want to borrow these vestments and wear them at his next opening. I include a slide of David modeling a stunning Chiapas skirt in front of Frida Kahlo's Blue House in Coyoacán. He told me the guard kept shouting, "Hey, you can't do that here. Don't put on that skirt." But he did anyway.

Here is David Zamora Casas, who not only decorates himself, but his entire house; the Anti-Oppression Church of Folk Art is a building swathed in cloth and statues and original art. It's something to look at. I especially like his sculptures. I have one of his Virgen de Guadalupes made of found objects, bones and barbed wire and ironwork, in my backyard.

Here's my friend Ito Romo. Not only is he an artist, he is a

Ito and me, Torres Taco Heaven

writer as well. And he's a great cook. Lately he's become influenced by Mexican funeral wreaths. Now he's creating spiritual pieces influenced by his recent interest in Buddhism and issues on the border.

I paused in front of these green ceramic pots during my museum tour. They're not valuable, I'm told, but they're certainly beautiful. They say something about Isabella Stewart Gardner and her love of beauty. And I thought my friend Terry Ybáñez would love them too. She'd love to break them! She uses shards of pottery and antique plates and anything you give her to frame her paintings. We've worked together on book covers and a children's book. But her work lately has been influenced by Mexican pottery decorated with mirrors, as well as by the roofs of Mexican buildings studded with broken glass to keep out thieves. It's a lucky thing Terry recycles items, because I break a lot of dishes.

Segment of a mural honoring Emma Tenayuca, by Terry Ybáñez. (This building was sold in 2015, and no doubt this wall will disappear due to gentrification.)

This is one of Terry's murals at the Quick Wash Laundromat on South Presa Street, in San Antonio. It tells the story of Emma Tenayuca, the labor organizer who helped the San Antonio pecan shellers in the 1930s, most of whom were Mexican women. I thought, *Wouldn't it be nice if Isabella Stewart Gardner were still alive; she could get Terry to do a mural on the outside wall for all the people who clean this museum.*

Among the artists whose work hangs in my home is the last artist I want to mention, Angel Rodríguez Díaz. He does a lot of

The Protagonist of an Endless Story,
by Angel Rodríguez Díaz

self-portraits as well as portraits, and I thought if Isabella were alive she might commission a portrait. Especially after she saw mine, *The Protagonist of an Endless Story*. It embarrassed me to have it in my home, because it looked like I'd commissioned it. It was hanging in a public space, my office, which happened then to be my living room. You could see it when you drove by. I knew what the neighbors were probably thinking—*Oh, that woman!* So I was relieved when the Smithsonian purchased it, and it left my house for the National Portrait Gallery in Washington, D.C.

And, of course, I'm wearing one of the outfits from my collection of vintage Mexican textiles. It just starts out with one dress, and then the next thing you know . . . Well, maybe that's what Isabella said.

iv. *Naciste bajo una estrella.*
(You were born under a star.)
—MY FATHER

Whenever anything good happens in my life, my father is quick to remind me I was born lucky, and I guess it's true. I'm lucky to be the daughter of *un tapicero* whose appreciation for cloth taught me to love textiles from an early age and to honor one's craft. I'm also the daughter of an intelligent, self-taught woman whose passion for collecting trained me to single out the remarkable from the ordinary through an internship of estate sales, thrift shops, flea markets, and, yes, weekly visits to museums.

Like Isabella Stewart Gardner, I too am a collector. In the course of my years in Texas, I've drawn near me an extraordinary collection of friends whose creativity inspires my own. They each teach me to take the time to admire what no one else might see, to trust what delights and uplifts the spirit. This community travels with me as I wander these opulent rooms. And this in turn allows me to redefine beauty on more generous terms.

I want to close with a quote from Jorge Luis Borges's *Seven Nights:* "Beauty is a physical sensation, something we feel with our whole body. It is not the result of a judgment. We do not arrive at it by way of rules. We either feel beauty or we don't."

Guadalupe the Sex Goddess

Our Lady, by Alma López

Artist Alma López was inspired to create a feminist Guadalupe after reading the following selection. When exhibited
in Albuquerque, it ignited a religious war that drew commentary from almost everyone, including the New Mexican
archbishop. Maybe a contemporary Willa Cather is needed to
capture what happened, because the press and protesters vili-

fied Alma's artwork as a "bikini-clad Virgin" instead of seeing its intention—a woman empowered by the goddess in herself. Both Alma and the exhibition's brave curator, Tey Marianna Nunn, were harassed to the point of needing police protection. Worst of all, they were not allowed to explain their perspective as one of celebration, not defamation. Fortunately, a detailed account of the hysteria has appeared since in *Our Lady of Controversy: Alma López's "Irreverent Apparition,"* edited by Alicia Gaspar de Alba and Alma herself, which I highly recommend.

I n high school I marveled at how white women strutted around the locker room, nude as pearls, as unashamed of their brilliant bodies as the Nike of Samothrace. Maybe they were hiding terrible secrets like bulimia or anorexia, but to my naive eye then, I thought of them as women comfortable in their skin.

You could always tell us Latinas. We hid when we undressed, modestly facing a wall, or, in my case, dressing in a bathroom stall. We were the ones who still used bulky sanitary pads instead of tampons, thinking ourselves morally superior to our white classmates. "My mama said you can't use tampons till after you're married." All Latina mamas said this, yet how come none of us thought to ask our mothers why they didn't use tampons *after* getting married?

Womanhood was full of mysteries. I was as ignorant about my own body as any female ancestor who hid behind a sheet with a hole in the center when husband or doctor called. Religion and our culture, our culture and religion, helped to create that blur, a vagueness about what went on "down there." So ashamed was I about my own "down there" that until I had my first period I had no idea I had another orifice called the vagina; I thought my period would arrive via the urethra or perhaps through the walls of my skin.

No wonder, then, that it was too terrible to think about a doctor—a man!—looking at you down there when you could never bring yourself to look. *¡Ay, nunca!* How could I acknowledge my sexuality, let alone enjoy sex, with so much guilt? In the guise of modesty my culture locked me in a double chastity belt of ignorance and *vergüenza,* shame.

I'd never seen my mother nude. I'd never taken a good look at myself either. Privacy for self-exploration belonged to the wealthy. In my home a private space was practically impossible; aside from the doors that opened to the street, the only room with a lock was the bathroom, and how could anyone who shared a bathroom with eight other people stay in there for more than a few minutes? Before college, no one in my family had a room of their own except me, a narrow closet just big enough for my twin bed and an oversized blond dresser we'd bought in the bargain basement of *el Sears.* The dresser was as long as a coffin and blocked the door from shutting completely. I had my own room, but I never had the luxury of shutting the door.

I didn't even see my own sex until a nurse at the Emma Goldman Clinic in Iowa City showed it to me. "Would you like to see your cervix? Yours is dilating. You must be ovulating. Here's a mirror, take a look." When had anyone ever suggested I take a look or allowed me a speculum to take home and investigate myself at leisure!

I'd been to only one other birth control facility prior to the Emma Goldman Clinic, and that was the University of Iowa Medical Center across town. I was a twenty-one-year-old grad student far (for me) from home for the first time. Before Iowa, I'd been afraid and ashamed to seek out a gynecologist and become responsible for my own fertility; but now that I was contemplating new partners, I was even more afraid of becoming pregnant. Still, I agonized about making a gyne appointment for weeks. Perhaps the anonymity and distance from my family allowed me finally to take control of my life. I remember wanting to be fearless like the other women around me, to be able to have sex when I wanted, but I was too afraid to explain to a would-be lover how I'd had sex with only one other man in my life, and we'd practiced withdrawal. Would he laugh at me? How could I look anyone in the face and explain why I couldn't go see a gynecologist?

One night a classmate I liked too much took me home with him. I meant all along to say something about how I wasn't on anything, but I never quite found my voice, never the right moment to cry out, "Stop, this is dangerous to my brilliant career!" Too afraid to sound stupid, afraid to ask him to take responsibility too, I said nothing, and I let him take me like that with nothing protecting me from motherhood but luck. The days that followed were torture, but fortunately on Mother's Day my period arrived, and I celebrated my non-maternity by making an appointment with the family planning center.

When I see pregnant teens, I can't help but think that could've been me. In high school I would've thrown myself into love the way some warriors throw themselves into fighting. I was ready to sacrifice everything in the name of love, to do anything, even risk my own life, but thankfully there were no takers. I was enrolled at an all-girls school. I think if I had met a boy who would have me, I would've had sex in a minute, convinced this was love. I have always had enough imagination to fall in love all by myself, then and now.

I tell you this story because I'm overwhelmed by the silence regarding Latinas and our bodies. If I, as a graduate student, was shy about talking to anyone about my body and sex, imagine how difficult it must be for a young girl in middle school or high school living in a home with no lock on the bedroom door, perhaps with no door, or maybe with no bedroom, no information other than misinformation from the girlfriends and the boyfriend. So much guilt, so much silence, and such a yearning to be loved, no wonder young women find themselves having sex while they are still children, having sex without sexual protection, too ashamed to confide their feelings and fears to anyone.

What a culture of denial. Don't get pregnant! But no one tells you how not to. If you can't control your fertility, you can't control your destiny. No wonder Church, State, and Family want to keep you in the dark.

This is why I was angry for so many years every time I saw la Virgen de Guadalupe, my culture's role model for brown women like me. La Lupe was damn dangerous, an ideal so lofty and unrealistic it was laughable. Did boys have to aspire to be Jesus? I never saw any evidence of it. They were fornicating like rabbits while the Church ignored them and pointed us women toward our destiny— marriage and motherhood. The other alternative was *puta*hood.

In my neighborhood I knew only real women, neither saints nor whores, naïve and vulnerable *huerquitas* like me who wanted desperately to fall in love, with the heart and soul. And yes, "down there" with the *panocha*, too.

As far as I could see, la Lupe was nothing but a Goody-Two-Shoes meant to doom me to a life of unhappiness. Thanks, but no thanks. Motherhood and/or marriage were anathema to my career. But being a bad girl—that was something I could use as a writer, a Molotov to toss at my papa and el Papa who had their own plans for me. I took the wicked route and wrote poetry with titles like *My Wicked Wicked Ways* and *Loose Woman*.

Discovering sex was like discovering writing. It was powerful in a way I couldn't explain. Like writing, you had to go beyond the guilt and shame to get to anything good. Like writing, it could take you to deep and mysterious subterranean levels. With each new depth I found out things about myself I didn't know I knew. And, like writing, for a slip of a moment it could be spiritual, the cosmos pivoting on a pin, could empty and fill you all at once like a Ganges, a Piazzolla tango, a tulip bending in the wind. I was no one, I was nothing, and I was everything in the universe little and large—twig, cloud, sky. How had this incredible energy been denied me!

When I look at la Virgen de Guadalupe now, she is not the Lupe of my childhood, no longer the one in my grandparents' house in Tepeyac, nor is she the one of the Roman Catholic Church, the one I bolted the door against in my teens and twenties. Like every woman who matters to me, I have had to search for her in the rubble of history. And I have found her. She is Guadalupe the sex goddess, a goddess who makes me feel good about my sexual power, my sexual energy, who reminds me I must, as the writer and Jungian Clarissa Pinkola Estés so aptly put it, "[speak] from the vulva . . . speak the most basic, honest truth," and write from my *panocha*.

In my research of Guadalupe's pre-Columbian antecedents, the she before the Church de-sexed her, I found Aztec Mother Earth Tonantzin, and inside Tonantzin a pantheon of other mother goddesses. I discovered Tlazolteotl, the goddess of fertility and sex, also referred to as Totzin, Our Beginnings, or Tzinteotl, goddess of the rump. *Putas,* nymphos, and other loose women were known as "women of the sex goddess." Tlazolteotl was the patron of sexual passion, and though she had the power to stir you to sin, she could also forgive you and cleanse you of your sexual transgressions via her priests who heard confession. In this aspect of confessor Tlazolteotl was known as Tlaelcuani, the filth eater. Maybe you've seen her; she's the one sold in the tourist markets

Mexico City Zócalo, 1985

even now, a statue of a woman squatting in childbirth, her face grimacing in pain. Tlazolteotl, then, is a duality of maternity and sexuality. In other words, she is a sexy mama.

To me la Virgen de Guadalupe is also Coatlicue, a bare-breasted creative/destructive force dressed in a serpent skirt and a lei of human skulls, hearts, and hands. When I think of her colossal statue in the National Museum of Anthropology in Mexico City, unearthed several times, then reburied because it was too frightening to look at, I think of a woman enraged, a woman as tempest, a woman *bien berrinchuda*, and I like that. La Lupe as *cabrona*. Not silent and passive, but silently gathering force.

Most days I, too, feel like the creative/destructive goddess Coatlicue, especially the days I'm writing, capable of fabricating pretty tales with pretty words, as well as doing demolition work with a volley of *palabrotas* if I want to. I am the Coatlicue-Lupe whose square column of a body I see in so many Indian women, in my mother, and in myself each time I check out my thick-waisted, flat-assed torso in the mirror.

Coatlicue, Tlazolteotl, Tonantzin, la Virgen de Guadalupe. They are each telescoped one into the other, into who I am. And this is where la Lupe intrigues me—not the Lupe of 1531 who appeared to Juan Diego, a humble indigenous man who would become a saint because of this miraculous encounter, but the one of the 1990s who has shaped who we are as Chicanas/*mexicanas* today, the one inside each Chicana and *mexicana*. Perhaps it's the Tlazolteotl-Lupe in me whose *malcriada* spirit inspires me to leap into the swimming pool naked or dance on a table with a skirt

Basílica de la Virgen de Guadalupe, Tepeyac, 1995

on my head. Maybe it's my Coatlicue-Lupe attitude that makes it possible for my mother to scold, "No wonder men can't stand you!" Who knows? What I do know is this: I am obsessed with becoming a woman comfortable in her skin.

I can't attribute my religious conversion to a flash of lightning on the road to Laredo or anything like that. Instead, there have been several lessons learned subtly over a period of time. A depression and near suicide in my thirty-third year. Thich Nhat Hanh's writing that has brought out the Buddha-Lupe in me. My weekly peace vigil in 1993 for my friend Jasna in Sarajevo. The books of the theorist Gloria Anzaldúa. A crucial trip back to Tepeyac in 1985 with the writers Cherríe Moraga and Norma Alarcón. Drives across Texas talking with other Chicanas. And research for the story "Little Miracles" that would force me back inside the Church from which I'd fled.

My Virgen de Guadalupe is not the mother of God. She *is* God.

Tepeyac, 1985

She is a face for a god without a face, *una indígena* for a god without ethnicity, a female deity for a god who is genderless, but I also understand that for her to approach me, for me to finally open the door and accept her, she had to be a woman like me.

Once, watching a porn film, I saw a sight that terrified me. It was the film star's *panocha*—a tidy, elliptical opening, pink and shiny like a rabbit's ear. To make matters worse, it was shaved and looked especially childlike and unsexual. I think what startled me most was the realization that my own sex has no resemblance to this woman's. My sex, dark as an orchid, rubbery and blue-purple as *pulpo*, an octopus, does not look nice and tidy, but otherwordly. I do not have little rosette nipples. My nipples are big and brown, like the Mexican coins of my childhood.

When I see la Virgen de Guadalupe I want to lift her dress as I did my dolls' and look to see if she comes with *chones*, and does her *panocha* look like mine, and does she have dark nipples too? Yes, I am certain she does. She is not neuter like Barbie. She gave birth. She has a womb. *Blessed art thou and blessed is the fruit of thy womb* . . . Blessed art thou, Lupe, and, therefore, blessed am I.

¡Que Vivan los Colores!

My Purple House, 1997; photo by the late Rick Hunter, for an article
in the *San Antonio Express-News*

The hysteria resulting from my painting my house periwinkle erupted the spring of 1997. Because I was in the middle
of writing my novel *Caramelo,* I wasn't able to properly write
about the incident until I'd finished the book. *House & Garden*
solicited the piece, and it appeared in April 2002. I used some
of my novel's unused "buttons," text all dressed up with no
place to go, to open and close the piece, as well as notes from
my research for my hearing with the San Antonio Historic and
Design Review Commission.

During the "purple" flare-up, I got lots of letters from folks
all over town, the country, and beyond. Inmates in prison

wrote to tell me they were watching my back. Schoolchildren
sent me wise letters of support. I even got a phone call from
a great-grand-descendant of Davy Crockett's, who was fighting a similar battle in Dallas. He had this to say to me: "Go,
Sandra, go!"

Who knew colors would kick up such a ruckus? Because
the Texas sun fades violet to blue, the house formerly known
as purple was painted over and is currently a shade of Mexican
pink. Folks still wander about the neighborhood and ask, "Do
you know where the purple house is?"

I'm writing this preface as my Texas home is about to be
put up for sale. I leave with no regrets and with the certainty
that I'll create a spiritual refuge elsewhere.

I f the universe is a cloth, then all humanity is interwoven with
different-colored threads. Pull one string, and the whole cloth
comes undone. That is why I believe in Destiny. Not the "destiny"
of European origin. But la Divina Providencia *de las Américas.*
Make the sign of the cross and kiss your thumb. Each person who
comes into your life affects your *destino,* and you affect theirs.

A friend of mine went to Mexico and was so overwhelmed by a
vendor's wares, she couldn't make up her mind. The colors made
her dizzy, drove her crazy. Exasperated, she finally appealed to
the shopkeeper. "Which colors go well together, do you think?"
"Señora," he said gently, as if he were talking to a child, "let me
teach you something. All colors go well together."

Color is a language. When I moved to San Antonio, I assumed
everyone here was bilingual, but when I painted my Victorian
house in the historic King William neighborhood a twilight shade
of blue-violet, the Historic and Design Review Commission raised
a red flag. They wanted me to choose from an approved palette

of colonial colors that included Surrey beige, Sèvres blue, Hawthorne green, Frontier Days brown, and Plymouth Rock gray— *colores tristes* in my opinion, and ugly.

To some, my "Purple House" needs no translation. Carmen Caballero's third-grade class at Ball Elementary, San Antonio, wrote me letters of support. "In my opinion," one little girl wrote in formal Spanish, "you should leave your house purple because San Antonio was once Mexico." Memories are nudged awake. An old man selling *paletas* from a pushcart remembers. "Of course there were purple houses, right here in La Villita," he says, citing a neighborhood a few blocks from my home. "There were houses of many colors when I was young: *fresa, limón, sandía, lima . . .*" He names colors as if he were naming flavors from his ice cream stock.

"Vibrant—it gives energy!" A blond jogger shouts her approval without stopping.

"Why are our Mexican colors okay for our city's Fiesta, but not for our own houses?" a local radio deejay asks his listeners.

The Mexican architect Luis Barragán has said that the sky is the true facade of a house. I moved here from the Midwest, yet felt I'd come home. Light, the transparent light of Mexico. Clouds so white it hurts to look at them, like linen puffed and drying on a clothesline. Sky and clouds don't need papers to cross the border.

When I lived in Provincetown, Massachusetts, a native told me houses are painted to match the sky. If this is true worldwide, then I was raised in Chicago neighborhoods where buildings are the color of bad weather. Tundra ice, tornado pewter, tempest gray, and do-not-go-gently-into-that-blizzard white.

I painted my home in San Antonio the colors of my Mexican memories. I chose strong colors, *colores fuertes,* because the light is *fuerte*. I wanted something soothing that would draw together earth and sky, and nourish it—jacaranda violet with turquoise trim. At twilight, with the clouds aflame and the sun setting behind it, my house sizzles and sparkles, looks absolutely gorgeous. To me.

Perhaps all houses are drawn from nostalgia. A local architect claims the Alamo doors remember blue paint. The San Antonio missions had elaborate designs imitating tiles inside and out. Even the building that now houses the San Antonio Conservation Society sported a joyful hue of pink stucco before O'Neil Ford "restored" San Antonio to fashionably acceptable white. History, after all, is layer upon layer of stories. What one considers history depends on who is telling the story and what story they consider telling.

To some, my periwinkle home screams *rascuache,* the term for making something from readily available materials. An old tire transformed into a planter. A shed patched with hubcaps. A toy airplane made from a beer can. Poverty is the mother of invention.

Once, when I was little, my mother pasted a travel poster in our kitchen with Karo corn syrup because we didn't have glue. Now, that's what I call *rascuache.*

Colores alegres, happy colors, as opposed to sad colors. *Colores fuertes,* as opposed to weak. Colors that look, as my mother would say, like they were boiled for too long. *Chillante,* literally screaming. Vibrant colors, sensuous, intense, violent, frightening, passionate. Is that blue beautiful because it reminds you of Tiffany's, or the Blessed Virgin Mary? Is it an Hermès orange or a Jarritos soft drink orange? It all depends on your memory.

The grande dame of Mexican letters, Elena Poniatowska, says that in Mexico "the people set the colors to fight like roosters:

all colors are enemies, and in the end the winner of the battle is art itself, because opposites attract each other and end up embracing."

The border is locked in a passionate embrace of north and south, of desire and rage, and from this coupling a new culture has erupted. I was told that my house was "not appropriate to history," and that the issue was "not about taste" but about "historical context." But my point is this: Whose history?

Mexicans love color so much, everything is awash with it, including themselves. Long before punk rockers, pre-Columbian women dyed their hair green, yellow, and red. Even today the Nahua women of Tetelcingo, Morelos, a town known for its witchcraft, dye their hair green. Maybe, like punk rockers, to make themselves more powerful.

Mexicans have such faith in color, if you visit the markets at the end of the year, you'll see mobs rushing to buy red or yellow underwear before midnight. If it's money you want in the incoming year, make sure you're wearing yellow underwear at midnight. But if it's love you're after, remember to wear red. And if you're especially greedy and desire both, you're condemned like me to welcome the new year in two pairs of *chones*.

Color is a story. An inheritance. Were the San Antonio missions *rascuache* because they imitated the elaborate Moorish tiles they could not afford? Nobody wants to live like they're poor, not even the poor. The poor prefer to live like kings. That's why they paint their houses with the only wealth they have—spirit.

Mango yellow, papaya orange, cobalt blue. When colors arrive from "the nobodies who don't create art, but handicrafts, who don't have culture, but folklore," as Eduardo Galeano sardonically says of the poor, they don't count, they're not valuable until a Rockefeller or a Luis Barragán borrows them and introduces them into the homes of the rich and gives them status.

Recent research on the distressed colors popularly known as the "Santa Fe look" confirms that in their time the colors were much brighter than we know them. The tones we think of as authentic are actually stronger colors that have faded with age and weather. Originally, the hues were as intense as the contemporary colors of Mexico. The local Southwest version waters it down to sorbet, perhaps because the real thing is too strong for the palettes and palates of the timid.

Although Mayan blue pigment has defied 1,400 years of sun and is still as intense as ever, the glory of my morning-glory house has already faded, settling to the soft color of a chambray work-shirt, a disappointment to the curious searching for the Barney purple of their imagination.

Two years after the original request for permission, the wise urban planning director found the Solomonic solution: submit the colors the house had faded to since the original paint job, and, lo and behold, the faded colors were deemed "historically accurate."

My house is still the most intense house on the block, but it looks *un poco triste* to me now. Next time I'd like to try a *rosa mexicano,* a color historically documented in my neighborhood, and on the historic king's row of showcase mansions.

Destiny works in strange ways.

When I imagine la Divina Providencia, I think of *una indígena* weaving bare-breasted in the comfort of her courtyard, a back-strap loom tied to a tree. She is sitting on the ground upon a woven *petate,* carefully separating the threads from their groups, distributing them evenly with the aid of a maguey spine, threads pulled into a tight V with her big toe. Or she is seated on a low stool, legs shamelessly akimbo, cotton skirt gathered and tucked under her crotch. Yes, this is how I like to think of her.

La Divina Providencia is mapping the motion of our lives like moon and sun across the thirteen layers of sky and nine of night, weaving a design larger than our lives, too intricate for the eye to follow, but every thread woven with clarity, purpose, and pattern.

My house in 2014, renamed Casa Rosa

Tenemos Layaway, or, How I Became an Art Collector

Franco Mondini-Ruiz was on the board of the Blue Star Arts Space in San Antonio. Then as now, he could never get his fellow artists to understand issues of race and class. So in an effort to get a dialogue going, Franco convinced me to speak at a show he curated at the Blue Star called *The Purple House,* an installation of some of my art pieces and the objects surrounding them. This was after the Purple House brouhaha as described in the previous chapter. During that time, strangers would knock on my door and ask to come inside. *Sigh,* I padlocked the front gate forever after.

I think it's important to add that I wrote this during a period I felt most at home in San Antonio after several years of feeling like a carpetbagger, when I'd finally found my spiritual family and my home still made me feel private, secure, and safe. (But not for long.)

This story was performed in November of 1998 at the Blue Star with pieces of creative writing interspersed to make my point, though I include only one poem here. I also had an opera singer friend sing "Júrame" at an appropriate moment, and I wish we could reproduce that here, but you can Google the song for yourself and get the vibe.

A house for me has been a lifelong dream. Owning one, having one, retreating to a space one can call one's own, where a radio or TV isn't blaring, and someone isn't knocking on the other side of a door saying, "Come on out of there!" A house for me is a space to decide whether I want to be sad and not turn on the lights, to sleep until noon or beyond, read a book propped up by fringed pillows, shut off the ringer of the phone, wear my pajamas all day, and not venture farther than the backyard fence if I feel like it. A house is the right to leave my hair uncombed, walk around barefoot, be rude. I don't want to *quedar bien,* that terrible syndrome of *las mujeres.* I like the civility of incivility. If someone rings the doorbell, does that mean I have to answer it? If someone says hello, do I have to grin like a geisha? I like the military chin-flick of the men. I see you, you see me. A house for me is this freedom to be. To go back to bed after breakfast. Peruse mail order catalogs while in the tub. Eat pancakes for dinner. Study *The New York Times* while ironing. A house is about the safety and privacy of doing what others might think odd, or eccentric, or wrong, and as I live alone and there is no one to tell me "You can't do that!" it's the richest indulgence I know next to writing.

We don't have a model for what it means to be a Latina and a woman of letters, except for the genius nun Juana Inés de la Cruz, and even she was forced by the Church to stop writing. No thank you. Joining a nunnery is a high price to pay for being allowed a room of one's own. We don't have a blueprint for how to tell *la familia* we can't come to Sunday dinner because we're working on a novel, and no, we don't want to attend the nephew's birthday party. *¿Cómo? ¿Cómo que no vas a ir?* Moving far away from my family was my way of creating the space I needed to create. But now the fame of the house has brought the public to my door. My friend the painter Terry Ybáñez painted a beautiful sign for me that reads "Please Do Not Ring the Bell Unless You Have an Appointment. Peace, Respect, Compassion, Wisdom," and it's a lucky thing. I was about to post this poem I wrote on the front gate:

It Occurs to Me I Am the Creative / Destructive Goddess Coatlicue

I deserve stones.
Better leave me the hell alone.

I am besieged.
I cannot feed you.
You may not souvenir my bones,
knock on my door, camp, come in,
telephone, take my Polaroid. I'm paranoid,
I tell you. *Lárguense.* Scram.
Go home.

I am anomaly. Rare she who
can't stand kids and can't stand you.
No excellent Cordelia cordiality have I.
No coffee served in tidy cups.
No groceries in the house.

I sleep to excess,
smoke cigars,
drink. Am at my best
wandering undressed,
my fingernails dirty,

my hair a mess.
Terribly

sorry, Madame isn't
feeling well today.
Must
Greta Garbo.
Pull an Emily D.
Roil like Jean Rhys.
Abiquiu myself.
Throw a Maria Callas.
Shut myself like a shoe.

Stand back. Christ
almighty. I'm warning.
Do not. Keep
out. Beware.
Help! Honey,
this means
you.

We all need a place to be. To cry without someone asking, "What's wrong?" To laugh without explaining why. To scratch our butt without saying, "Oh, pardon me." We need a house to fly. To hear the heart speak. To listen in earnest and then, talk back.

When I'm at home writing, the house is absolutely silent, sometimes only partially lit, as if I wished to reduce the world to the printed page, and in a sense, I do. Sometimes my house is lonely, but mostly I enjoy the aloneness. Aloneness is a luxury, like grief. Something society tries to kill. "Don't be sad." "Why is this door locked? What are you *doing* in there!" For a writer, both loneliness and grief serve their purpose of allowing one the heart dialogues. Quoting the poet Gwendolyn Brooks: "I like being alone, but I don't like being lonely." A hazard of the trade. I have come to understand even loneliness can be whittled into something useful. A poem. A paragraph. A page if I'm lucky.

A house for me is about permanence against the imperma- nence of the universe. Someplace to store all the things I love to collect. *Rebozos,* shoes, hats, gloves, a wardrobe that resembles a female impersonator's. Someplace to centralize all the books and storage-unit boxes from the ten years when I meandered like a cloud. A place to hold the art treasures I've purchased from the many artist friends I know.

When my father was dying, I needed to return to the stillness of my own home and look at my walls the way the thirsty return to water. There was such a pain in my belly that I couldn't make sense of the world until I came home and just stared at the walls. The mango against the pink, the green against the yellow, a vase of magenta carnations beside an ocher painting, a wood sculpture against an Ave Maria blue. The art soothed me, comforted me, was a way of seeing the world in an orderly, calm way amid the chaos and cruel noise of those days.

I think this is why artists live the way they do. Arranging and rearranging the little objects of every day until there is a beauty that heals. That's why I like visiting the houses of my artist friends. I walk around and admire a stone, a photo next to a doll, a bowl of feathers and shells, with the awe of one visiting a church. This is true of the San Antonio artists I know, Anne Wallace and her lovely austerity with wood and unpainted furnishings, the colors and cloth of the home of Rolando Briseño and Angel Rodríguez Díaz, the passion and surprising juxtaposition of the tiny still lifes of toys and saints and salt shakers on the shelves and windowsills of the house of Terry Ybáñez. Because it matters a great deal if when you look up you see something that pleases the eye and

Altar para los hombres, by Terry Ybáñez

delights the heart, even if that something is only a teapot next to a sugar bowl. My house is an homage to this sensitivity and respect for things of the spirit.

When I was in elementary school, we were required to attend daily Mass before class each morning. It was a ritual that bored me beyond belief. But what saved me from fainting was the building, a modern 1960s creation with a wall filled with triangles of stained glass from top to bottom, each one different from the next. While the miracle of the Mass was going on, I couldn't take my eyes off that other miracle, a certain triangle of stained glass that made me shiver, a blue swirling into pink, like the tip of a cloud when the sun is setting. Sky blue pirouetting into a tender pink. It swirled inside my heart and made me happy in a way I couldn't understand then or explain. I didn't know it, but that blue next to pink was as holy as what was supposed to be going on at the altar. How come nobody told me an aria, a piece of stained glass, a painting, a sunset can be God too?

"Wait till you get your house," said my friend Liesel, who once worked in the German film industry. Her Greek house of the thirteen terraces is a kind of film set, high on a hill on a Greek island with a dramatic view of the Aegean. The Greeks think she's so German about everything, muttering about the garbage the wind blows onto her property, picking up everything the sky tosses onto her thirteen terraces, even an olive. "They stain the whitewash. You think I'm crazy. Just you wait till you get your house, it will become your lover."

She was right. My house has become the beloved. When I drive away on a trip, I look over my shoulder and am filled with regret. When I return, my heart leaps when she's in sight. Any nick on her walls, or split in her floorboards, or curled paint causes me to cringe. Adorning her is my pleasure. Furniture like a Carlota empress. Paintings like a Versailles. Unlike some people who buy a painting to match a couch, I upholster the furniture to match the paintings, in the jewel tones of ball gowns—royal blue, lemon yellow, emerald green. Like the sumptuous silks and grandiose skies of Angel Rodríguez Díaz's paintings. Whatever my odalisque desires, nothing is too grand for her.

What color to paint the exterior of such a beauty? Beige? White? Evergreen? Pleeeease! I consider a Mexican pink, a Greek cobalt, am tempted by a joyous Caribbean papaya, a '40s seafoam green, but decide finally on a soothing periwinkle inspired by a photo of a house in India. Periwinkle is a pretty color. I'd seen periwinkle houses in Mexico, only there they called it jacaranda, after a tree that bursts into flower like a blue gas flame.

A house decides its own name. Once I thought of baptizing my home "Rancho Ahí Te Wacho," but no matter how hard I imagine it, she's no *rancho*. Community and local scandal have dubbed her "the Purple House." "The Purple House" is fine by me, though she's more lavender than purple, a morning glory in the morning glory, a faded workshirt blue in the hard Texas midday light, a throbbing ultraviolet when day dissolves into dusk.

I think of the Purple House, and it makes me think of that other house, la Casa Azul, the Blue House of Frida and Diego. And though I admire Frida's house, and Frida's paintings, and Frida's clothes and furniture and toys, though not Frida the martyr, the Blue House is too serious a comparison. My house is more Pee-wee's Playhouse than Frida's Blue House. I love the Playhouse's craziness; say the secret word and everyone jumps up and down yelling—yayyy! I like its joy, its whimsy and inventiveness. I don't realize how much it's inspired me until after I take a good look at my house with its niches and cupboards peopled with plaster saints and clay *putas,* its shelves of Mexican toys, its sense of humor juxtaposing high and low art, its operatic over-the-top drama and tongue-in-cheek camp.

I say my style of home decorating is inspired by the intense still lifes of Terry Ybáñez, who in turn says she is inspired by my altars. Virgen de Guadalupes huddled with Buddhas. A pre-Columbian Coatlicue next to a Cantinflas toy. Mango walls next to a Veracruz pink.

"Let's imagine a literary salon, in Mexico, in the thirties," Franco Mondini-Ruiz says. "Let's imagine this is the house of someone who was once rich during the Porfiriato, but lost it all in the revolution and has survived with only a few family heirlooms. Let's imagine the living room of artist Chucho Reyes, the bedroom of Dolores del Río, the dining room chairs of Emiliano Zapata's *cuartel.*" We laugh and have a good time inventing vignettes, arranging furniture to tell a story, reminding each other how the cluttered houses of our mothers both inspire and haunt us. "My mother saves everything!" "No, *my* mother saves everything; did I ever tell you about my mother and the thousand Cool Whip containers?"

Something of my mother and my father seeps into my way of seeing a house. My mother's excellent thrift-store finds that she hid from my snobby Mexico City father. My father's designer fabrics he brought home from his upholstery shop, elegant leftovers from his fancy North Shore clients. With these we redid our thrift-store furniture, we reinvented our lives, though sometimes there wasn't enough fabric to go around. Father fixed it; covered the front in one fabric, the back in a coordinating other; he was ahead of his times.

You can tell I've been poor; I over-glamorize my body, my house. I take my house personally. I take my art collection personally, too. Overcompensation perhaps. I recognize it in some houses, in some people who are like me. A house for me is a space to reinvent oneself, like putting on a new dress.

Once there really was a nun who passed by the Chicago brownstone we lived in and couldn't believe I lived in the ugly three-flat I was playing in front of. The place was a dump. A faded "Drink Fox Head Beer" advertisement was flaking off one side. You could tell the building had once been grand, grand enough to warrant renovation, but that would require so much money, and we lived in neighborhoods destined for the urban expansion of the University of Illinois. It made me realize forever after that people would mistake the landlord's neglect for our own sense of self-worth, and would allow me to see, forever after, how even the poorest of houses, the most beat up and scruffy and *fregadas,* the ones families rent but don't own, are sometimes the ones with the most pride. A tin of flowers in a lard can. A window full of cheerful Halloween decorations. A ton of Christmas lights even if the screen door is hanging like a broken jaw. "We may be poor, but you can bet we're proud."

I have lived such exaggerated pride. Been forced to mop stairwells with Pine-Sol, and can understand why the hole-in-the-wall taco joints also reek of Pine-Sol. "We may be poor, but you can bet at least we're clean."

Poverty has always had the stigma of dirtiness. That's why I couldn't wait to move into my own home, where the walls didn't shimmer at night with the lacquered bodies of cockroaches, shadows didn't scuttle along the floorboards. Imagine my surprise when I inherited cockroaches in my new house! And rats in the attic. Nobody told me. I didn't know. I associated cockroaches and rats with poverty. Just goes to show the democracy of *cucarachas y ratones*. Isn't the world amazing?

Across a table of *sopa de conchitas* at Torres Taco Haven, this question: "What is the Mexican American aesthetic?" A San Antonio architect is asking. He's trying to translate the private Mexican housescape to the public building. What is the Mexican American aesthetic? I think and then respond: "More is more."

My friend the late Danny López Lozano, once owner of Tienda Guadalupe, inspired an entire community of artists with this "more is more" aesthetic. Talk about style. More is more was not only Danny's way of decorating, but his way of living, of someone who had grown up poor and had to reinvent himself in a high-glam way. But it wasn't only about excess, it was about the juxtaposition of this excess. Like our mothers' china cabinets that house both prize English teacups and a porcelain Dumbo the elephant. A house like a layer cake, like the nine excavations of Troy. All the things one had gotten and been given in a lifetime.

I sometimes am overwhelmed at how much I've collected, and only can see the clutter when I've gone on a trip and come back after a long absence. Immediately, I vow to *not* buy more, to start selling things or store them away. I pull back only to replace the things I've stored with more *cositas*. More is more. *Más es más.* "*¡Qué bonito! Regálamelo.*" Yours.

I did not plan to become an art collector. I have more art than I have walls. But how can one stop from acquiring happiness, especially when happiness is so within reach? In San Antonio art is very cheap, several times cheaper than a framed poster, especially if one has the eye, as Danny López Lozano did, for seeing art where most people don't—a bouquet of aluminum foil roses, a grandmother's antique rosary, a little aluminum airplane made out of a Bud Lite beer can.

Art exists in the houses of the very poor, in the essence of their sense of color and life in creating with what they have, in the tire flower planters, and the chipped San Martín de Porres statue blurred from the kisses of the devout. We don't need to be a Rockefeller to see it. Or maybe we do need a Rockefeller, a mighty white man to hold it up, for all of us to wondrously look up from the dust of our lives and say, *"¡Qué bonito! Regálamelo."* Yours.

For a long time I couldn't afford to collect anything, not even unemployment. But in 1982 I won a fellowship, and with this I was able to travel. I lived in Provincetown for a summer working on *The House on Mango Street.* There were exhibits of art all summer in every shop, it seemed. One featured a series of striking woodcuts. I kept looking and looking at them. They reminded me of something familiar. The artist's biographical note stated she had studied with the Mexican artists, and here is where I found that point of connection. I was especially moved by a print called *Woman in the Moon.* It was seventy-five dollars. Seventy-five dollars! I had seventy-five dollars. "Should I buy it?" I remember asking my roommate and best buddy Dennis Mathis. "Buy it," Dennis said. It was my first art purchase, and I still love that *Woman in the Moon* as much as I did the first time I saw her, and as she is small, she has traveled with me to most of the cities I've lived in.

Woman in the Moon, woodcut by Tina Dickey

Not all my purchases have been good matches. I once went to a gallery here in San Antonio with a poet friend. She talked me into buying something I later gave away. I've since learned to trust my own instincts when it comes to love, whether it's a painting or a person. You can't fall in love because someone tells you to. If you love to look at something, and it keeps drawing you back, then follow that hunch. That's how it was when Terry Ybáñez sold me her first still life. She wasn't trying to sell it; I remember asking how much she was intending to ask for it. She thought for a little while, her paintbrush held in midair, and then said, "Two hundred and fifty," not realizing I was making mental calculations. "Two hundred and fifty! Do you have layaway?" Lucky for me, she did.

I've since met many artists, most of them are my friends, and all of them have layaway. Sometimes they have trouble paying the rent, and I buy a piece of art before they even make it. Sometimes buying a piece of art is preferable to lending them money, because if you lend them money, you may never see it again. But a piece of art is something wonderful that they can give you in exchange for helping them out. A lot of times this has been how I've been able to share some of my success. I win an award and I spend it here locally with local artists, and this enables them to continue living in San Antonio, to buy more art supplies and make more art, to buy a breakfast taco and keep on living. And so it goes and goes. It's simple.

And I'm grateful for having the artists around. They improve the quality of my life. Danny López Lozano used to say, "We live like millionaires." And he was right. We do live like millionaires, even when we don't have five bucks in our pockets. The artists realize it's as important to feed one's spirit as to feed one's belly. That's why sometimes Danny would dress the table with the finest china, with the Lalique crystal, with the linen tablecloth and napkins, with branches filched from the flowering tree in the empty lot across the street, even if we were just eating Church's fried chicken. We live like millionaires!

And I find it curious to see here in this gallery an art installation of a messy living room juxtaposed with the installation of my living room, which attempts to be very froufrou. The rich like to live like they're poor. The poor wish to live like kings.

The used furniture I've bought at Franco's Infinito Botánica store and reupholstered in French fabrics reminds me of the furniture showrooms in the barrio with the imitation Marie Antoinette couches, the couches of my *tías,* reupholstered with leftover fabric and covered with plastic covers against the exuberance of kids.

That sense of having been poor allows me to understand the artists who are poor too, poor but educated, and therefore with tastes better, in my opinion, than the rich, who often only have their wealth, but are poor when it comes to imagination.

My artist friends are poor but talented, and therefore blessed or doomed to live like millionaires, with a joie de vivre and a grief that is a passion. They live hand to mouth, most without health insurance, most without a regular paycheck, doing what they do after having made great personal sacrifices, serving on committees and boards, volunteering at the community fairs, donating their art for good causes, generous to the point of foolishness.

The other night at the Purple House victory party, listening to Janis De Lara singing a cappella at the Acapulco Drive Inn, I realized our lives are very rich indeed. A life blessed with beauty and things of the spirit. "We live like millionaires!" Danny would say. No, Danny, we live *mejor*. We live like artists.

Thanksgiving at Danny López Lozano's
high-glam apartment, 309 Madison Street,
San Antonio

An *Ofrenda* for My Father on Day of the Dead

My personal altar for my father

This story came of its own accord, uncommissioned, though I was to first publish it in the *Los Angeles Times,* on October 26, 1997, and the *San Antonio Express-News,* on November 2, 1997. At the same time I created an altar for my father in my home since it was the first Day of the Dead after his death. Later I would write an *ofrenda* and install an altar for my mother when her time came. Both story and altar served the same purpose: nourishment, clarity, and transformation at a time when my spirit was dying.

M i'ja, it's me, call me when you wake up." It was a message
left on my phone machine from my friend José De Lara.
But when I heard that word *"mi'ja,"* a pain squeezed my heart.
My father was the only one who ever called me this. Because my
father's death is so recent, the word overwhelmed me and filled
me with grief.

"Mi'ja" (MEE-ha) from *"mi hija"* (me EE-ha). The words translate as "my daughter." "Daughter," "my daughter," "daughter of
mine," they're all stiff and clumsy, and have nothing of the intimacy
and warmth of the word *"mi'ja."* "Daughter of my heart," maybe.
Perhaps a more accurate translation of *"mi'ja"* is "I love you."

With my father's death the thread that links me to my other
self, to my other language, was severed. Spanish binds me to my

ancestors, but especially to my father, a Mexican national by birth who became a U.S. citizen by serving in World War II. My mother, who is Mexican American, learned her Spanish through this man, as I did. Forever after, every word spoken in that language is linked indelibly to him. Can a personal language exist for each human being? Perhaps all languages are like that. Perhaps none are.

My father's Spanish, particular to a time and place, is gone, and the men of that time are gone or going—Don Quixote with a hammer or pick. When I speak Spanish, it's as if I'm hearing my father again. It's as if he lives in the language, and I become him. I say out-of-date phrases that were part of his world. *Te echo un telefonazo. Quiúbole. Cómprate tus chuchulucos. ¿Ya llenaste el costalito? Que duermas con los angelitos panzones.*

There is stored in my father's Spanish, the way a spider might be sealed in amber, a time and place frozen just out of reach, but that I can hold up to my eye to make the world more golden. Intrinsic in Mexican Spanish is a way of looking at all things in the cosmos, little or large, as if they are sacred and alive. The original indigenous languages may have disappeared, but not the indigenous worldview. This native sensibility transposes itself into the English I write.

As a writer, I continue to analyze and reflect on the power words have over me. As always I'm fascinated with how those of us who live in multiple cultures and the regions in between are held under the spell of words spoken in the language of our childhood. After a loved one dies, your senses become oversensitized. Maybe that's why I sometimes smell my father's cologne in a room when no one else does. And why words once taken for granted suddenly take on new meanings.

When I wish to address a child, a lover, or one of my many small pets, I use Spanish, a language filled with affection and familiarity. I can liken it only to the fried-tortilla smell of my mother's house or the way my brothers' hair smells like Alberto VO5 when I hug them. It just about makes me want to break down and cry.

The language of our *antepasados,* those who came before us, connects us to our center, to who we are, and directs us to our life-work. Some of us have been lost, cut off from this essential wisdom and power. Sometimes our parents or grandparents were so harmed by a society that treated them ill for speaking their native language, they thought they could save us from that hate by teaching us to speak only English. Those of us, then, live like captives, lost from our culture, ungrounded, forever wandering like ghosts with a thorn in the heart.

When my father was sick, I watched him dissolve before my eyes. Each day the cancer that was eating him changed his face, as if he were crumbling from within and turning into a sugar skull, the kind placed on altars for Day of the Dead. Because I'm a light sleeper, my job was to be the night watch. Father always woke

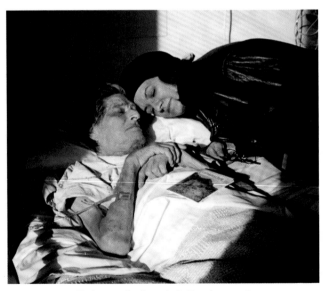

Father at the hospital, October 1996

several times in the night choking on his own bile. I would rush to hold a kidney-shaped bowl under his lips, wait for him to finish throwing up, the body exhausted beyond belief. When he was through, I rinsed a towel with cold water and washed his face. *"Ya estoy cansado de vivir,"* my father would gasp. *"Sí, yo sé,"* I know. But the body takes its time dying. I have reasoned since then that the purpose of illness is to let go. For the living to let the dying go, and for the dying to let go of this life and travel to where they must.

Whenever anyone discusses death they talk about the inevitable loss, but no one ever mentions the inevitable gain. How when you lose a loved one, you suddenly have a spirit ally, an energy on the other side that is with you always, that is with you just by calling their name. I know my father watches over me in a much more thorough way than he ever could when he was alive. When he was living, I had to telephone long distance to check up on how he was doing, and if he wasn't watching one of his endless telenovelas, he'd talk to me. Now I simply summon him in my thoughts. *Papá.* Instantly I feel his presence surround and calm me.

I know this sounds like a lot of hokey new-age stuff, but really it's old age, so ancient and wonderful and filled with such wisdom that we have had to relearn it because our miseducation has taught us to name it "superstition." I have had to rediscover the spirituality of my ancestors, because my own mother was a cynic. And so it came back to me a generation later, learned but not forgotten in some memory in my cells, in my DNA, in the palm of my hand that is made up of the same blood of my ancestors, in the transcripts I read from the great Mazatec visionary María Sabina García of Oaxaca.

Sometimes a word can be translated into more than a meaning; in it is a way of looking at the world, and, yes, even a way of accepting what others might not perceive as beautiful. *"Urraca,"* for example, instead of "grackle." Two ways of looking at a black bird. One sings, the other cackles. Or *"tocayo/a,"* your name twin, and, therefore, your friend. Or the beautiful *"estrenar,"* which means to wear something for the first time. There is no word in English for the thrill and pride of wearing something new.

Spanish gives me a way of looking at myself and the world in a new way. For those of us living between worlds, our job in the universe is to help others see with more than their eyes during this period of chaotic transition. Our work as bicultural citizens is to help others to become visionary, to help us all to examine our dilemmas in multiple ways and arrive at creative solutions—otherwise we all will perish.

When you see a skeleton, what does it mean to you? Anatomy? Satan worship? Heavy-metal music? Halloween? Or maybe it means—Death, you are a part of me, I recognize you, I include you in my life, I even thumb my nose at you. Today on Day of the Dead, I honor and remember my *antepasados,* those who have died and gone on before me.

I think of those two brave women in Amarillo[*] who lost their jobs for speaking Spanish, and I wonder at the fear in their employer. Did she think they were talking about her? Didn't she understand that speaking another language is another way of seeing, a way of being at home with one another, of saying to your listener, "I know you, I honor you. You are my sister, my brother, my mother, my father, my family." If she had learned Spanish—or any other language—she would have been admitting, "I love and

---

[*] In 1997 in Amarillo, Texas, a small insurance agency hired two women clerks who were bilingual in English and Spanish to deal with their Spanish-speaking clients. Their employer became paranoid when they spoke Spanish to each other and asked them to sign an English-only pledge, which they refused to do. They were fired. The two women felt insulted, while their boss felt they were "whispering to each other behind our backs."

respect you, and I love to address you in the language of those you love."

This Day of the Dead I make an offering, *una ofrenda,* to honor my father's life and to honor all immigrants everywhere who come to a new country filled with great hope and fear, dragging their beloved homeland with them in their language. My father appears to me now in the things that are most alive, that speak to me or attempt to speak to me through their beauty, tenderness, and love. A bowl of oranges on my kitchen table. The sharp scent of a can filled with *xempoaxóchitl,* marigold flowers, for Day of the Dead. The opening notes of the Agustín Lara bolero *"Farolito."* A night sky filled with moist stars. *"Mi'ja,"* they call out to me, and my heart floods with joy.

Holding a photograph of my father in a San Antonio
Day of the Dead procession

Un Poquito de Tu Amor

I'm not a writer who can meet a deadline. It pains me that this is so, but there it is. I admire journalists who can whip out a story in time to make a visible difference during world events. Elena Poniatowska, Studs Terkel, Eduardo Galeano, Alma Guillermoprieto, Gabriel García Márquez. But I'm not of that breed. Sometimes folks come up to me and ask, "Why don't you write about . . . ?" I can't explain my process. I just know when given a topic, I can only try, but I give no guarantees. "It's like fishing," I explain. "I can get up early, mend the nets, get my boat ready, and row myself to an area where there are plenty of fish, but I can't guarantee my catch. I'm just the fisherman, not the creator of fish. It's a matter of waiting." So when this story tugged at my line, I was surprised when I reeled it in and grateful when it appeared in the *Los Angeles Times*, on February 22, 1998.

When my father died last year a piece of my heart died with him. My father, that supreme sentimental fool, loved my brothers and me to excess in a kind of over-the-top, rococo fever, all arabesques and sugar spirals, as sappy and charming as the romantic Mexican boleros he loved to sing. *"Give me just a little bit of your love at least, give me just a bit of your love, just that . . ."* "Music from my time," Father would say proudly, and I could almost smell the gardenias and Tres Flores hair oil.

Before my father died, it was simple cordiality that prompted

Father and me dancing at my brother
Al Jr.'s wedding

me to say, "I'm sorry," when comforting the bereaved. But with his death I am initiated into the family of humanity. I'm connected to all deaths and to their survivors: *"Lo siento,"* which translates as both "I am sorry" and "I feel it" all at once.

Lo siento. Since his death, I feel life more intensely.

My father, born under the eagle and serpent of the Mexican flag, died beneath a blanket of stars and stripes, a U.S. World War II veteran. Like most immigrants, he was overly patriotic, exceptionally hardworking, and, above all, a great believer in family. Yet often I'm aware that my father's life doesn't count, he's not "history," not the "American" politicians mean when they talk about "American."

I thought of my father especially this holiday season. The day before Christmas, 1997, forty-five unarmed Mayans were slain while they prayed in a chapel in Acteal, Chiapas, twenty-one of them women, fourteen children. The Mexican president was shocked and promised to hold all those responsible accountable. The Mexican people aren't fools. Everybody knows who's responsible, but it's too much to wish for the Mexican president to fire himself.

I know the deaths in Chiapas are linked to me here in the United States. I know the massacre is connected to removing native people from their land, because although the people are poor, the land is very rich, and the government knows this. And the Mexican debt is connected to my high standard of living, and the military presence is necessary to calm U.S. investors, and the music goes round and round and it comes out here.

I've been thinking and thinking about all this from my home in San Antonio, as fidgety as a person with *comezón,* an itch I can't quite scratch. What is my responsibility as a writer in light of these events? As a woman, as a *mestiza,* as a U.S. citizen who lives on several borders? What do I do as the daughter of a Mexican man? Father, tell me. *Ayúdame,* help me, why don't you? *Lo siento.* I've been searching for answers. On Christmas, I'm reverberating like a bell.

In my father's house, because my father was my father— "Hello, my friend!"—our Christmas dinners were a global feast, a lesson in history, diplomacy, and the capacity of the stomach to put aside racial grievances. Our holidays were a unique hybrid of cultures that perhaps could happen only in a city like Chicago, a bounty contributed by family and intermarriage, multiethnic neighborhoods, and the diversity of my father's upholstery shop employees.

To this day, a typical Christmas meal at our home consists first and foremost of tamales, that Indian delicacy that binds us to the pre-conquest. Twenty-five dozen for our family is typical, the popular red tamales, the fiery green tamales, and the sweet pink tamales filled with jam and raisins for the kids. Sometimes they're my mother's homemade batch—"This is the last year I'm going to make them!" But more often they're ordered in advance from someone else willing to go through all the trouble, most recently from the excellent tamale lady in front of Carnicerías Jiménez on North Avenue, who operates from a shopping cart.

Father's annual contribution was his famous *bacalao,* a codfish stew of Spanish origin, which he made standing in one spot like a TV chef—"Go get me a bowl, bring me an apron, somebody give me the tomatoes, wash them first, hand me that knife and chopping board, where are the olives?"

Every year we're so spoiled we expect—and receive—a Christmas tray of homemade pirogi and Polish sausage, sometimes courtesy of my sister-in-law's family, the Targonskis, and sometimes from my father's Polish seamstresses, who can hardly speak a word of English. We also serve Jamaican meat pies, a legacy from Daryl, who was once my father's furniture refinisher but has long since left. And finally, our Christmas dinner includes the Italian magnificence from Ferrara Bakery in our old Taylor Street neighborhood. Imagine if a cake looked like the Vatican. We've been eating Ferrara's pastries since I was in the third grade.

But this is no formal Norman Rockwell sit-down dinner. We eat when we're inspired by hunger or by *antojo,* literally "before the eye." All day pots are on the stove steaming, and the microwave is beeping. It's common to begin a dessert plate of cannoli while someone next to you is finishing breakfast, pork tamales sandwiched inside a loaf of French bread, a *mestizo* invention thanks to French intervention.

History is present at our table. The doomed emperor Maximiliano's French baguette as well as the Aztec corn tamales of the Americas, our Andalusian recipe for codfish, our moves in and out of neighborhoods where we were the brown corridor between Chicago communities at war with one another. And finally a history of intermarriage and of employees who loved my father enough to share a plate of their homemade delicacies with our family even if our countries couldn't share anything else.

Forty-five are dead in Acteal. My father is gone. I read the newspapers, and the losses ring in my heart. More than half the Mexican American kids in this country are dropping out of high school—more than half!—and our politicians' priority is to build bigger prisons. I live in a state where there are more people sentenced to death than anywhere else in the world. Alamo

A moment after the Cisneros Family Christmas, with pastries still on the table in my mother's basement kitchen, Keeler house; I'm standing on the far right, second row.

Heights, the affluent white neighborhood of my city, values Spanish as a second language beginning in the first grade, yet elsewhere lawmakers work to demolish bilingual education for Spanish-dominant children. Two hours away from my home, the U.S. military is setting up camp in the name of bandits and drug lords. But I'm not stupid; I know who they mean to keep away. *Lo siento.* I feel it.

I'm thinking this while I attend a Latino leadership conference between the holidays. I don't know what I expect from this gathering of Latino leaders exactly, but I know I don't want to leave without a statement about what's happened in Acteal. Surely at least the Latino community recognizes that the forty-five are our family.

"It *is* like a family," one Arizona *político* explains to me. "But understand, to you it may be a father who's died, but to me it's a distant cousin."

Is it too much to ask our leaders to lead?

"You're too impatient," one Latina tells me, and I'm so stunned I can't respond. A wild karaoke begins, and a Chicano filmmaker begins to preach: "There's a season to play and a season to rage." He talks and talks till I have to blink back the tears. After what seems like an eternity, he finally finishes by saying, "You know what you have to do, don't you?"

And then it hits me, I *do* know what I have to do.

I will tell a story.

When my brothers and I were in college my mother realized investing in real estate was the answer to our economic woes. Her plans were modest: to buy a cheap fixer-upper in the barrio that would bring us income. After months of searching, Mother finally found something we could afford, a scruffy building on the avenue with a store that could serve as Father's upholstery shop and two apartments above that would pay the mortgage. At last my mother was a respectable landlady.

Almost immediately the family on the third floor began paying their rent late. It wasn't an expensive apartment, a hundred dollars, but every first of the month, they were five or ten dollars short and would deliver the rent with a promise to pay the balance the next payday, which they did. Every month it was the same: the rent minus a few dollars promised for next Friday.

Mother hated to be taken advantage of. "Do they think we're rich or something? Don't we have bills too?" She sent Father, who was on good terms with everybody. "You go and talk to that family, I've had it!"

And so Father went, and a little later quietly returned.

"I fixed it," Father announced.

"Already? How? What did you do?"

"I lowered the rent."

Mother was ready to throw a fit. Until Father said, "Remember when ten dollars meant a lot to us?"

Mother was silent, as if by some *milagro* she remembered. Who would've thought Father was capable of such genius? He was not by nature a clever man. But he inspires me now to be creative in ways I never realized.

I don't wish to make my father seem more than what he was. He wasn't Gandhi; he lived a life terrified of those different from himself. He never read a newspaper and was naive enough to believe history as told by *la televisión*. And, as my mother keeps reminding me, he wasn't a perfect husband, either. But he was kind and at some things extraordinary. He was a wonderful father.

Maybe I've looked to the wrong leaders for leadership. Maybe what's needed this new year are a few outrageous ideas. Something absurd and genius like my father, whose generosity teaches me to enlarge my heart.

Maybe it's time to lower the rent.

"Dame un poquito de tu amor . . ." Ever since the year began that song has been running through my head; my father just won't let up. *Lo siento.* I feel it.

Papá, Buddha, Allah, Jesus Christ, Yahweh, la Virgen de Guadalupe, the Universe, the God in us, help us. Give us just a little bit of your love at least, give us just a little bit of your love, just that . . .

Eduardo Galeano

I was asked to write a foreword for the reissue of Eduardo Galeano's *Days and Nights of Love and War.* Who was I to introduce Galeano? Galeano is celebrated across the Americas and beyond. Twice exiled, from his homeland Uruguay and then from Argentina because of his political writing, he wrote *Days and Nights* while living as a refugee in Spain. Venezuelan president Hugo Chávez gave a copy of Galeano's *Open Veins of Latin America* to President Barack Obama, no doubt to have the United States see history from the point of view of the other America, and that woke everyone up who hadn't heard of Galeano before. After wrestling with the task, I finally realized the best way to get past my writer's block was to create vignettes inspired by Galeano's own favorite form. In the same year that I wrote this introduction, 1999, the Lannan Foundation awarded Galeano the Prize for Cultural Freedom in recognition of "extraordinary and courageous work [that] celebrates the human right to freedom of imagination, inquiry and expression."

While this book was in production, Galeano passed away, on April 13, 2015.

I have been in the company of the man I consider my teacher only a handful of times and always too briefly. In Boston we shared a stage. It was an old theater, like the one where Lincoln was shot. There was no microphone, or if there was, it didn't work. I had to shout to be heard. I read as if I were angry. It was the only way. In the back of my head, it occurs to me the writer Eduardo Galeano is in the audience listening to me. This thought makes my blood freeze.

In the spring of '91 while teaching in Albuquerque, I was asked if I would escort you for the day. You wanted to go to Acoma and needed a driver; you don't drive. I don't like to drive, but if you had asked me to drive you home to Montevideo, Uruguay, I would've said yes. It was a straight shot west to that mythical city high up on a mesa. Poor Eduardo! I chattered like a monkey the entire trip. You must've been exhausted. It's not half as tiring to talk as it is to listen.

I believe certain people, events, and books come to you when they must, at their precise moment in history. You arrived sent by "Saint Coincidence," as the poet Joy Harjo calls it. Saint Coincidence led me first to your book *Memory of Fire* in '87. That was the year I wanted to die and did die, but Divine Providence resurrected me.

————

Once before I'd met you at a book signing, but that was only briefly. The line meandered as sluggishly as the Rio Grande. When you finally came into view, I saw why. You talked to everyone. Every one. Not chatter, but dialogue. Next to your name you drew little pictures of a pig and a daisy. You hugged people; some you even kissed!

Back then I made the mistake, as only the naive can, of confusing the books with the author. When I met you again this year, I'm happy to report I was wiser.

The book is the sum of our highest potential. Writers, alas, are the rough drafts.

————

This time we spend the day driving around my city on a scavenger hunt of sorts, for various items you were asked to take back home to Montevideo. One of them makes me laugh—a collapsible piñata, one that squashes down for easy transport and later can be opened and filled. You're certain we can find one if we only look. I haven't the heart to tell you there is no such thing except in the minds of poets and inventors.

————

When I read your work what I find remarkable is my inability to classify what I'm reading. Is this history? And if so, it seems to me to be the best kind, full of gossip, full of story. Your books read like fable, fairy tale, myth, poem, diary, journal, but certainly not the dull lines of historical writing. And then I understand. You're an acrobat, Eduardo. You're a storyteller.

———

You have a list of things to buy. We go to my favorite vintage shop where you buy nothing and you watch me buy everything. We stop at a supermarket to buy you cans of jalapeños to take home. Band-Aids and fluorescent Post-it notes catch your eye, and these we buy too. We run to find CDs for your children, tequila for your agent, and a tailor to have your jeans hemmed. We eat breakfast tacos at Taquería No Que No.

———

By your own admission you call yourself a chronicler, but this doesn't say exactly what you do, what you give to writers like me. We've traded stories of how overwhelming it is to write, and it's a great relief to hear someone else say how strenuous it is to compose a sentence, a short paragraph, to rewrite it thirty, forty times. It gives me *ánimo* to hear about how each book becomes more difficult for you. Because with each book your standards are raised.

———

Carranza's Meat Market is where we stop next for *barbacoa* Tex-Mex. It amuses you because of the railroad across the street. "What poetic justice," you say. "Mexican president Carranza was plagued by the Zapatistas bombing the railroads, and now here are the railroads across the street plaguing his descendants."

———

I think, when I look at you, how did you do it, remain human, after everything? What is left after so many goodbyes, after everything?

After much pain, much fear? I'm not a writer in exile. I've never been exiled from anything, except maybe a bar or two.

I can't imagine being in exile.

———

I look and can't find you in the books you write. You do a Sally Rand fan dance. I find you only in this book—*Days and Nights of Love and War*. Only here do I catch glimpses of you refracted in the mirror of other faces, dreams, stories of other dreamers, stories of other storytellers.

———

You write: "I've known few people who have survived the tests of pain and violence—a rare feat—with their capacity for tenderness intact."

———

You don't talk about yourself, Eduardo. You talk about my house, my dogs, the book I'm writing, and sometimes for a wisp of a moment you mention you. But only by inference. On our way to run errands you say, "I didn't expect so many trees and hills here. San Antonio is very pleasant. It looks like a good town to walk in." "Oh, do you like to walk?" "I walk all the time," you say. "Blocks and blocks." And I try to imagine you walking through the streets of Montevideo, through Buenos Aires, through Calella de la Costa, Spain, where you've written this book.

I imagine you walking through all the cities where you've lived exiled from your last life. I imagine you drinking in bars and eating as you do here with me, *con gusto*. I gather from sharing beer and food with you a little of who you are. I see you riding trains and buses. The waiter fills your glass with beer, a woman hands you change. People talk to you without knowing who you are.

People like to talk to you because you like to listen. You are a writer, you are a witness.

————

You once told me a writer can write of life only if they've experienced death. You weren't talking about yourself, but I thought of you and your first death at nineteen chronicled in *Days and Nights of Love and War.* Your body was already in the morgue, until someone, "Saint Coincidence" perhaps, chanced to notice you were still breathing. Since this death and the subsequent deaths and resurrections, you write with life. One way to conquer death.

————

Your memory startles me. Your attention to detail. You quote poems as easily as you do history. On the ride to Acoma your face furrows into Xs when you grill me about a short story of mine. "What did you mean here: 'I believe love is always eternal. Even if eternity is only five minutes'?" And I explain myself. "Ah," you say, "is that it?" Silence. Then you add, "You love like a man."

————

Love resuscitates the living dead, don't you think? For others, it's laughter. For writers, the pen is our savior. For some the needle, I suppose, or the bottle, or perhaps that rare elixir: poetry. I don't know how it is for others, for those without words, I mean. I can only imagine. For me, there are the writers like you, who remind me why I write.

————

"And what about love, Eduardo?"
    "Love? The Brazilian poet Vinícius de Moraes says it best. *No es*

infinito pero es infinito en cuanto dura. It's not infinite, but it's infinite while it lasts."

I make you write this down for me, and you do, adding your signature pig.

———

We walk into a shop full of piñatas. Hundreds of piñatas. Piñatas shaped like superheroes and cartoons, like soldiers and like Chihuahuas, but no collapsible piñatas. At least you and I are in agreement. These piñatas are *bien feas,* truly ugly. The best kind is the old-fashioned piñata. The one shaped like a star.

———

You teach me to remain faithful to the word. To revere the syllable as a poet does, to remain attentive to writing as if one's life, several lives, depended upon it.

This is what I want. To believe one can write to change the world.

To change the world.

———

I do not believe, Eduardo, you are as you claim an atheist. You believe in "Saint Coincidence," the power of love, and in *brujos:* that religion called superstition by the uncoverted and spirituality by the devout. In short, you believe in humanity.

———

On that first visit to Albuquerque you had a hard time reading the English translations of your work. With one vignette in particular, you're obsessed with the English translation, how it doesn't ring as true as the original Spanish. "We have to revise it," you plead.

You make me sit down with you at the Albuquerque airport and get to work. You insist. The little furrows on your forehead don't disappear until we've gone over the vignette and revised and revised and revised.

––––––––

After hearing you speak, we don't sleep for days. Some of us want to write like you. Some of us want to be you. Our crush is laughable. Television producers, journalists, university professors, cashiers, lesbian lawyers, dentists, opera singers, students, writers, retired schoolteachers, nurses, gay painters, and straight architects. We are in love with your words, with the deep voice saying them, with the way you speak English, the way you speak Spanish.

Admiration is a love potion.

––––––––

In *Days and Nights of Love and War,* you write, "I have known the machinery of terror from the inside and that exile has not always been easy. I could celebrate that at the end of so much sorrow and so much death, I still keep alive my capacity for astonishment at marvelous things, and my capacity for indignation at infamy, and that I continue to believe the advice of the poet who told me not to take seriously anything that does not make me laugh."

––––––––

A table full of San Antonio artists and poets have come to the Liberty Bar to have an encore of Eduardo after his reading. A penniless painter pulls like a rabbit from a hat a gift he's made for you that evening. He had to run home to make it.

It's a collapsible piñata!

You're overjoyed! You laugh like a child. Greedy and grateful.

————————

You write: "I thought I knew some good stories to tell other people, and I discovered, or confirmed, that I had to write. I had often been convinced that this solitary trade wasn't worthwhile if you compare it, for example, to political activism or adventure. I had written and published a lot, but I hadn't the guts to dig down inside and open up and give of myself. Writing was dangerous, like making love the way one should."

————————

Eduardo, I love your books because you write like a woman.

Infinito Botánica

There are so many stories about Franco Mondini-Ruiz. Some he invented himself, and some we were lucky enough to have witnessed, and some became San Antonio legend. Franco is part artist, part eccentric, part genius, part clown, part demon. Sometimes all at the same time. When his collection of sculptures and stories were featured in book form, *High Pink: Tex-Mex Fairy Tales*, he asked to include a poem I'd written for him years before. But I asked if I could write the introduction, too. I was grateful; Franco, and before him Danny López Lozano, were part of an arts scene in San Antonio that made me feel, finally, at home. Their art happenings in the '90s were revolutionary gatherings, terrifically inclusive, and brought down the apartheid walls of class, color, and sexuality existent in San Antonio for generations. By the time I finished this introduction, on September 11, 2004, the party was definitely over.

Amor, dinero, y salud, y el tiempo para gozarlos.
(Love, money, and health, and the time to enjoy them.)
—Mexican *dicho* painted on the side of Infinito Botánica's
building, South Flores Street, San Antonio, Texas

I first met Franco Mondini-Ruiz in the kitchen of his Geneseo Street house. He was living the life of a successful lawyer then. I had my hands in sudsy water and was furiously washing dishes the moment he poked his head through the kitchen doorway and introduced himself. His houseguest had invited us over for an impromptu party, and I remember our panic trying to get the house clean again before Franco walked in from an out-of-town trip.

There was no need to worry, I'd later find out. Franco's house was always full of strangers. He never locked the doors. Often beautiful boys fell asleep there, and more often beautiful boys ripped him off. He lived like an Italian movie: part Fellini, part Pasolini. This was part of *el mundo* Mondini, a chapter of my life that was to run its course during the decade of the '90s.

Falling into Franco's life was like falling down Alice in Wonderland's rabbit hole. The house on Geneseo was famous for parties where wealthy little old ladies in gold lamé might appear, as well as six-foot-tall transvestites and a parade of live chickens.

But Franco's most remarkable feat would be the alchemy of Infinito Botánica, a crumbling Mexican magic shop filled with folk medicine as well as high art. It was the only place in the city where a working-class person might hobnob with a millionaire. Rich Houston ladies shopped alongside tatooed *vatos,* big Botero-esque babes from the south-side dyke bars, Mexican nationals dressed in impeccable designer wear, and Mexican illegals sweaty from hard labor, the neighborhood Catholic priest. Everyone was welcome. In a sense, it was like one of Franco's parties, high low, or high *rascuache.**

The predecessor of this high-camp living was a man who had inspired us all and introduced us to each other. Danny López Lozano of Tienda Guadalupe Folk Art. It was Danny who provoked a generation of Chicano artists to relook at the *bueno, bonito, y*

---

* "High *rascuache*" comes from the brilliant imagination of the art critic Tomás Ybarra-Frausto, who coined the phrase to name objects that are at once funky and glamorous, like a plaster Virgen de Guadalupe statue covered in Swarovski crystals.

Franco at his glorious *botánica*

rascuache of San Antonio and transform it into glamour. The gatherings at his shop on South Alamo Street, as well as at his parties at his home, became our salon. If anyone was our mother, it was Danny, and we belonged devotedly to the House of Guadalupe.

When Danny died of throat cancer in 1992, it was up to others to carry the torch. Franco stepped in with Infinito Botánica, on South Flores Street. Other artists followed, living upstairs or next door, so that when an arts event occurred, it involved several open studios and the space between. Anything could happen and often did. Performances on the sidewalk spilling onto the street. Backyard cookouts featuring feasts more magnificent than Moctezuma's. A spontaneous eruption of Pancho Villa moustaches painted on the women and Frida eyebrows on the men.

Some of us aren't speaking to each other anymore, but for a time not only were we speaking, we were singing arias. Whatever inspired one of us was sure to inspire us all. An outbreak of Buddha art. Day of the Dead altars. Maria Callas look-alike nights. Paquita la del Barrio. Oh, honey, do I have to tell you?

Franco taught us to play. At the Liberty Bar, the name wasn't just a name, it was a way of life. We might compete for the same boys: "You can have him after me." A fight might break out over *mole*—from a jar versus from scratch. But we did see the world through the same rose-tinted glasses called Mexican nostalgia.

Franco taught me to see beauty in pink cupcakes, plastic champagne cups filled with colored water, Mexican *pan dulce* adorned with pre-Columbian artifacts. I still have the Marie Antoinette living room set I bought at Infinito, full of woodworms and horsehair stuffing, chairs so uncomfortable they're not for sitting.

That was then. Before 9/11. Before we started getting harassed for looking like the Arab Jews we are. We were escape artists in our escapades, looking for a shortcut to Berlin or Buenos Aires, trying to make high glam from whatever we had on hand. Those times. As a drunk woman so aptly put it at the final Infinito party, "It's the end of an error."

El Pleito/The Quarrel

My friends are highly competitive. After I'd written an intro for the artist Franco Mondini-Ruiz's book *High Pink: Tex-Mex Fairy Tales,* Rolando Briseño asked if I'd write something for his upcoming art book *Moctezuma's Table,* which would feature his paintings about food. I'm not a writer who can write on assignment, but I said I'd give it a try. It's a tricky business; when a friend asks you to write about them, it's like asking you to create their portrait. I warned Rolando, "It might not be a pretty picture."

Moctezuma's Table: Rolando Briseño's Mexican and Chicano Tablescapes was published by Texas A&M University Press in 2010.

It was the night Astrid Hadad sang at the Guadalupe Theater in San Antonio. She had a spectacular show, complete with bandoliers across her corseted *chichis,* papier-mâché pyramids and cacti, sequined skirts, a holster, pistols that fired blanks, and jokes that hit their targets on both sides of the border. Well, she was the best thing to ride into San Antonio in a long time. We still talk about that night even now though it was years ago.

Astrid Hadad is a Mexican-Lebanese performance artist from el D.F. (Mexico City). She and I once had our photo taken *nariz a nariz,* because with her Lebanese profile and my Aztec/Arab one, we could be twins, I'm not lying.

My nose is the one on the left.

After her show, we invited Astrid to the only twenty-four-hour restaurant we're not ashamed of, Mi Tierra. With its sugary trays of *pan dulce* and Mexican candy, enough twinkling lights to illuminate a city, *papel picado* flags fluttering overhead, strolling *músicos,* and a room where it's Christmas all year round, it's as campy as Astrid.

It was in the shimmering Christmas Room where they seated our party. The table was longer than the Last Supper, with the lucky ones at the center next to Astrid, and the ones who got there early and weren't thinking seated at the no-man's-land at the end, like Judas. We were the *tontos* seated at the end.

Now, you have to know this was when Astrid was really famous. Maybe you haven't heard of her, but anyone who lives in Mexico or watches Mexican television would know that nose anywhere. She had risen from singing her political *feminista* numbers in cafés and bars, where I first saw her, to appearing in a popular telenovela. I

Mi Tierra Restaurant, the Christmas Room

wish I could tell you the name, but to tell the truth I never knew it. So this happened when she was on television, and Astrid Hadad was on everyone's tongue, from the mex-intelligentsia to the *pobre* who offered to wash your windows at the stoplight.

I don't know why everyone wants to go to dinner with a *famosa,* because you never get to talk to the guest of honor, and even if you do, she's tired after a show where she's been belting them out, and to make matters worse, that night she was coming down with something. "My throat hurts," Astrid said, reaching into her purse and bringing out her own medicine, a tequila she swore she never traveled without. And again I wish I could tell you the name, but you know how I am. Unless I write it down, forget it.

It was time finally to order dinner. The waiter was having a hell of a time with so many folks seated at such a long table, and with a woman who looked like a cross between Cleopatra and Vampira slugging back tequila from her own *botella,* well, imagine.

Rolando Briseño to my right, Ito Romo to his right,
and my best friend, Josie Garza, on his right

Then it was our turn to be humble and act like groupies, after
that show where she knocked us out with songs like *"Un Calcetín"*
and *"Mala,"* we were ready to genuflect right then and there and
kiss her red high heels with the spurs. And to make matters even
better, she was whip-smart and well read, a woman of tremendous intelligence, not the vapid *vedettes* of Mexican television.

So we're at Mi Tierra restaurant in el Mercado, right? It's probably just past midnight, the beginning of the evening for me, but
in sleepy, *pueblerino* San Antonio, the middle of the night. We're
here because this is one of the few spots open, and because they

serve drinks, and even though the place is flooded with tourists in the day, after midnight the locals pile in for a bowl of *menudo* for their *cruda*, or *pan dulce* and Mexican hot chocolate after a *velorio*, or to slurp up a big bowl of tortilla soup after a night out, and I mean big, even bigger than your head.

Here we are, then, the writer/artist Ito Romo, the visual artist Rolando Briseño, and me, and I don't know who else besides Astrid and her musicians, but the table is filled with a whole lot of hangers-on hanging on. I remember Ito decides to order *enchiladas de mole,* and that's where the whole *pleito* begins.

More or less the conversation that night, the way I remember it:

ROLANDO: [in an incredulous tone, as if he were about to bite into cat *caquita*] You're going to order *enchiladas . . . de mole!* Here? You wouldn't catch me ordering *mole.* Forget it, I bet they make it from a jar. You could never get me to eat them in a million years. In my house we grew up with my mother making *mole* FROM SCRAAATCH. [This last part was with an accompanying Jackie Gleason hand gesture and leer.]

ITO: *A poco.* [And here he starts to laugh in a typical Ito *risa,* with his shoulders hunched like a vampire, and a giggle rising out of him like a gurgling fountain overflowing.] What a liar you are, Rolando! Your mother made jar *mole* from Doña María like everyone else's mother from here to Torreón.

ROLANDO: My mother made *mole* FROM SCRAAATCH. Not from a jar. I can't BELIEVE your family would eat *mole* from a jar!

ITO: Aw, come on. You're trying to say your mother dried the *chiles,* and ground them up, and took days and days to

make *mole* from scratch? You've got to be kidding! Who do
you think we are to believe such a story?

ROLANDO: My mother would never THINK of making *mole*
from a jar. What are you TALKING about!

ITO: Rolando, how do you have the nerve to say such things.
She NEVER made *mole* from a jar?

ROLANDO: Never.

And like that and like that. So that the way it ended, they were
furious with each other before the *enchiladas* even arrived, and
they haven't talked to each other decently since, even though
that was the same night Astrid belted out a song for dessert that
had everyone, including the kitchen help, flooding the Christmas
Room with applause.

But that was a long time ago. Over a decade, to be precise. I
recently invited myself to *mole* dinner at Rolando's house. This
was because I had fresh *mole* that *padrinos* from Mexico City had
brought in a cooler in their car, a *mole* dark and moist like a heart
freshly sacrificed in an Aztec ritual. And besides, everyone knows
I don't cook.

It was a splendid dinner, with several courses beautifully pre-
sented. Beneath an elegant chandelier, the table shimmered with
Rolando's grandmother's century-old china and fiftieth wedding
anniversary silver.

But when the main course arrived, it was green *mole* Rolando
finally decided to serve, not the red *mole* that had traveled all the
way from Mexico City.

"Wow!" I oohed and aahed. "And how long did it take to prepare the *mole*?" I asked.

"Oh, it was easy," he said, brushing the air with his hand. "I
made it from a jar."

PILÓN/BONUS TIDBIT

Though I admit to having reconstructed dialogue, this story is true. There are witnesses to back up my claim. Rolando, however, insists my account is nothing but *puro cuento,* pure story. But that, dear reader, is another *pleito.*

To Seville, with Love

After the European book tour of *Caramelo*, I was invited to write for *The New York Times*'s *Sophisticated Traveler* magazine soon after my return to the States. I could go anywhere I wanted, but I was so tired, the only place I wanted to travel to was my bed. Fortunately, I keep notes in a journal, save business cards, glue candy wrappers and restaurant napkins in my notebook, document graffiti on my camera, and from this "button" jar of images that snagged my eye and ear and a few questions to my travel companion, I was able to re-create the following after the fact. It includes a lot of shopping tips that may be out-of-date now, but the emotions are still current. The article first appeared in print on November 16, 2003.

Since the conquest, Mexico has had a crush on Spain. That's why I never believed my Mexican family's boasts about our Spanish patriarch, a composer of waltzes who supposedly once performed for the Mexican president. I assumed it was *puro cuento*, just another story. Until Uncle Enrique Arteaga stepped forward with my great-great-grandfather Luis Gonzaga's baptism certificate from San Esteban, a church in the old part of Seville.

I've inherited something from my family, those nomads who came and went and were forever homesick for what they left behind. My father for the lost Mexico City of his youth. My great-great-grandfather for the Andalucía of his memories, perhaps.

And me, hiding out on the border searching for the homeland of the imagination. I've since been filled with a desire to travel somewhere that might explain and answer the question "Where are you from?" and, in turn, "Who are you?" Isn't this why all writers write, or is it just those of us who live on borders?

So when a book tour transports Liliana Valenzuela, the translator of the Spanish editions of my books, and me from Texas to Spain, we arrange a weekend vacation to Seville before heading home.

On that very weekend, a soccer tournament claims every hotel room in town. Instead of the quaint pension of our dreams, we find ourselves in Nervión, a throbbing neighborhood of shops, a sports stadium, and an endless zoom of traffic. We can't complain, our hotel is Euro-chic and quiet.

It's a short cab ride or a long hot walk to the old part of the city. We walk, hoping to be mistaken for natives and not the Mex-Tex and Tex-Mex aliens we are. We're as mesmerized by Seville as the two Indian captives Columbus brought back with him from the New World. Shop windows filled with the ordinary fascinate us—door locks and bolts of serious twine, confections of baby clothes as exquisite as whipped pastries, hams lined up like soldiers, a delightful chaos of hard rolls. Here and there, on anonymous apartment buildings, enigmatic graffiti:

"READ ME WHEN YOU FORGET THAT I LOVE YOU"

"BREAD WITH TOMATO"

"PAPERS FOR EVERYONE"

"What does *that* mean?" I ask Liliana.

"It's about immigration," Lili answers matter-of-factly.

The old part of town begins when streets narrow into alleys, and we have to stand sideways to let cars pass. Walls are papered with signs for bullfights, language schools, student housing, and flamenco shows. How is it we've timed our excursion right in the middle of siesta? We're starving, and it's as hot as Texas, a heat that can make a horse faint. And it's only May.

The world is so quiet we can hear a spoon clink against a glass. Somewhere behind iron grilles and geraniums, someone is washing dishes. I imagine my grandmothers in houses like this, a child upstairs pretending to sleep, a husband snoring in a dark bedroom. To stave off the heat, they unfurl curious window shades, like jute rugs, no doubt the same since the time of Cervantes. And I wonder where I could buy some to take home to Texas.

In front of the beautiful Casa de Pilatos, a nobleman's mansion, a vendor sells tourists paper cones of sugared almonds, like the ones my father always craved and bought in small doses each payday at *el Sears*. Can someone inherit a craving? I wonder. I buy in memory of my father, and perhaps in memory of ancestors who craved sugared almonds too.

The sun has made a little hat on our heads and we're in a terrible mood, but by diligence or providence, we stumble upon a church, austere and stocky as a fortress. San Esteban of my ancestors, finally! It's closed. Of course. It's Saturday. What were we thinking? We were thinking like Americans. Lili takes a picture of me in front of the gothic doors, and I sigh and promise to come back before leaving.

A few blocks down and in the nick of time, a tapas bar raises its metal curtain and rescues us from perishing. The bartender at La Bodega treats us like long-lost kin and introduces us to his Virgen de Guadalupe. Seville is devoted to over fifty images of la Virgen—la Virgen del Rocío, la Virgen de la Macarena, la Virgen de los Remedios. And here, her pictures are featured on the wall like celebrity photos in American restaurants.

Because we don't know what to order, we ask the bartender for his recommendation, and he serves us an Especial Bodega, a sandwich of serrano ham, goat cheese, a smoked mackerel called "melva," anchovies, and mussels, on a crusty bread drizzled with olive oil. It's 1.65 euros at the table, or 1.50 euros standing. We stand. With a cold glass of beer, it's the cheapest and best meal yet.

At home, my mother would complain when we'd "eat standing like horses," but in Seville everyone except the elderly eats at the bar. We dine under an array of ham legs dangling comically above our heads like piñatas. The young marrieds next to us hand-feed a fussy toddler in a stroller. "This is probably how tapas got invented," Lili says. "Some housewife said, 'Enough! It's too hot to cook, we're going out!'"

Just beyond La Bodega, Lili and I discover la Plaza de la Alfalfa, a tiny neighborhood square, not blessed with looks, but with good shops. "And why is this plaza called alfalfa?" I ask. "Well, at one time I suppose they sold alfalfa for the animals," a local says, shrugging. *Puro cuento,* nothing but story, I think.

La Esmeralda is a boutique only wide enough to hold two or three customers at a time, but a treasure box of costume jewelry styled with enough Moorish influence, they look like the antiques *las majas* wore in the paintings in the Prado.

Across the street, the wide selection at Mayo, a shop specializing in flamenco shoes, tempts me to buy, even though I dance like a donkey.

It's next door, at Ángeles Berral, where we finally find what we need to transform ourselves into proper *majas*. Flamenco wear—dresses, silk roses, hair combs, earrings, and *mantones* and *mantillas* with exquisite hand-knotted fringe. Here the staff addresses you as *"guapa,"* good-looking, and, with amazing expertise, selects colors and patterns to help you create your *nuevo* look.

Tucked behind the plaza is Compás Sur, a shop devoted exclusively to flamenco music. Esperanza Fernández, the latest Ketama, campy Martirio, the legendary Conchita Piquer, they're all here. The shopkeeper is knowledgeable and helpful. Except when we ask where we can hear live authentic flamenco. Then he's as vague as everyone else in Sevilla. After a little thought, he recommends El Sol Café Cantante.

Since the time of Caesar, Seville has been a crossroads. Cultures may clash elsewhere, but here they thrum. At El Sol Café Cantante, located near El Rinconcillo, the oldest tapas bar in town, they put on a short, sweet, and snappy show with a sinewy dancer who turns out to be a Swede studying flamenco on a government grant. Her guitarist is Dutch. It's here at the bar where I discover *un zumo y tinto,* a popular summer drink. One part red wine, one part fresh o.j., one part sparkling water. Lots of ice. This will work well in Texas, I think.

Well, that's that, yawning and catching a cab to call it a night. But just as our taxi winds past an alley in the old quarter, the roar of flamenco music snaps us to attention. *"Your mother,* niña, *your mother, doesn't want me to see you . . . she won't even let you hang your clothes to dry on the roof . . ."*—a popular hit by Los Romeros de la Puebla. "Stop the car!" The taxi screeches to a halt, we tumble out, delighted to find ourselves in a plaza with an open-air recital of one of the dance academies. The little plaza is a flurry of polka dots. Good thing we thought to wear our new shawls and earrings from la Plaza de la Alfalfa.

The dancers are gum-chewing little girls and teens, but their mamas have gone to a lot of trouble to dress them and arrange their hair as if they were queens. What kind of hair gel do you suppose they use, and how do they get those flawless chignons? We take our seats among the relatives on the wooden folding chairs. This isn't a professional show like the one we've just seen, but it's charming, filled with the thrill and pride only family can feel for their own.

By midnight, kids are slouched and snoring on laps and shoulders. Still the party goes on, and, it seems, just as a cab swoops us up, the amps are turned up even louder. It is, after all, Saturday night.

Sundays are for church and family dinner in Mexico City, in San Antonio, Texas, and here in Seville. Out of obligation as out-of-towners, we visit the famed La Giralda, the main cathedral, swarming with tourists. It's like being inside a box of bees. I can't stand it and am forced to flee. Later I'll brush up on my Seville homework and realize Columbus is asleep here, brought back from his first burial site in Havana. And later I'll regret I didn't know all his papers are here too. On Palm Sunday, 1493, he returned to Seville with his booty from the New World, treasures, plants, animals, and two Indians who survived the journey, reluctant tourists, well, why do I have to tell you? You know the rest of the story. *I* am the rest of the story!

Lili and I take a refreshing carriage ride through María Luisa Park. I know, a bit corny, but the only sensible thing to do during the savage siesta hour. After being deposited downtown, we set off in search of a book fair, only to find again we are thinking like Americans. It's closed. We walk over to Triana, the birthplace of flamenco, just across the Guadalquivir River, in search of authentic music.

But in Triana it's like the day the earth stood still. Only pastry shops are open. We buy ice cream cones and miniature flamenco dancers and meander down the Triana streets amused by a sign in a shop that rents lockers: "Dear Customers, We beg you, please do not leave fish inside the lockers. —The Management."

It's here in Triana, by accident or on purpose, that we hear something honest and heartbreaking. From a closed bar— Antigua Taberna la Cava—the sounds of *palmas* and of men's and women's voices rising like black silk, the metal curtain half shut to block out the sun. All we can see is the dimpled hand of a child sitting on the cool tile floor.

Who cares that our feet hurt? Who cares that we're leaning against a building in full sun? This is it. The real *duende,* when the performer is simply a medium and the song sends shivers down your spine. We're in rapture. Until the child's hand shifts and a curly head pokes out from under the metal curtain to look up at us. We flutter off as startled as pigeons.

Monday is my last day for guerrilla shopping, and our neighborhood of Nervión is a great convenience. The streets are filled with shops, and everybody crazy about polka dots. I didn't bring a purse with me on this trip, or even a wallet, because Spain has such wonderful leather goods. El Corte Inglés has it all—soft Italian driving moccasins and, of course, Spanish espadrilles. In the music department I find Los Romeros de la Puebla with their catchy hit *"Tu madre, niña, tu madre,"* and La Mala Rodríguez, a Spanish hip-hop singer.

Around a sale bin, knowledgeable old women and I stand opening fans next to our ear, listening for the good ones that flick open like a switchblade. Fans are not only practical gifts to pack, in Texas, as in Seville, they're necessities.

On my last day I make it back to la Plaza de la Alfalfa to try once more to get inside San Esteban Church. I knock and knock, and finally someone opens. "I've come from across the ocean . . ." But there's a funeral tonight, they're busy, come back another day. Then the door thumps shut, and I'm left feeling like Dorothy at the door to Oz. Muddied with grief, I don't know what to do. Until the door swings open again with another man, who takes pity and lets me in.

San Esteban is small and dark and cool as a cave, and smells like all churches, like candle wax and tears. A weepy Madonna dominates the front altar. "Is that the patron of this church?" "No, that's la Virgen de los Desamparados. Here is the patron of this church," the man says, directing me to a splendid golden Madonna radiating in a niche off the main altar: "la Virgen de la Luz."

The Virgen of the Light. *La luz!* Here, one hundred and fifty years ago, my ancestors prayed and lit candles. I light one too before leaving, but my heart is already filled with light.

I make my way back toward la Plaza de la Alfalfa and try one more Bodega Special sandwich—oh, all right, I had two!—and attempt to get to that enticing shop around the corner, Callejuela, with frothy flamenco dresses in its windows. I'd been back twice, but it was always closed. It reminds me of home, of San Antonio, where shops open when they feel like it, or close if it rains. I'm lucky this time; the shop door swings open gaily when I push it.

"That dress in the window, the copper one with the pale blue dots, how much?"

"Seven hundred euros."

This is more than twice the amount of the off-the-rack flamenco dresses I saw at El Corte Inglés. Alas, though my profile is Andalusian, my torso is pure Mexican. Seven hundred euros isn't bad for a custom-made dress, I convince myself.

"I'd like one just like that, please."

"Oh, but I can't sell you a dress today," the saleswoman says. "The woman who takes measurements isn't here. You'll have to come back tomorrow."

"Tomorrow! But I leave tomorrow. And I won't come back till next year!"

"Well, then, come back next year."

I drag myself from the shop like a thirsty woman being denied water, and linger outside the window eyeing my dress: *"Your mother, niña, your mother, doesn't want me to see you . . ."*

It is as it should be. I leave Sevilla burning with *ganas,* desire. For a copper flamenco dress with sky-blue polka dots, for the archives with Columbus's papers on the New World, for authentic flamenco music, for a sandwich with anchovies, tuna, and goat cheese. I leave with perhaps the same regret in my heart as my great-great-grandfather Luis Gonzaga. And perhaps with the same vow: "I'll be back soon, Mamá, God willing."

A White Flower

I wanted to make a gift to a woman I admire. In gratitude. But I didn't know whether one could make gifts to one's therapist. What's allowed? It's a culture I wasn't familiar with, like traveling to a country where you don't speak the language. I no longer visit her as I did back in 2005 when I wrote this; I've since moved away. But I often think of her. She was my teacher and spirit guide for over a decade. She taught me how to understand my dreams and how to soar. In other times, she might've been a Mayan high priestess or an oracle at Delphi. This analogy would make her laugh, I think. But that's how I saw and still see her.

Every Tuesday I drive toward the most congested area of San Antonio at the most congested hour of the day, and, no matter how early I start, I arrive promptly late for my appointment with a woman I call the shameless shamaness. She doesn't call herself this. Her business card reads "Jungian Therapist."

A few months short of finishing my nine-year novel, I sought her out. I was as prickly as a snake after shedding its skin, as agoraphobic as a vampire in the day, as waterlogged as a blue maguey. I was frightened and sad beyond the reach of family and friends. I felt myself drifting away from society, like an unmoored boat swept away by subterranean seasons.

I'd been this ill before, and I knew what to do when I was this beyond-help blue. Seek out a *bruja*. I asked around, and somebody who was also heartsick and sad gave me her name.

At our first meeting I thought my shamaness looked exactly as a *bruja* should—wise and clever as a little white owl, benevolent as a television-show grandmother. My therapist listens and is paid to listen to my stories. In the beginning I felt I had to be entertaining. There is something odd for me still in telling a story one-on-one without getting a story back in return. It makes me feel guilty. As if I am being narcissistic hogging up the spotlight. As if I am being rude for not asking, "And you? How was *your* day?"

I think about her between sessions. When I dream an especially good dream, I'm as delighted to present it as a pupil delivering an apple. I'm curious about this woman who listens patiently to the latest episode of the story called my life. I want to ask her so many things, so many, but I think it's against the rules.

I would like to ask, for example, "Do you approve of me, or am I silly?" Even if she didn't approve, what does it matter? But it matters a lot. To me.

I would ask whether the stories I've told her are any good— worth repeating, worth remembering. That's how I define a good story.

Does she get tired listening to stories all day and all week, year after year? How does one stay healthy at the end of a day full of stories? Does one have to shake oneself off like a dog after its bath?

And. What did you eat for breakfast today? Do you believe in an afterlife? What about a before-life? Does your husband read to you? Does passion exist until death? Have you ever seen a ghost? Did you have a good childhood? What is the most remarkable thing you remember about giving birth? Do you own a dog? Are you happy? What has *la vida* taught you? Does your husband listen to the story of your life before you put out the light?

When I was a child, there really was a girl I knew whose name was Sally, and who would later inspire bits and pieces of the character of the same name in *The House on Mango Street*. She was in my class all through middle and junior high, but it wasn't until about midway that we actually began to talk to each other. I think it was only because we walked home the same way, and because she was mad at her best friend that day.

Her home was a half block before mine, on top of the corner grocery store. She invited me up, and I was allowed to walk through the big wide rooms of her apartment, an old Chicago-style building with wooden floors, high ceilings, and tall windows. I thought it was grand, but I could tell Sally didn't think so.

Then she stunned me by asking something I didn't expect: "Can I see your pajamas?" It was a strange request, but I was anxious for her to be my friend, so I took her home with me that instant.

Our two-story bungalow was tidy and full of spirit and, best of all, ours. Nothing luxurious, but I could tell Sally thought I was rich. Maybe it was our nice furniture that fooled her. Our father, after all, was an upholsterer. And we had art on the walls. A silk tiger our uncle Frankie brought back from Japan after he was in the service, and a set of paint-by-number geishas my mother had painted. Thanks to the previous owners, almost all our rooms were wallpapered, and some had carpeting. Sally didn't seem to notice the sweaty walls and drafty space heaters, the bedrooms without doors.

I led Sally to the little closet that was my room, tugged back the bedspread and pillow from my twin bed, and showed her my neatly folded pajamas. I didn't know for sure whether my pajamas disappointed or met her expectations. She didn't say anything, and I didn't say anything either, but I supposed she expected frilly silk and marabou feathers, not my flowered flannel.

After all these years, I think I finally get it. I would like to ask my therapist, "Can I see your pajamas?" It's as if I want to understand, in a shorthand way, who she really is.

When I'm on the road giving readings, I sign books after my performances. I'm aware that my audience has waited a long time to tell me something. I often feel like a therapist then. So I try to pay attention and make eye contact, to be as present as I can possibly be, because the business of listening is much more difficult than speaking.

One evening after a reading I gave at the National Museum of Mexican Art in Chicago, the line to meet the author was especially long and slow-moving. I could feel myself flagging.

"You used too much energy tonight, didn't you?"

I looked up and saw a woman who could've passed for my sister. A woman with a Mona Lisa grin that said, "I know you."

"You're a *bruja,* aren't you?" I blurted out. I could tell she was a good witch, one who works in the light. She smiled, and we recognized each other the way animals recognize their own kind.

"Okay, then," I said. "What can I do to recharge?"

This is what she told me: "When you get back to your room tonight, find a quiet space. I want you to close your eyes and imagine a white flower. Any kind will do, but it must be white. Imagine it as a bud. Now see it opening-opening-opening-opening. Imagine it in full bloom, as full and heavy as can be. Now blow all its petals away, so that nothing's left but the stem.

"That's for everyone you met and talked to today.

"Now I want you to imagine another white flower bud. See it opening again. Opening-opening-opening-opening. It's beautiful. Enjoy it. Inhale it. Savor it. This flower is for you."

Last month, after three years of being my therapist's patient, I received an unusual message on my phone machine. My therapist was canceling our appointments for the time being, a family emergency, she would get back to me. And when she finally did return after a month's absence, it was with the frank and calm announcement that her husband had died.

I wanted, then, to take care of my story listener. It was her turn to tell me a story, and it was my turn to listen. And finally I felt I could be of some use to her, that I could, for a change, give her something back for all she had given me. But I felt too shy to say this and couldn't find the language for all the things swirling inside me. The next time I saw her I brought a white orchid, luminous as the full moon.

The Japanese say it's a black cat that's necessary when one is in mourning. They say black cats absorb one's grief. This may be true, but I know from experience that white flowers know how to listen.

And because I could not say what I felt then, I say it here now. You are my white flower. I offer you this bouquet, to cleanse and soothe and salve you. These pages are for you.

Señor Cappuccino

I'm shy when forced to meet other writers. I suppose it's like this for lots of writers. We're an introverted species. And when we're herded into one another's company, what a jaded bunch we become! Nobody's less impressed that you're a writer than a roomful of writers.

And so it happened I found myself in just such discomfort for the 2005 Premio Napoli, where we were gathered like smiling beauty queens secretly sizing each other up. Maybe that's not so. Maybe that's just how I remember it. I remember sincerely desiring someone else to win. (This sounds like a lie, but it's true.) Most of the writers I met were cordial. But one writer had thoughts like a scimitar and was amusingly competitive. I laugh even now when I see his name in print.

Only Ryszard Kapuściński won everyone's respect and floated above the rabble. I wish I'd read his work before meeting him and not after. I lost an opportunity to ask him . . . to ask him what? I'd ask, "Does a writer have to live in a perpetual border in order to be able to see?"

The writer Ryszard Kapuściński died on January 23, 2007, at the age of seventy-four. The *New York Times* editorial of February 2nd featured a beautiful *homenaje* for this journalist, who wrote with the language of his senses and not, as the *Times* put it, the "everyday language of information that we use in the media."

He was a border crosser in every sense of the word, crossing genres as easily as he crossed countries, a Pole who followed his stories across continents, witnessing wars, witnessing the grief of the poorest of humanity. My partner and I were lucky to have met Señor Kapuściński, only briefly, but that was all we needed to see who he was. He never mentioned he was world famous, that he was a regular contributor to *The New Yorker, The New York Times, Granta,* that his several books—*Travels with Herodotus, Shah of Shahs, The Emperor*—had been translated into more than eighteen languages. He never said any of this, and it would be only after his death that I came to know his writing.

We met in September 2005 in Naples. He would win the Premio Napoli that year, surprisingly enough in the poetry category. We gathered in the foyer of the hotel where we were awaiting a representative from the Premio Napoli offices, and from that first meeting, Señor Kapuściński charmed us.

He was an older man, stocky as a prizefighter, with silver hair that stood straight up like brush bristles. I remember he contrasted sharply with the other invited writers, a flock of blackbirds, because he was dressed in pale colors that matched his hair. We spoke to each other in Spanish; Señor Kapuściński did not speak English. He talked about living in Mexico and in Latin America. What was remarkable was the way he listened. He looked at you when you spoke; his attention never floated above and beyond you, like most famous people I've met. He was so popular with all the writers present that by the end of the week whenever he climbed up on our motor bus, an involuntary cheer would rise. If there had been a vote for Mister Congeniality, I'm sure Señor Kapuściński would've won.

Finally our welcome committee arrived, a tiny creature as fragile as coral. She looked like a child to me, but this happens a lot now that I'm older. That day we were to visit several bookstores and community centers, since many people in Naples were reading and voting on our books. Did we want to walk or take a taxi to the plaza where the motor bus waited?

"It isn't far," the escort assured us, "just a few blocks."

That should've clued us all in. I know from experience that for Italians "a few blocks" could mean kilometers. It was also unfortunate that it was a hot autumn day, and though it was early morning, we would be walking uphill. To make matters worse, Señor Kapuściński was dressed formally in suit and tie. He voted to walk.

The Naples streets looked like opera sets to my eyes. We would cross an entranceway and peer into a courtyard laced with laundry hanging from balconies—those proud flags of the housewives— turn a narrow corner, and a plaza would suddenly bloom before us. We walked past stationery shops filled with ordinary but intriguing items—composition books, fountain pens, sand timers—a writer's heaven, and beyond to baroque monuments and splendidly stocked news kiosks. We dodged café tables where

Donatella Versace look-alikes smoked cigarettes and flicked their platinum manes. It was pleasant, and since we had a lot to talk about, we didn't complain. But after a while Señor Kapuściński began dabbing his face with his handkerchief and asking, "How many more blocks?"

Our child escort now seemed like someone sent from a horror film, the very picture of Death with her Cleopatra eyes and miniskirt. She kept luring us forward, promising, "It isn't far now, it's just up ahead."

We passed a stoop where an ancient woman in black sat silently selling holy pictures from a basket. I gave her my Guadalupe holy card from my wallet, and she kissed and kissed it, blessing me in Italian a thousand times.

With every block, Señor Kapuściński grew more flushed. At times he would stand still to make a point in a story as much as to catch his breath. My partner and I lagged behind to keep him company since by then the rest of the party was far ahead.

Finally Señor Kapuściński had had enough. "I thought she said it was just up ahead! This is an outrage!" "Yes, it's too much," we agreed. We sat down at the next outdoor café with him and ordered cappuccinos, pretending to be upset too, even though we were fine.

It took a while for our hostess to realize we'd mutinied. She came back for us, and by then Señor Kapuściński was calmer after he'd rested and had something to drink.

"But we're almost there," she said, and by then her claim was true. The bus was purring at the next plaza, just around the corner. But Señor Kapuściński had walked too many blocks for *un señor grande,* and his rage was real, though aimed at the wrong target. It wasn't the young hostess who had lied to him, but his own aging body.

I wanted then to take care of Señor Kapuściński. He reminded me of my grandfather, of my father, of all the men I've known who grow frustrated at the inadequacy of their aging bodies and blame it on you. "You see, you see what you made me do!"

I think it was then I dubbed him Señor Cappuccino, because in my mind he became, from then on, indelibly linked with that cup of coffee we shared together during our mutiny.

Señor Kapuściński laughed at his nickname, and when we said goodbye at the week's end, he promised to send and did indeed send me his poetry. In Polish, for my Polish eye doctor. He apologized and was sorry the book was not yet translated into English for me. He never mentioned his extraordinary body of work, as compact as poetry, in exquisite prose I would discover and fall in love with later for its ability to exceed journalism and invent a new genre: reportage with literary power—poetic and precise.

So much was he in my thoughts this new year, I had a friend buy a Mexican calendar for me to send him, even though the days of his life were already over. That was the same day I would learn of his death in the newspaper.

"What kind of Mexican calendar should I buy?" my friend asked that morning on the phone.

"Buy him a traditional one," I instructed. "It's for an elder, *un señor grande.*"

Señor Cappuccino's calendar arrived a few days later, when I'd almost forgotten about it. An Aztec warrior firing an arrow toward the sun.

Natural Daughter

Retrato de india cacique, 1757

In the spring of 2006, the San Antonio Museum of Art featured a show called *Retratos: 2,000 Years of Latin American Portraits.* It included a portrait of a chieftain's daughter, a woman straddling the Old World and the New, dressed in a baroque *huipil,* an indigenous tunic altered with Spanish lace, as much a product of the *mestizaje* as she was.

It's this woman I linger with and look upon when I'm invited to the show, and it's she I have in mind as I search for the subject of my lecture for the prestigious Rome summer arts festival, Festival delle Letterature, where I'm to read in the Roman Forum. I don't know what I'll write about, but somehow I know this painting is the route.

I've been invited along with the Olympians—José Saramago and Doris Lessing. The topic is "Natural/Artificial." Is writing this way natural? Isn't it artificial to be force-fed a title and then have to produce something that suits the theme? For weeks I wake and sleep in a frenzy. Are Saramago and Lessing having as difficult a time as I am?

We are at war. I want to say something that will help heal, help bring peace to the planet, to my listeners. I don't know what story I can tell that will be that powerful. I'm only one person, and I feel small to the task at hand. I always do. I'm only one writer, but I'm one of the writers they've invited.

I know that before I begin to write something, I need to ask for humility. I need to ask my father's spirit to come and help me. I need to ask for the story that has heart and soul, a story I feel in my body. What story is that? I haven't a clue.

I do what I always do when I'm lost: I take a nap.

When I wake, I ask myself this: What is the story we won't tell? And when is it time to tell it? Is it a natural story—that is, born of the truth? Or is it an artificial story, one we have to make up to fill in all the gaps because no one will tell us the truth? I have just enough of a story, but not enough. Maybe it's as I always suspected. The best stories are the ones we can't tell.

I'm Jacob wrestling the angel. "I will not let thee go except thou bless me." Day after day, week after week, I'm locked in a *lucha libre* with the Angel of Death. And when I finally finish, my back aches. She blessed me.

So why am I overwhelmed with grief?

B efore you and your brothers were born," my mother said to me, "before your father met me, he already had a kid in Mexico City. Illegitimately. With one of *las muchachas* who worked for your grandmother. A daughter."

It was 1995. We were at Presbyterian St. Luke's in Chicago, the hospital where I was born and where my father was under the knife having heart surgery. While we waited in the hospital lounge, my mother bared her own heart to me, her only daughter.

"Sometimes when we were in Mexico visiting, this woman and her daughter helped out with our laundry. You used to play with the girl. But you were little, you don't remember."

I didn't tell my mother then, but I *did* remember. The face of this girl, my natural sister, traveled back to me, *una paloma blanca* fluttering across the expanse of forty years.

And though my father survived the heart surgery and accompanied us in the world of the living for two more winters, he never mentioned his other daughter to me. I never mentioned her to him.

There are some questions a daughter can't ask a father.

I thought about this sister a lot as I wrote *Caramelo*. After my father died, I hesitated with whether to exploit this family secret as raw material for my story. I had to promise my father's spirit that in the end it would all turn out *bonito*. The novel was finished years ago. But she haunts me still.

I somehow thought after *Caramelo*'s publication my family would be forced to sit down and talk, finally, like a real family, with one person speaking and the others listening. I imagined my six brothers and me having a moment like in the telenovelas where the music rises and tears fall, but in the end we would all embrace.

But that didn't happen. We never talk about things that matter. We talk about breaded pork chops, the Chicago White Sox, the dog's skin rash, voices shouting over one another and no one listening.

And because I don't mention this woman, even thinking about her makes me feel like crying. So who could I seek out, who could tell me about her?

As Divine Providence would have it, when I telephone my mother in Chicago the following week, guess who's visiting from Mexico? Señor Juchi is sitting at my mother's kitchen table as if willed into being. Señor Juchi is a character in real life and in my novel. He's also my father's *compadre* from way back, from the Mexico City of their youth, after Father came back from serving in the U.S. Army in World War II.

The first thing Señor Juchi tells me about my half sister is: "I think you're mistaken."

He goes on: "I remember your father had a '41 Buick, a big yellow convertible. And good suits Señor Curiel the tailor made for him, and those expensive shoes. Italian leather. They cost a lot. He liked to dress good. Beautiful suits. Beautiful shoes. 1948, '49. I knew your uncle Little first, that's how I came to meet your father. Through Little. Little and I were still riding bicycles, and we would see your father come and go in that big 41 Buick of his. What a car! He liked those big-shouldered suits. What I remember was the 41 Buick. But a daughter? No, I think you're mistaken.

"A '41 Buick. Beautiful, but it gave him a lot of car problems."

Señor Juchi is a master storyteller. He takes his time when he should take his time. He slows the story almost to a halt when he has your interest, and then speeds the story along like a dancer pattering toward the footlights, pausing right before a furious final pirouette.

"This was around the time when this girl Silvia was my girlfriend when we were just *chamacos,* just kids. She was maybe fourteen, so let's see, maybe I was sixteen or so. These days Silvia takes care of my house in Juchitán when I'm in Mexico City. I let her stay there rent free, because she's old now and I feel sorry for her, but, oh, my wife is jealous! She thinks this woman and I have got something going on. Look, she was just my girlfriend a long time ago. When we were just *chamacos. Cha-ma-cos.* But I broke it off, because she was fooling around on me. I said, 'Silvia, I think it's to your benefit if you and I go our separate ways . . .' "

"But what does this have to do with my father?" I ask.

"Oh, well, that. No. I think you're mistaken."

After I interview her about the secret sister, my mother says, "So what else is new?"

It's been a decade since that first conversation we had in the hospital. I'm ashamed to say I was afraid of my mother's bad temper. She was angry with her mother-in-law for bringing the washerwoman around when *she* was there as the official wife. But this time, after she told me all she knew, which was about as much as I knew, she said, "That was the past. It doesn't have anything to do with me. So what else is new?" She sounds as blasé as if talking about the weather.

My mother doesn't like silences. She fills them up with "So what else is new?" Or with a detailed report of what she had for dinner. Or what she bought at the grocery store. Silences are to be filled in the way one stuffs a mouse hole with steel wool. That's what my mother's lists of food and talk that is just talk are all about. Syllables to fill the void, so the real stories that slink about in the dark won't come out and spook us.

I wonder about my mother. And I wonder about myself and my own curiosity, my nagging need to poke under the bed with a broom.

———

Señor Juchi calls me back a few days later: "I spoke with your mother about the girl. She said she didn't think it was true."

I'm surprised at my mother lying to him so coolly and ask, "Did she get upset?"

"No. But she did say this: 'If he has a daughter, she's probably in Korea, because that's where he was stationed between the wars.'"

Then he tosses this Molotov: "And I managed to get ahold of your uncle Old. Old said he doesn't know anything about your father and any illegitimate daughter. But . . ."

And here he pauses for effect.

"He did confess to having an illegitimate daughter himself! A girl he sees on Mexican television because she's a newscaster."

Before hanging up, he gives me this advice: "Look, the person you should really ask is your aunt Baby Doll. She and your father were always close."

But when I do summon the courage to call Father's favorite sister, they tell me she's in Mexico. How is it when she lived in Mexico she was always visiting the U.S., and now that she lives in Chicago, you can never find her, because she's in Mexico City!

Maybe the antidote to my fever is to *not* think about her, like Mother: "That was before he met me. It doesn't have anything to do with me."

———

I telephone my oldest brother late at night when I know I'm sure to find him. He's a doctor and rarely home. He tells me a story, but not the one I'm looking for.

"You know the story of our Tía Esmeralda in Mexico, don't you? How she was pretty, the prettiest of all her pretty sisters, right? She's a black widow."

"What do you mean?"

"She killed all her husbands."

"What! But *how?*"

"Well, *I* don't know," he says. "Poison maybe."

"But what about the family secret about our half sister?"

"Oh that," he says flatly. "I already knew. Papa told me in the car. He was already sick when he told me."

"And what did *you* say?"

"What *could* I say? I was in shock!"

"The girl used to play with us," I say. "Remember?"

"No, I don't."

"But *you* were the one who made up the game to see if she wore underwear."

"How do you remember those things?" he says.

"How do you forget?"

––––––––

I think if I think the thought, my lost sister will materialize and tell me the story of her life. The one without our father. If she stayed behind in Mexico, it's probable she never learned to read and write. It's possible she made her living as a laundress like her mother. If she had children, maybe they made their way north to the border and crossed over. And maybe that crossing was safe and uneventful, or maybe it was dangerous and fatal, or worse. It's always worse for women, isn't it?

And if her children made it over to this side, I *know* how difficult their lives are here. Especially now after 9/11 when politicians want to build a wall around the country.

And I think about the recent immigrant rights marches and the sign one man carried: IF YOU DEPORT ME, WHO WILL BUILD THE WALL?

––––––––––

Brother Number Two and I exchange emails under the subject "The Missing Sister," like a mystery story from Sherlock Holmes.

Brother writes, *She might be related to us, but she's a stranger to me. Anyway, the way I see it, I have a lot of relatives I already know that I barely have time for as it is. What do you expect to get from all this?*

I don't know, I write back immediately, *I'm a writer. It's my job to think about things. I live my life facing backward.* I don't tell him all of this bothers me because I was Father's favorite. His *reina.* How come Father lavished all this love on me and none on her?

My brother writes, *Why don't you ask Aunt Baby Doll? She loves to talk about the past.*

If I could find her, I write back, *but she's an unreliable witness. You know how she always covered up for Father.*

My brother suggests I ask our father's friends. But most of them are gone already, crossed over the final border to the other side, where, as New Mexican poet Levi Romero puts it, *"quizás están muy contentos allá en la gloria / porque no llaman ni escriben."* They must be very happy over there in heaven, because they don't call or write.

My father's *compadres.* Even the ones who might be alive, how to find them? Drifters who worked both sides of the border, a little upholstery, a little buying here and selling there. Who knows what they did over there. They were never home, their wife and kids stashed conveniently on the other side. Sure, they sent money home. Some of them went to church every Sunday.

Just a bunch of ne'er-do-wells, big talkers, nothing-but-story. Bullshitters. The kind of guys like Fellini's *I Vitelloni*. Just a bunch of big mama's boys. Babies with suits.

———

Everyone warns me not to revisit the story about the laundress's daughter, because it's not fiction anymore.

Now it's dirty laundry.

———

"You just want the dirt on Papa."

Brother Number Three is home when I call. He and our two youngest brothers, the twins, manage the upholstery shop my father left behind. It's Saturday. Brother is minding the kids while his wife is out.

"You just want the dirt," he insists.

"No, I just want to know what you think."

"I think everybody has secrets."

"Not me," I say. "My life is an open book." But as soon as I say this, I wonder if it's true.

Brother admits he knew. Cuco, one of Father's upholstery buddies, told him.

"Remember Cuco?" he asks. "He's the only upholsterer I knew who wore a suit to work, like a businessman. A fat man with slick hair hammering chairs in his white shirt and tie. After Papa got sick, I used to hang around with Cuco and listen to his stories, stories about the war, stories about the relatives. He's the one that told me Aunt Oralia had a fling with Uncle Paco before she married his brother."

"You're lying!"

"That's what he said. He was a good guy for stories, I tell you that."

My brother adds, "Mama didn't like him, though, said he was a bad influence. Mama always suspected Papa was having an affair with one of his seamstresses. Well, the seamstress was nothing to look at, but I don't know. I think, well, I went through things in my own life. But I'm good with my wife and my kids, you know. It's different once you become a father."

"That's the point," I say. "You have a daughter you're crazy about. Think about *her*."

"Wait, I'm not so sure Cuco is dead. I'll ask this guy who sells Poly-Foam. He would know. And you should try getting ahold of Aunt Baby Doll."

He promises to call me back. But then he doesn't.

———

Brother Number Two says Father was always running away from his problems. I think about this for a while and consider its truth. When the washerwoman was pregnant, Father ran to Korea. And when Mother was pregnant with her firstborn in Chicago, Father ran back home to Mexico City. But he was scolded by his own father, who reminded him, "We are not dogs." And Father returned with his tail between his legs to Mother in Chicago, and he married her.

———

I think a lot about the reasons for my obsession while I'm driving the car, while I'm waiting at a red light. Maybe it's about abandonment. It's because I was abandoned by lovers when I was writing *Caramelo,* not once but twice. It's because I know the worst thing in the world isn't having someone leave you by death. That, after all, is not their fault. But to have someone leave of their own volition, to have someone you love alive, existing on the planet, but choosing not to share any part of that living with you.

The weakness isn't having the child. It's abandoning it.

To me abandonment is worse than death.

―――――

Why do you suppose Grandfather didn't insist Father fulfill his obligation to the washerwoman? Was it because she was Indian? Mexico glorifies its Indian past, but the contemporary situation is another story. Indians are the ones who work the worst jobs, who are at the bottom of the social ladder. You only have to watch Mexican television to see all the stars are as white as Hollywood. It's the mixed-bloods, the *mestizos,* who play the part of Indians even in the telenovelas. I don't know of any Indians who play Indians. And when there is a role for an Indian, it's a bit part as a servant, or in a Stepin Fetchit role that ridicules Indians. In Mexico the worst kind of insult is to call someone *un indio.*

―――――

The washerwoman's daughter. My father's natural daughter. What kind of father was he to her? It's like a telenovela. Did the mother fall in love with my father in his good suits and yellow convertible? Or did my father simply help himself to what was close at hand? He wouldn't have had a hard time. My father was always a charmer.

I wonder what she felt, this washerwoman, watching my mother and her kids, watching us, watching me play, while her own daughter with the same face as my father, the darker daughter, had to work.

We were always *amolados,* always traveling from Chicago to

Father in Korea

Mexico City and back on a shoestring. No seat belts. No credit cards. No stopping. Bologna sandwiches for dinner.

Sometimes my father was so sleepy he'd swerve across the line. A truck would honk. That's when my mother would jerk awake and scream, "Alfredo! You could've killed us!" And then we'd pull over to the side of the road and let Father join us for a snooze.

He couldn't resist babies. He borrowed them from their mothers at the supermarket just so he could get a chance to hold them. He honked and waved at kids when his car paused at Stop signs. "Watch out!" we'd warn him. "Somebody's going to think you're a pervert." He didn't care. He was a lover of children even as a young soldier. Photos of him in Korea holding crying toddlers, hugging street kids, three or four in each arm. My father was always a man who loved kids. He raised seven of them.

Above all else. Above anyone, everyone. Including his wife. My father adored kids. How could the man I knew be the same one to walk away from a daughter?

————

I should've asked my father when he was alive. After lying on the operating table having a quadruple bypass, he had almost two more years of life.

My family suffers stories no one dares to tell.

The grandmother who had a child from another liaison before she married my grandfather. The uncle who ran off with the army payroll. The cousin in Philadelphia who shot his wife in a fit of jealousy and had the rest of his life in prison to regret his bad temper. The maternal great-grandmother who, despite being ugly, married five times and thus is suspected by this descendant of being good in bed.

We don't talk about these things. Father would get angry if I even mentioned them.

So how was I to ask?

I should've asked.

————

Brother Number Four says he knew because of *Caramelo*. He's a geologist. His wife was born in Mexico, so they go back and forth a lot. It's because they've witnessed what it is to be poor over there. Every time they go, they visit an orphanage and bring gifts, donate a little money. This brother is the only one who says he wouldn't mind trying to find our sister.

"But how do we find her?" he asks. "Hire a detective?"

"I don't know," I say. "I don't know."

————

Sister, maybe your mother saw an opportunity.

I don't blame her.

Maybe she fell in love with his words, his big-shouldered suits, the fine car, the good shoes. Maybe he was the only gentleman who ever looked at her.

Or maybe he just used her. A player like the ones I fell in love with and imagined myself in love with for years.

I'd fall for a suit and a tie every time. A nice car. A good profession. An apartment in a neighborhood that was glamorous. Not like my neighborhood, which looked like a mouth with open sores.

Maybe she thought he'd come to rescue her, like the stories in the telenovelas. Deliver her from the rooftop room and install her in a home of her own.

———

I want to see you, and I do see you, everywhere, in all the women I meet when I travel to Mexico or Bosnia or Italy. I see you in all the women, the poorest of the poor. That spring day in Sarajevo, an unforgettable picture of misery: a Roma woman with terror on her face, standing on the curbside, ignored, offering for sale half-dead lilacs wilting in the miserable heat. The *indígena* in the Tepoztlán market begging me to please buy another bag of *chocolate* even though I'd already bought one: *"Por favorcito,* it's not going well for me today. *Por favorcito."* In Rome the Polish refugee knitting hats on the curb of Piazza Mazzini, her wares spread on a little card table; the Peruvian nannies afraid to talk to me, homesick but afraid to complain, sunning their little charges in the pebbled park of the Gianicolo; the Asian women at Piazza Navona, silk scarves draped from their arms as if they were the goddess Kwan Yin, each desperately shouting lower and lower prices just to make a sale. At Union Square, San Francisco, the homeless woman who says, "Thank you. You're the first person all day who looked me in the eye and treated me like a human being."

Everywhere, no matter where I go, I see you.

———————

My phone machine. Brother Number Five: "Got your message. Call me back."

———————

The U.S. Census form arrives by mail, and I find myself confused by the most basic question.

"What are we?" I call out to Ray, my partner, who is working in his study. "What shall I put down for what we are?"

We don't agree with being classified as "Hispanics," that slave name I connect with presidents who never even bothered to ask us what we call ourselves. What's in a name? Everything. If it doesn't really matter, why won't "wetback" do?

"Sweets, what shall I put down for what we are?"

Ray and I decide after some conversation to check off "other."

But then the census form insists on details and offers ethnic categories.

We claim "indigenous" because we don't know how to explain it in one word.

But after I check off "indigenous," the next question baffles us even more: *What tribe?*

"Ray, what tribe are we?" I say, shouting toward the next room. "What?"

"They want to know what tribe we are. What shall I say?"

After some discussion we agree to write in *"mestizo."*

———————

Brother Number Five calls. Says, "I don't know anything."

Then a knocking on the phone cuts us off, as if our father doesn't like us discussing his sins.

———————

Brother Number Six, the youngest, comes to visit me in San Antonio with his wife and kid. Because they're tourists, we consider the horse and carriages parked next to the Alamo. We're eating ice cream sundaes and we hesitate. But the driver says, "Sure you can bring your ice cream on board." So we climb up.

I'm enjoying my caramel sundae and the ride when the driver, a big country woman from outside Dallas, starts talking about genealogies. How she's one-sixteenth Cherokee and one-fourth I-don't-know-what, and on and on. She is the color of boiled milk.

Somehow it pisses me off for her to claim to be Indian. So many Americans claim to be Indian, but I don't see them volunteering to assist their natural brothers on the reservation.

It might be the canvas sack collecting horse *caquita* under the horse's tail, or it might be the story she's telling, but my caramel sundae starts tasting like horse manure.

After I've had enough, I finally speak up and say, "Well, we're Indian too!"

She twists around from her seat in front of the carriage and says, "Oh yeah?" in a smart-alecky tone, and then, just like the U.S. Census, she asks, "What tribe?"

"What tribe? Well, I don't know," I say. "Our families fled Mexico during the Mexican Revolution. But all you have to do is look at our faces."

My sister-in-law is the color of coffee with not enough milk, my brother and I the color of *café con leche,* the child the color of a cappuccino. My brother, his wife, their child, and me, we look like Mexicans, Arabs, Jews, Moors, Sicilians, American Indians, East

Indians, Turks, Greeks, Palestinians, Roma, Egyptians, Pakistanis, Iraqis, Iranians, Afghanis. We look like what we are.

And who the hell knows what that is.

———————

Aunty shrieks like a parrot when I tell her why I'm calling. She calls the woman and the daughter both *esa chamaca*, that youngster. All the characters in her story are *esa chamaca, ese fulano, este ratero, esa sinvergüenza*. That youngster, that so-and-so, this thief, that shameless one. I'm not certain if she's talking about the mother, the daughter, an older daughter, the man the mother took up with, or the man my natural sister ran off with.

"Now wait a second, Aunty. *Who* stole *what* money?"

"She robbed me," Aunty goes on without answering. "I'm certain *por Dios Santo* she was not your father's daughter. How could he be the father if he was in Korea when she was pregnant?"

Then she goes on: *"La chamaca Luz . . ."*

Luz! My memory was right about the mother's name.

"She was a clubfooted servant . . ."

Funny, I hadn't remembered her clubfoot, but, yes, I do remember now the little polka of her gait, the way she labored under the tin bowls of wet laundry.

" . . . a good washerwoman, excellent, but she did not wash her own body. How could a man as delicate as your father take up with a woman who was dirty and smelly?"

My aunt calls the washerwoman *mugrosa*, dirty, and *apestosa*, smelly, but I saw her as dusty and worn out from labor. I suppose if you had to hobble about washing clothes and pulling loads through a wringer washer on the rooftop in the summer heat, you'd be smelly too.

"She had two girls, an older one, Teresa, from another man, of course. And a younger girl whose name I can't remember.

Because they were the kind of women who would get involved with anyone.

"Yes, she had a fellow who lived up there on the roof with her. But after the younger one was born, the *sinvergüenza* left them, and your grandmother would find her work. Your grandmother was just trying to be kind. Do you think she would've had her around had she known the gossip?"

"But I remember the girl, and she looked just like my father, only darker."

"What are you saying! She didn't look like your father! She went with us to Acapulco. You have photos of her."

I'm astounded. In *Caramelo* I invented just this scenario. I thought I made up several parts of my novel, but later someone tells me that this, and other things too, really happened. The things I think I imagined are true, and the things I remember as truly happening . . . ? But maybe it's the older girl who was my

Family trip to Acapulco, c. 1964

father's daughter. After all, my father came home periodically on leave.

Aunty goes on with her story, still talking about the younger girl. "Somebody put the idea in her head about your father. That girl tried to get money from us after you'd all gone back to Chicago, and when she couldn't, she robbed us. I didn't call the police because of her mother. But let me look for the photos of Acapulco. And the letters from your father in Korea. I'll look and we'll set this all straight."

Is it only a good story, not a true one? And if it is true, is it too ugly for fiction, made dirty with theft and accusations, blackmail and bigotry, the same prejudices one class, one race, has about another?

Then Aunty proceeds to unravel another family secret, one she thinks I don't know. I do, but I want to hear how she will tell it. It's about when "the grandfather" was a colonel in the Mexican army, stationed on the coast at Tampico. He had a mistress there who was *el amor de su vida* . . . But this is *my* version of the story, not Aunty's.

"Mamá moved us there for two years to keep an eye on him. One day Little and I discovered that so-and-so talking to Father at the barracks. We chased her with sticks all the way back to her door, so she would leave him alone. Father was so mad he sent us back to Mexico City after that."

Aunty chuckles with pride over her victory over *la fulana* even though it happened more than a half century ago.

I want to ask her about her father. Didn't she think she should've beaten him up too? But I don't bring up this detail since she seems so pleased with herself.

Poking under the bed, all I've found is other people's dirt. Everyone has told me something I didn't know, or that they didn't know I knew.

I wonder, Are all stories like this? The natural events much more complicated than the artificial story each of us weaves where we are the heroes, in the center of the universe.

Aunty tells me, "I went to visit your father at the hospital at the end and told him. 'Look, you're not the father of that girl. When Luz was pregnant, you were in Korea. The dates don't coincide. So there!'"

And then, as if she knows how I feel, Aunty adds to me, "You have nothing to feel guilty about."

"And then?"

"What do you mean?"

"What did Father *say* when you told him?"

"Nothing. That's the end of the story. What else could he say?"

Then it's my turn to say nothing.

A Girl Called Daydreamer

For decades the only childhood report card that survived my nomadic wanderings was the one from fifth grade, a testament to shame and sorrow. This uninspiring collection of marks at least allowed me to tell a good story as a successful writer, since I used it often as a visual aid in my lectures to younger audiences, many of them fifth graders themselves with dull report cards. Other school evaluations would float up from the wreckage of my mother's shoe-box archives and attest to academic improvement later. But at the time I wrote the following, my terrible fifth-grade report card was all I had to remind me of my childhood panic of school. I remember I'd wake up sick with fear, often bleating, "Ma, I don't want to go to school today." "So don't go," she'd say without a "How come?" or "You better." God knows why she was lenient with me. Maybe she intuited my unhappiness. I felt *susto*, terror, from third grade through sixth. This memory is so strong, it overwhelms me every time I visit an elementary school to speak even now. Thankfully, it wears off once I start talking.

This lecture was first delivered at the downtown San Antonio Public Library in October 2007 to an auditorium of middle and high school students. The occasion was the second San Antonio reunion of los MacArturos, the Latino MacArthur fellows. Our first MacArturo event had happened a decade earlier. I shared the program this time with the president of the Farm Labor Organizing Committee, Baldemar Velásquez, a great oral storyteller, and that P. T. Barnum of booksellers,

Reubén Martínez, who made our jaws drop when he gave away
a crisp hundred-dollar bill to the student who could remember
the name of the library director. I learned a lot from Reubén
about making an unforgettable impression.

When I was in fifth grade, my teacher, Sister Mary Regina
Immaculata of the Holy Ghost Most High, asked to see
my mother. This was a big deal. It meant I had done something
awful. But I couldn't remember what awful thing I'd done.

"Now what?" Mother said, disgusted. Dinner would be late.
She would have to walk over to my school and walk back, and I'd
have to go with her. My two older brothers would be ordered to
take care of the four younger; the last time they'd done that, the
twins had wound up at the police station, and they were only five
years old. Father would come home from work tired, hungry, and
with his feet throbbing. Mother, in a terrible mood, would hurl

words at anyone who got in her way. Thanks to me, the world was thrown into chaos.

The complaint from Sister Mary Regina Immaculata of the Holy Ghost Most High was this: "Your daughter is a daydreamer."

What could I say? It was true. When my teacher called on me, I seldom knew where we were. But it was also true that the class was a mix of forty-seven noisy kids from a mix of grade levels, too much for one tired teacher to deal with. Often in a day there were moments when you could drift away on a daydream, and often I took that route, staring out the window at a cloud, a coral geranium petal, or at Salvador, the boy who sat in front of me, whose wrinkled shirt and dirty collar made me wonder why his mama didn't take better care of him.

I thought and thought about Salvador a lot back then and imagined he lived with a family of little brothers, and maybe these little brothers made his mama too busy to send Salvador to school in a clean, pressed shirt. I imagined Salvador getting up early to help with the babies. I was sure I knew where Salvador lived, over on Western Avenue near Flournoy Street, in a Chicago neighborhood worse than ours, near my aunt Timo, who, like the woman who lived in a shoe, had so many children she didn't know what to do.

And just when I could imagine Salvador tumbling out of bed and dressing himself in his wrinkled shirt, helping his mama feed the babies cornflakes from a tin cup, combing his hair with water, rushing to get to school, this was exactly when the teacher would call on me. I don't remember much else about that fifth-grade year except things I wish I could forget. "Daydreamer." A word worse than a stick or a stone. It broke more than bones.

I felt ashamed to raise my hand for the rest of the school year, until, by Divine Providence, our pipes froze the following winter and we had to move to another neighborhood, another school, one with kind, compassionate lay teachers and nuns who discovered I was an artist and writer. But before that bright eureka, I hid inside myself and drew and wrote in secret, never volunteering an answer in class because I assumed if I thought of it, it *must* be wrong.

My fifth-grade report card

It's funny, with all of the moves in my life, that horrible report card from fifth grade survived to remind me who I used to be. I have only to look at the constellations of Cs and Ds to remember how others saw me, and how I once saw myself. Too bad there was no grade for art, or I would've gotten an A. Too bad there was no credit for the seven or eight books I borrowed every week from the public library. Who knew this was important to bring to the attention of someone like Sister Mary Regina Immaculata of the Holy Ghost Most High?

In the fortieth year of my life, I received a MacArthur fellowship, the so-called genius grant, which is like an Academy Award for the story of your life. (That's how I explained it to my mother, who didn't understand at first.) What it finally made me realize was this: I have always been a daydreamer, and that's a lucky thing for a writer. Because what is a daydreamer if not another word for thinker, visionary, intuitive—all wonderful words synonymous with "girl."

A House of My Own

To write this introduction for the twenty-fifth anniversary of my first book, *The House on Mango Street,* I knew I had to search for a photo from that time. If I stared at it long enough, I'd have my story. But who was that woman in the photo? She wasn't me, I wasn't her. It was as if I were writing about someone else, and this inspired me to write in both the third and first person. I also wanted to set straight many biographical facts. Thus, the specific addresses where I'd lived. I was surprised my mother appeared in the writing. But how could she not? I finished it on May 26, 2008, less than a year after her crossing. Her spirit was still nearby.

The young woman in this photograph is me when I was writing *The House on Mango Street*. She's in her office, a room that had probably been a child's bedroom when families lived in this apartment. It has no door and is only slightly wider than the walk-in pantry. But it has great light and sits above the hallway door downstairs, so she can hear her neighbors come and go. She's posed as if she's just looked up from her work for a moment, but in real life she never writes in this office. She writes in the kitchen, the only room with a heater.

It's Chicago, 1980, in the down-at-the-heels Bucktown neighborhood before it's discovered by folks with money. The young woman lives at 1814 North Paulina Street, second-floor front. Nelson Algren once wandered these streets. Saul Bellow's turf was over on Division Street, walking distance away. It's a neighborhood that reeks of beer and urine, of sausage and beans.

The young woman fills her "office" with things she drags home from the flea market at Maxwell Street. Antique typewriters, alphabet blocks, asparagus ferns, bookshelves, ceramic figurines from occupied Japan, wicker baskets, birdcages, hand-painted photos. Things she likes to look at. It's important to have this space to look and think. When she lived at home, the things she looked at scolded her and made her feel sad and depressed. They said, "Wash me." They said, "Lazy." They said, "You ought." But the things in her office are magical and invite her to play. They fill her with light. It's the room where she can be quiet and still and listen to the voices inside herself. She likes being alone in the daytime.

As a girl, she dreamt about having a silent home, just to herself, the way other women dreamt of their weddings. Instead of collecting lace and linen for her trousseau, the young woman buys old things from the thrift stores on grimy Milwaukee Avenue for her future house-of-her-own—faded quilts, cracked vases, chipped saucers, lamps in need of love.

The young woman returned to Chicago after graduate school and moved back into her father's house, 1754 North Keeler, back into her girl's room with its twin bed and floral wallpaper. She was twenty-three and a half. Now she summoned her courage and told her father she wanted to live alone again, like she did when she was away at school. He looked at her with that eye of the rooster before it attacks, but she wasn't alarmed. She'd seen that look before and knew he was harmless. She was his favorite, and it was only a matter of waiting.

The daughter claimed she'd been taught that a writer needs quiet, privacy, and long stretches of solitude to think. The father decided too much college and too many gringo friends had ruined her. In a way he was right. In a way she was right. When she thinks in her father's language, she knows sons and daughters don't leave their parents' house until they marry. When she thinks in English, she knows she should've been on her own since she was eighteen.

For a time father and daughter reached a truce. She agreed to move into the basement of a building where the oldest of her six brothers and his wife lived, 4832 West Homer. But after a few months, when the big brother upstairs turned out to be Big Brother, she got on her bicycle and rode through the neighborhood of her high school days until she spotted a second-floor apartment with fresh-painted walls and masking tape on the windows. Then she knocked on the storefront downstairs and convinced the landlord she was his new tenant.

Her father can't understand why she wants to live in a hundred-year-old building with big windows that let in the cold. She knows her apartment is clean, but the hallway is scuffed and scary, though she and the woman upstairs take turns mopping it regularly. The hall needs paint, and there's nothing they can do about that. When the father visits, he climbs up the stairs muttering with disgust. Inside, he looks at her books arranged in milk crates, at the futon on the floor in a bedroom with no door, and whispers, "Hippie," in the same way he looks at boys hanging out in his neighborhood and says, *"Drogas."* When he sees the space heater in the kitchen, the father shakes his head and sighs. "Why did I work so hard to buy a house with a furnace so she could go backward and live like this?"

When she's alone, she savors her apartment of high ceilings and windows that let in the sky, the new carpeting and walls white as typing paper, the walk-in pantry with empty shelves, her bedroom without a door, her office with its typewriter, and the big front-room windows with their view of a street, rooftops, trees, and the dizzy traffic of the Kennedy Expressway.

Between her building and the brick wall of the next is a tidy, sunken garden. The only people who ever enter the garden are a family who speak like guitars, a family with a southern accent. At dusk they appear with a pet monkey in a cage and sit on a green bench and talk and laugh. She spies on them from behind her bedroom curtains and wonders where they got the monkey.

Her father calls every week to say, *"Mi'ja,* when are you coming home?" What does her mother say about all this? She puts her hands on her hips and boasts, "She gets it from me." When the father is in the room, the mother just shrugs and says, "What can I do?" The mother doesn't object. She knows what it is to live a life filled with regrets, and she doesn't want her daughter to live that life too. She always supported the daughter's projects, so long as she went to school. The mother who painted the walls of their Chicago homes the color of flowers; who planted tomatoes and roses in her garden; sang arias; practiced solos on her son's drum set; boogied along with the *Soul Train* dancers; glued travel posters on her kitchen wall with Karo corn syrup; herded her kids weekly to the library, to public concerts, to museums; wore a button on her lapel that said, "Feed the People Not the Pentagon"; who never went beyond the ninth grade. *That* mother. She nudges her daughter and says, "Good lucky you studied."

The father wants his daughter to be a weather girl on television, or to marry and have babies. She doesn't want to be a TV weather girl. Nor does she want to marry and have babies. Not yet. Maybe later, but there are so many other things she must do in her lifetime first. Travel. Learn how to dance the tango. Publish a book. Live in other cities. Win a National Endowment for the Arts award. See the northern lights. Jump out of a cake.

She stares at the ceilings and walls of her apartment the way she once stared at the ceilings and walls of the apartments she grew up in, inventing pictures in the cracks in the plaster, inventing stories to go with these pictures. At night, under the circle of light from a cheap metal lamp clamped to the kitchen table, she sits with paper and a pen and pretends she's not afraid. She's trying to live like a writer.

Where she gets these ideas about living like a writer, she has no clue. She hasn't read Virginia Woolf yet. She doesn't know about Rosario Castellanos or Sor Juana Inés de la Cruz. Gloria Anzaldúa and Cherríe Moraga are cutting their own paths through the world somewhere, but she doesn't know about them. She doesn't know anything. She's making things up as she goes.

When the photo of the young woman who was me was snapped, I still called myself a poet, though I'd been writing stories since grammar school. I'd gravitated back to fiction while in the Iowa poetry workshop. Poetry, as it was taught at Iowa, was a house of cards, a tower of ideas, but I can't communicate an idea except through a story.

The woman I am in the photo was working on a series of vignettes, little by little, along with her poetry. I already had a title—*The House on Mango Street*. Fifty pages had been written, but I still didn't think of it as a novel. It was just a jar of buttons, like the mismatched embroidered pillowcases and monogrammed napkins I tugged from the bins at Goodwill. I wrote these things and thought of them as "little stories," though I sensed they were connected to one another. I hadn't heard of story cycles yet. I hadn't read Ermilo Abreu Gómez's *Canek,* Elena Poniatowska's *Lilus Kikus,* Gwendolyn Brooks's *Maud Martha,* Nellie Campobello's *My Mother's Hands.* That would come later, when I had more time and solitude to read.

The woman I once was wrote the first three stories of *House* in one weekend at Iowa. But because I wasn't in the fiction workshop, they wouldn't count toward my MFA thesis. I didn't argue; my thesis adviser reminded me too much of my father. I worked on these little stories on the side for comfort when I wasn't writing poetry for credit. I shared them with colleagues like the poet Joy Harjo, who was also having a hard time in the poetry work-

Joy Harjo in Iowa City

shop, and the fiction writer Dennis Mathis, a small-town Illinois native, whose paperback library was from the world.

Little-little stories were in literary vogue at the time, in the '70s. Dennis told me about the Japanese Nobel Prize winner Kawabata's minimal "palm of the hand" stories. We fried omelets for dinner and read García Márquez and Heinrich Böll stories aloud. We both preferred experimental writers—all men back then except for Grace Paley—rebels like ourselves. Dennis would become a lifelong editor, ally, and voice on the phone when either one of us lost heart.

The young woman in the photo is modeling her book in progress after *Dream Tigers* by Jorge Luis Borges—a writer she'd read since high school, story fragments that ring like Hans Christian Andersen, or Ovid, or entries from the encyclopedia. She wants to write stories that ignore borders between genres, between written and spoken, between highbrow literature and children's nursery rhymes, between New York and the imaginary village of Macondo, between the United States and Mexico. It's true, she wants the writers she admires to respect her work, but she also

Dennis Mathis and me in Iowa

wants people who don't usually read books to enjoy these stories too. She *doesn't* want to write a book that a reader won't understand and would feel ashamed for not understanding.

She thinks stories are about beauty. Beauty that is there to be admired by anyone, like a herd of clouds grazing overhead. She thinks people who are busy working for a living deserve beautiful little stories, because they don't have much time and are often tired. She has in mind a book that can be opened at any page and will still make sense to the reader who doesn't know what came before or comes after.

She experiments, creating a text that is as succinct and flexible as poetry, snapping sentences into fragments so that the reader pauses, making each sentence serve *her* and not the other way round, abandoning quotation marks to streamline the typography and make the page as simple and readable as possible. So that the sentences are pliant as branches and can be read in more ways than one.

Sometimes the woman I once was goes out on weekends to meet with other writers. Sometimes I invite these friends to come to my apartment to workshop each other's work. We are black, white, Latino. We are men and we are women. What we have in common is our sense that art should serve our communities. Together we publish an anthology—*Emergency Tacos,* because we finish our collaborations in the early hours before dawn and gather at the same twenty-four-hour *taquería* on Belmont Avenue, like a multicultural version of Hopper's *Nighthawks* painting. The *Emergency Tacos* writers organize monthly arts events at my brother Keek's apartment—Galería Quique. We do this with no capital except our valuable time. We do this because the world we live in is a house on fire and the people we love are burning.

The young woman in the photograph gets up in the morning to go to the job that pays the rent on her Paulina Street apartment.

She teaches at a school in Pilsen, her mother's old neighborhood on Chicago's South Side, a Mexican neighborhood where the rent is cheap and too many families live crowded together. Landlords and the city take no responsibility for the rats, trash that isn't collected often enough, porches that collapse, apartments without fire escapes, until a tragedy happens and several people die. Then they hold investigations for a little while, but the problems go on until the next death, the next investigation, the next bout of forgetting.

The young woman works with students who have dropped out of high school but have decided to try again for their diplomas. She learns from her students that they have more difficult lives than her storyteller's imagination can invent. Her life has been comfortable and privileged compared to theirs. She never had to worry about feeding her babies before she went to class. She never had a father or boyfriend who beat her at night and left her bruised in the morning. She didn't have to plan an alternative route to avoid gangs in the school hallway. Her parents didn't plead with her to drop out of school so she could help them earn money.

How can art make a difference in the world? This was never asked at Iowa. Should she be teaching these students to write poetry when they need to know how to defend themselves from someone beating them up? Can a memoir by Malcolm X or a novel by García Márquez save them from the daily blows? And what about those who have such learning problems they can't even manage a book by Dr. Seuss, but can weave a spoken story so wondrous, she wants to take notes? Should she give up writing and study something useful like medicine? How can she teach her students to take control of their own destiny? She loves these students. What should she be doing to save their lives?

The young woman's teaching job leads to the next, and now she finds herself a counselor/recruiter at her alma mater, Loyola

University on the North Side, in Rogers Park. I have health benefits. I don't bring work home anymore. My workday ends at 5 p.m. Now I have evenings free to do my own work. I feel like a real writer.

At the university I work for a program that no longer exists, the Educational Opportunity Program, that assists "disadvantaged" students. It's in keeping with my philosophy, and I can still help the students from my previous job. But when my most brilliant student is accepted, enrolls, and then drops out in her first semester, I collapse on my desk from grief, from exhaustion, and feel like dropping out myself.

I write about my students because I don't know what else to do with their stories. Writing them down allows me to sleep.

On the weekends, if I can sidestep guilt and avoid my father's demands to come home for Sunday dinner, I'm free to stay home and write. I feel like a bad daughter ignoring my father, but I feel worse when I don't write. Either way, I never feel completely happy.

One Saturday the woman at the typewriter accepts an invitation to a literary soiree. But when she arrives, she feels she's made a terrible mistake. All the writers are old men. She has been invited by Leon Forrest, a black novelist who was trying to be kind and invite more women, more people of color, but so far, she's the only woman, and he and she the only coloreds.

She's there because she's the author of a new book of poetry—*Bad Boys* from Mango Press, the literary efforts of Gary Soto and Lorna Dee Cervantes. Her book is four pages long and was bound together on a kitchen table with a stapler and a spoon. Many of the other guests, she soon realizes, have written *real* books, hardbacks from big New York houses, printed in editions of hundreds of thousands on actual presses. Is she really a writer, or is she only pretending to be a writer?

The guest of honor is a famous writer who went to the Iowa Writers' Workshop several years before she got there. His latest book has just been sold to Hollywood. He speaks and carries himself as if he were the Emperor of Everything.

At the end of the evening, she finds herself searching for a ride home. She came on the bus, and the Emperor offers to give her a lift home. But she's not going home, she's got her heart set on a movie that's showing only tonight. She's afraid of going to the movies alone, and that's why she's decided to go. Because she's afraid.

The famous writer drives a sports car. The seats smell of leather, and the dashboard is lit like an airplane cockpit. Her own car doesn't always start and has a hole in the floor near the accelerator that lets in rain and snow, so she has to wear boots when she drives. The famous writer talks and talks, but she can't hear what he is saying, because her own thoughts are drowning him out like a wind. She doesn't say anything, doesn't have to. She is just young and pretty enough to feed the famous writer's ego by nodding enthusiastically at everything he says until he drops her off in front of the cinema. She hopes the famous writer notices she is going to see *Gentlemen Prefer Blondes* alone. To tell the truth, she feels miserable walking up to the box office by herself, but she forces herself to buy the ticket and go in because she loves this movie.

The theater is packed. It feels to the young woman as if everybody is there with somebody, except her. Finally, the scene where Marilyn sings "Diamonds Are a Girl's Best Friend." The colors are cartoon-wonderful, the set deliciously campy, the lyrics clever, the whole number is pure old-style glamour. Marilyn is sensational. After her song is over, the audience breaks into applause as if this were a live performance, though sad Marilyn has been dead years and years.

The woman who is me goes home proud of having gone to the movies alone. *See? It wasn't that difficult.* But as she bolts the door of her apartment, she bursts into tears. "I don't have diamonds," she sobs, not knowing what she means, except she knows even then it's not about diamonds. Every few weeks, she has a messy crying jag like this that leaves her feeling shipwrecked and awful. It's such a regular occurrence she thinks these storms of depression are as normal as rain.

What is the woman in the photograph afraid of? She's afraid of walking from her parked car to her apartment in the dark. She's afraid of the scuffling sounds in the walls. She's afraid she'll fall in love and get stuck living in Chicago. She's afraid of ghosts, deep water, rodents, night, things that move too fast—cars, airplanes, her life. She's afraid she'll have to move back home again if it turns out she really isn't brave enough to live alone.

Throughout all this, I'm writing stories to go with that title, *The House on Mango Street*. Sometimes I write about people I remember, sometimes I write about people I've just met, often I mix the two together. My students from Pilsen who sat before me when I was teaching, with girls who sat beside me in another classroom a decade before. I pick up parts of Bucktown, like the monkey garden next door, and plop it down in the Humboldt Park block where I lived during my middle and high school years—1525 North Campbell Street.

Often all I have is a title with no story—"The Family of Little Feet"—and I have to make the title kick me in the behind to get me going. Or sometimes all I've got is a first sentence—"You can never have too much sky." One of my Pilsen students said I said this, and she never forgot it. Good thing she remembered and quoted it back to me. "They came with the wind that blows in August . . ." This line came to me in a dream. Sometimes the best ideas come in dreams. Sometimes the worst ideas come from there too!

Whether the idea came from a sentence I heard buzzing around somewhere and saved in a jar, or from a title I picked up and pocketed, the stories always insist on telling me where they want to end. They often surprise me by stopping when I had every intention of galloping along a little further. They're stubborn. They know best when there's no more to be said. The last sentence must ring like the final notes at the end of a mariachi song— *tan-tán*—to tell you when the song is done.

The people I wrote about were real, for the most part, from here and there, now and then, but sometimes three real people would be braided together into one made-up person. Usually when I thought I was creating someone from my imagination, it

Norma Alarcón

turned out I was remembering someone I'd forgotten or someone standing so close I couldn't see her at all.

I cut apart and stitched together events to tailor the story, gave it shape so it had a beginning, middle, and end, because real-life stories rarely come to us complete. Emotions, though, can't be invented, can't be borrowed. All the emotions my characters feel, good or bad, are mine.

———————

I meet Norma Alarcón. She's to become one of my earliest publishers and my lifetime friend. The first time she walks through the rooms of the apartment on North Paulina, she notices the quiet rooms, the collection of typewriters, the books and Japanese figurines, the windows with the view of freeway and sky. She walks as if on tiptoe, peering into every room, even the pantry and closet, as if looking for something. "You live here . . . ," she asks, "alone?"

"Yes."

"So . . ." She pauses. "How did you do it?"

———————

Norma, I did it by doing the things I was afraid of doing so that I would no longer be afraid. Moving away to go to graduate school. Traveling abroad. Earning my own money and living by myself. Posing as an author when I was afraid, just as I posed in that photo you used on the first cover of *Third Woman Magazine.*

And, finally, when I was ready, after I'd apprenticed with professional writers over several years, partnering with the right agent. My father, who sighed and wished for me to marry, was, at the end of his life, much more gratified I had my agent, Susan Bergholz, providing for me rather than a husband. "*¿Ha llamado Susan?*" he

My literary agent, Susan Bergholz, in front
of Danny López Lozano's Tienda Guadalupe
Folk Art shop, San Antonio

asked me daily, because if Susan called it meant good news. Diamonds may do for a girl, but an agent is a woman writer's best
friend.

I couldn't trust my own voice, Norma. People saw a little girl
when they looked at me and heard a little girl's voice when I
spoke. Because I was unsure of my own adult voice and often
censored myself, I made up another voice, Esperanza's, to be my
voice and ask the things I needed answers to myself—"Which
way?" I didn't know exactly, but I knew which routes I didn't want
to take—Sally, Rafaela, Ruthie—women whose lives were white
crosses on the roadside.

At Iowa we never talked about serving others with our writing. It was all about serving ourselves. But there were no other examples to follow until you introduced me to Mexican writers, Sor Juana Inés de la Cruz, Elena Poniatowska, Elena Garro, Rosario Castellanos. The young woman in the photograph was looking for another way to be—*"otro modo de ser,"* as Castellanos put it.

Until you brought us all together as U.S. Latina writers—Cherríe Moraga, Gloria Anzaldúa, Marjorie Agosín, Carla Trujillo, Diana Solís, Sandra María Esteves, Diane Gómez, Salima Rivera, Margarita López, Beatriz Badikian, Carmen Ábrego, Denise Chávez, Helena María Viramontes—until then, Normita, we had no idea that what we were doing was extraordinary.

———

I no longer make Chicago my home, but Chicago still makes its home in me. I have Chicago stories I've yet to write. So long as those stories kick inside me, Chicago will still be home.

Eventually I took a job in San Antonio. Left. Came back. And left again. I kept coming back lured by cheap rent. Affordable housing is essential to an artist. I could, in time, even buy my own first house, a hundred-year-old home once periwinkle, but now painted a Mexican pink.

Two years ago my office went up in my backyard, a building created from my Mexican memories. I am writing this today from this very office, Mexican marigold on the outside, morning-glory violet on the inside. Wind chimes ring from the terrace. Trains moan in the distance all the time; ours is a neighborhood of trains. The same San Antonio River tourists know from the River Walk wends its way behind my house to the missions and beyond until it empties into the Gulf of Mexico. From my terrace you can see the river where it bends into an S.

White cranes float across the sky like a scene painted on a lacquered screen. The river shares the land with ducks, raccoons, possums, skunks, buzzards, butterflies, hawks, turtles, snakes, owls, even though we're walking distance to downtown. And within the confines of my own garden there are plenty of other creatures too—yappy dogs, kamikaze cats, one lovesick parrot with a crush on me.

This is my house.

Bliss.

October 24, 2007. You come down from Chicago for a visit, Mama. You don't want to come. I make you come. You don't like to leave your house anymore, your back hurts, you say, but I insist. I built this office beside the river for you as much as for me, and I want you to see it.

Once, years ago, you telephoned and said in an urgent voice,

My office in San Antonio

"When are you going to build your office? I just saw Isabel Allende on PBS and she has a HUGE desk and a BIG office." You were upset because I was writing on the kitchen table again like in the old days.

And now here we are, on the rooftop of a saffron building with a river view, a space all my own just to write. We climb up to the room I work in, above the library, and out to the balcony facing the river.

You have to rest. There are industrial buildings on the opposite bank—abandoned granaries and silos—but they're so rain-rusted and sun-bleached, they have their own charm, like public sculptures. When you've recovered your breath, we continue.

I'm especially proud of the spiral staircase to the rooftop. I'd always dreamt of having one, just like the houses in Mexico. Even the words for them in Spanish are wonderful—*una escalera de caracol*, a snail ladder. Our footsteps clang on each metal step, the dogs following so close we have to scold them.

"Your office is bigger than in the pictures you sent," you say, delighted. I imagine you're comparing it to Isabel Allende's.

"Where did you get the drapes in the library? I bet they cost a pretty penny. Too bad your brothers couldn't upholster your chairs for you and save you some money. Boy, this place is niiiiice!" you say, your voice sliding up the scales like a river grackle.

I plop yoga mats on the rooftop, and we sit cross-legged to watch the sun descend. We drink your favorite, Italian sparkling wine, to celebrate your arrival, to celebrate my office.

The sky absorbs the night quickly-quickly, dissolving into the color of a plum. I lie on my back and watch clouds scurry past in a hurry to get home. Stars come out shyly, one by one. You lie down next to me and drape one leg over mine like when we sleep together at your home. We always sleep together when I'm there.

At first because there isn't any other bed. But later, after Papa dies, just because you want me near. It's the only time you let yourself be affectionate.

"What if we invite everybody down here for Christmas next year?" I ask. "What do you think?"

"We'll see," you say, lost in your own thoughts.

The moon climbs the front-yard mesquite tree, leaps over the terrace ledge, and astonishes us. It's a full moon, a huge nimbus like the prints of Yoshitoshi. From here on, I won't be able to see a full moon again without thinking of you, this moment. But right now, I don't know this.

You close your eyes. You look like you're sleeping. The plane ride must've tired you. "Good lucky you studied," you say without opening your eyes. You mean my office, my life.

I say to you, "Good lucky."

For my mother, Elvira Cordero Cisneros
July 11, 1929–November 1, 2007

An *Ofrenda* for My Mother

My altar installation for my mother at the National Hispanic
Cultural Center, Albuquerque

I was in the room the moment my mother died. She was in
intensive care hooked up to machines that were keeping her
alive. I was on a cot asleep in the same room when the nurse
shook me and said, "She's going." We'd been waiting for this
moment for forty-eight hours and maybe all our lives, but it
was still a surprise. It was dark out, November 1st, just before
sunrise. There wasn't time to call anyone else except my
brother Lolo, who had camped out in the hall. My mother's
doctor had said she was brain dead, but the nurses in ICU
talked to her gently as if she were still present, as did we.

I'd been there when my friend Danny López Lozano's spirit

crossed. I wasn't in the hospital room with him, but in my backyard after receiving the news. I was trying to meditate, but I didn't know how and was making a mess of it. My mind kept straying from Danny to whether I'd remembered to defrost the chicken. Then I was filled with guilt and tried again to think of Danny and only Danny. I mention this because I know I didn't bring on what happened next. The strangest thing. I felt a heat at the crown of my head, as if someone had broken an egg and the yolk flowed down slow as honey, but warm as a fever. It wasn't just the heat that startled me, but the overwhelming emotion that came with it. A feeling of joy so intense it made me cry. It moved through me vertically. By the time it entered my torso moving to my feet, the top of my head was already cooling down. It scared me as it was happening. *What is this?* I thought. Then I realized it was Danny's spirit *despidiéndose,* I'll be seeing you, I'm fine, don't be sad, don't worry, tell the others. And by the time I understood, my body went back to its normal temperature. He was gone.

That's why in the ICU room with my mother, I was ready like a baseball player waiting for a fly ball. My mother was a force of nature, so I was expecting a tsunami. Instead I almost didn't notice the hovering emotion that moved about the room like moonlight shimmering on water. It was gentle and tender and sweet sweet sweet. Not like my mother at all. And it didn't travel through me from crown to feet. It was as soft as a mouth and barely perceptible, like a moth fluttering just beyond reach. "Do you feel that?" I asked Lolo, but he just frowned. "Grab her hands, tell her she can go," I said. I was excited the way I imagine you're excited when you're witnessing a birth; you can't believe it's happening. I felt like that, as if I were in a sacred room, lucky to help her to die, just as she had helped me to be born. "You have no idea," I said to Mother. "No idea what you did in this life." It cracked my heart in two to think this pure love was my mother all along, underneath all that bravado, under the thunder and rage. How had she gone from *that* to the woman I knew? Then the shimmering dimmed, then faded, and we were left alone.

This story first appeared in print in *Granta*'s Chicago issue, in December 2009.

I became a writer thanks to a mother who was unhappy being a mother. She was a prisoner-of-war mother banging on the bars of her cell all her life. Unhappy women do this. She searched for escape routes from her prison and found them in museums, the park, and the public library.

As a child she lived in the parish of St. Francis of Assisi in Chicago, off Roosevelt Road and South Halsted Street, close enough

My mother (*left*) and Frances Casino

My mother as a bridesmaid in
her teens

to downtown she could walk there. I have a photo of her as a very young girl on the steps of a Chicago museum with her best friend, Frances. I know my mother often ran off all day with her friends and paid her younger sisters to do her chores. She did not know what awaited her in her life, and if she had she might've run farther than the museum.

Because my mother needed to fortify her spirit, Saturdays were reserved for the library, Sundays for the concerts in Grant Park or visits to the many Chicago museums. I used to think this was for our sake, but now I realize it was for hers. She loved opera, Pearl Buck novels, and the movie based on *A Tree Grows in Brooklyn.* Later she would ditch Pearl Buck for Noam Chomsky, but in the beginning she read fiction. I know she dreamt of becoming some sort of artist—she could sing and draw—but I'm sure she never dreamt of mothering seven kids.

I think she married my father because he rescued her from a house with peeling paint and beds crowded with sisters and bedbugs. At least this is what my father reminded her when they argued. He came from Mexico City and spoke an impeccable Spanish as stiff and formal as the beautiful suits he wore. He was a gentleman, and I imagine my mother saw him as cosmopolitan and sophisticated. She did not know he was a dreamer and would give her seven kids and an unimaginative life.

My mother was the beauty of the family, used to being spoiled by her eldest sister. If there was one thing my father knew how to do, it was how to spoil a woman. He believed women want words more than anything, and he had a lot of them. *Mi cielo. Mi vida. Mi amor.* So for a little while she must have been happy. I have a photo of them dancing and kissing. It's obvious they're in love. But it didn't last very long and was replaced with a more durable, daily love, and the words were replaced with more durable, daily words, too.

My parents before they married, at a Chicago party

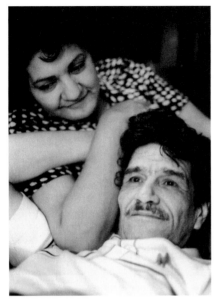

My parents

My mother and me

"*¿Vieja, donde estás?*" Where's my old lady?

"*¡No me llames vieja, yo no soy vieja!*" Don't call me "old lady," I'm not old!

Sundays Father chauffeured us wherever Mother directed. A classical concert in the park, while he snored on a blanket under a tree. The Brookfield Zoo or a Grant Park museum. "I'll wait here," Father would say, and slide onto a bench. He would've preferred to stay home reading his Mexican magazines in bed or soaking his feet after a week of bobbing like a prizefighter around the sofas and chairs he upholstered. But Mother complained she had to get out of that house or go crazy.

On Saturdays I walked with Mother to the library. For me, the library was a wonderful house. A house of ideas, a house of silence. Our own house was like that of the cook's in *Alice in Wonderland,* a lot of shouting and shattering of dishes. Would someone hand me a baby and would the baby turn into a pig? Anything could happen in this kitchen. It was a nightmare, and I was condemned to the lowest job of scullery maid, because I was too daydreamy to learn how to cook. The rice burned on me— an expensive mistake. So I was ordered to cut potatoes into little squares, or scrub pans, or set the table, or anything else Mother thought of while she was busy banging pots and yelling.

Hell was a kitchen. Hell was having to go to the supermarket every Friday with her. Sometimes Father drove us. Usually we walked there and back with a collapsible shopping cart and a red wagon. It was a cross, buying groceries for our army. Neither Mother nor I enjoyed it.

Sometimes my father and mother went to the Randolph Street market to buy eggs and vegetables wholesale for the nine of us. Sometimes my mother walked down North Avenue, beyond Humboldt Park, to the day-old bakery to buy us sweet bread. On Sundays after scavenging the flea market at Maxwell Street, we stopped for Mexican groceries on 18th Street; *carnitas* and *chicharrón* served on hot tortillas with dollops of sour cream and sprigs of cilantro. These Sunday dinners were one of the few times Father "cooked." He stood over the cutting board and chopped like a Japanese chef, humming while he worked, until the *carnitas* were diced to his liking.

Father was meticulous. He liked to remind everyone he was from a good family, the son of a Mexican military man and the grandson of a pianist who was also an educator, but Father's appreciation of the finer things in life did not extend beyond nightclubs. He loved dance halls and cabarets, the big bands of Xavier Cugat, Pérez Prado, and Benny Goodman, the sultry voice of Peggy Lee singing Lil Green's "Why Don't You Do Right?"—whose lyrics "Get out of here and get me some money too" always made him laugh. He was a good dancer and a sharp dresser. And then he got married.

Like everybody we knew, we took road trips from Chicago to Mexico to visit family. In Mexico we didn't have to ask Father to drive us to museums; the past and the present were all around us. We witnessed paper Judases exploding on Holy Week, saw Aztec pyramids sprouting in the middle of downtown, watched dancers swing like birds from a giant pole planted in front of the cathedral, listened to ancient music played on drums and conch shells in the central plaza. Art was in the paper flags fluttering above us at a fiesta, in the mangoes sliced like roses and served on a stick, in the cheap trinkets we bought with our Sunday allowance at the market, in the pastel wafer candies studded with pumpkin seeds. Art was a way of being.

On these vacations, Father caught up on his reading. His library consisted of Mexican comic books and pocket-sized *fotonovelas* printed in a dark chocolate ink on paper so cheap it was used as toilet paper by the poor. When Father was done with his little books, he'd turn them over to me, and I painted over the ladies' chocolate-tinted mouths with a red-lead pencil dipped in spit. This is how I learned to read in Spanish.

Father also had a private library, a secret stash of *¡Alarma!* magazines, whose covers were so savage, Mother forced him to keep them under the mattress in brown paper bags. *¡Alarma!* featured sensational stories about everyday Mexican events—yet another bus drives off a cliff, yet another quake swallows a village, yet another machete murder. All with detailed photos. Mexicans love staring at death. I wasn't allowed to read these magazines, but once in a while I did catch a headline when Father was reading in bed. "Wife Kills Husband and Serves His Head in Tacos."

Back in Chicago, Mother painted geishas in paint-by-number sets in the kitchen after her housework was done. She made fake flowers with crepe paper until she grew real flowers from seeds she sent away for. She sewed stuffed toys and doll clothes, designed theater sets and created puppets. But it wasn't enough. Mother felt duped by life and sighed for the life that wasn't hers. Father watched television in bed, content, chuckling, calling out for pancakes.

—There's no intelligent life around here, Mother said out loud to no one in particular.

When she was in a bad mood, which was often, she threw sharp words like knives, wounding and maiming the guilty and the innocent.

—Your mother, Father complained to me, near tears.

Sick and tired, miserable, Mother raged and paced her cell. We tiptoed around her feeling gloomy and guilty.

I understood Father. He understood me. Neither of us understood her, and she never understood us. But that didn't matter. A stack of pancakes. A paycheck. A bouquet of dandelions. A ride to the Garfield Park Conservatory. A box of popcorn from "the Sears." A language for the words we couldn't say.

Resurrections

It occurs to me there's a global conspiracy to keep me in the dark about certain simple truths. This is in regards to getting older and fatter, and other transmogrifications of aging, like losing your parents. Did someone forget to tell me, or was I not listening? I ask, "How come nobody told me?" almost on a daily basis.

And so this piece was finished in 2011 and turned into the epilogue for my book *Have You Seen Marie?*, a story about the loss of a cat named Marie and the loss of a mother, with a cast of characters that included real San Antonio friends and neighbors—Reverend Chavana, the widow Helen, Cowboy Dave, Bill and Roger.

Normally, I wouldn't feel the need to add an epilogue, because I said what I wanted to say in the story. But there were some things I wanted to add as the author that couldn't be said as the protagonist, things that might help others through their own time of mourning.

I n Mexico they say when someone you love dies, a part of you dies with them. But they forget to mention that a part of them is born in you, not immediately, I've learned, but eventually, and gradually. It's an opportunity to be reborn. When you're in between births, there should be some way to indicate to all, "Beware, I am not as I was before. Handle me with care."

The real Bill and Roger (Sánchez and Solís) posing for the book

I live in San Antonio on the left bank of the river in an area of the city called King William, famous for its historic homes. South of Alamo Street, beyond King William proper, the San Antonio River transforms itself into a wildlife refuge as it makes its way toward the Spanish missions. Behind my house the river is more creek than river. It still has its natural sandy bottom. It hasn't been covered over with concrete yet. Wild animals live in the tall grass and in its waters. My dogs and I can wade across and watch tadpoles and turtles and fish darting about. There are hawks and cranes and owls and other splendid winged creatures in the trees. It is calming and beautiful, especially when you're sad and in need of big doses of beauty.

In the spring after my mother died, a doctor wanted to prescribe pills for depression. "But if I don't feel," I said, "how will I be able to write?" I need to be able to feel things deeply, good or bad, and wade through an emotion to the other shore, toward a rebirth, of sorts, a return to the living. I knew if I put off moving through grief, the wandering between worlds would only take longer. Even sadness has its place in the universe.

I wish somebody had told me then that death allows you the chance to experience the world soulfully, that the heart is open like the aperture of a camera, taking in everything, painful as well as joyous, sensitive as the skin of water.

I wish somebody had told me to draw near me objects of pure spirit when living between births. My dogs. The trees along the San Antonio River. The sky and clouds reflected in its water. Wind with its scent of spring. Flowers, especially the sympathetic daisy.

I wish somebody had told me love does not die, that we can continue to receive and give love after death. This news is so

Ester Hernández

astonishing to me even now, I wonder why it isn't flashed across the bottom of the television screen on CNN.

I wrote the story *Have You Seen Marie?* in the wake of death—*poco a poco,* slow by slow, little by little. A writer who had come to visit had lost her cat—Marie. The real Marie eluded capture for over a week, but searching for her forced me during those days to meet neighbors, and the idea for a book came about.

Some people who heard me perform early versions of *Have You Seen Marie?* out loud thought it was for children, but I wrote it for adults, because something was needed for people like me who suddenly found themselves orphans in midlife. I wanted to be able to make something I could give those who were in mourning, something that would help them find balance again and walk toward their rebirth. Since I've long admired her work, and because she'd recently lost her own mother, too, I knew that the artist Ester Hernández would be right as the illustrator for the story.

Ester flew out from California to San Antonio on a scouting mission. Neighbors and their kids posed for us and got involved in the project: we included real people, houses, and places almost as if we were creating a documentary, and this book became a collective community effort.

I liked the idea of the pictures telling another story about the people of San Antonio, of cultures colliding and creating something new. Folks with blond hair, a German last name, and a Spanish first name inherited from a Mexican grandmother several generations back. Tex-Mexicans with Arab and indigenous features and a Scottish surname. Ultra-devout Catholics with Sephardic roots. Stories the Alamo forgets to remember.

We are a village, of sorts, with big houses and little houses, home to trust-fund babies as well as folks who have to take the bus to buy their groceries. We have houses with American flags and homemade signs. "God Bless Private Manny Cantú." "Bring Home the Troops Now." "Please Don't Let Your Dog Poop On My Yard."

I wanted both the story and the art to capture the offbeat beauty of the *rascuache,* things made with materials readily at hand, funky architecture and funky gardens, creative ways of making do, because it seems to me that this is what is uniquely gorgeous about San Antonio.

I knew as I wrote this story that it was helping to bring me back to myself. It's essential to create when the spirit is dying. It doesn't matter what. Sometimes it helps to draw. Sometimes to plant a garden. Sometimes to make a Valentine's Day card. Or to sing, or assemble an altar. Creating nourishes the spirit.

I've lived in my neighborhood for over twenty years, longer than I've lived anywhere. Last April, just as folks brushed a new coat of paint on their porches and trimmed their gardens for the annual King William parade, my neighbor, Reverend Chavana, passed away unexpectedly. His family surprised me by asking if I'd write his eulogy. I can't make a casserole, but I felt useful during a time when I usually feel useless, and I was grateful.

There is no getting over death, only learning how to travel alongside it. It knows no linear time. Sometimes the pain is as fresh as if it just happened. Sometimes it's a space I tap with my tongue daily like a missing molar.

Say what they say, some may doubt the existence of God, but everyone is certain of the existence of love. Something is there, then, beyond our lives, that for lack of a better word I'll call spirit. Some know it by other names. I know it only as love.

Ten Thousand

Once, many years back, I attended a Modern Language Association conference in Chicago during Christmas break with Norma Alarcón as driver. On the way home we were stuck in bumper-to-bumper downtown traffic. Norma was upset. To lift her spirits, I started to read to her from a book I'd picked up at the conference, a reissue from an international series. Just like that, the miserable Chicago traffic and weather disappeared, and we found ourselves on the beaches of Indonesia. When our car started moving again we groaned, sorry we had to put the book away.

What a catalog of things this writer documented, a world filled with ten thousand things, all of them extraordinary. I especially liked how the narrator talked to you as if she were in the room. Was the author borrowing from the spoken stories of the Javanese, or perhaps from an ancestor? Now as then, it seems to me this book demands to be read out loud. It has the curious ability to resonate within you for a lifetime, like the very best poetry.

My first "finished" version of this piece is dated August 26, 2008, but I abandoned it until now.

A woman named Maria Dermoût lived in the Molucca Islands near Java a long time ago. She lived there and fell in love with all island things, even though she was Dutch and not of the island. But as the saying goes, *"¿Si los gatitos nacen en el horno, son* *gatitos o son bizcochos?"* Just because the kittens are born in the oven doesn't mean they're biscuits.[*]

So this kitten, Maria, became Javanese by choice and not simply chance, and by choice loved Java intimately. She was busy. She was a mother, after all, and then a grandmother. By the time she was done with the ten thousand distractions of being both, she finally had a little time of her own and could profess her love of all things Javanese by taking up her pen. Which she did by the time she was sixty-three, or at least she began publishing then.

Dermoût wrote two novels. Only two. But one book exquisitely done is worth fifty not worth remembering. Her first is called *Days Before Yesterday* or *Yesterday* depending on which edition you read. But the one I want to tell you about is *The Ten Thousand Things*. And it really does contain ten thousand things sweeping across a geography like Noah collecting all the animals. Tree snails with white shells like porcelain fruit. The giant octopus with its eight grasping arms, who lived in a hollow in the rocks waiting for the fishermen to forget. A flock of noisy, gleaming birds drinking from a moss-covered cistern in a forest that smells of spice trees.

But not just the animals. The myths and stories too. Pearls from the sea that are tears we will have to cry ourselves, and pearls from the earth disinterred from the graves of the dead, which are never to be worn at all, else they bring death with them. The slave bell that rang whenever a proa came or left—if someone remembered to ring it. The open-sea wind different from the sighs of the land wind, and the storm wind called Baratdaja. The waves, one behind the other, behind the other, behind the other—"the father, the mother, and the child—can you hear it?"

---

* I found this in *There Are No Madmen Here,* but author Gina Valdés isn't sure if it's Mexican in origin or a family invention. I've been told that in Maine folks use a similar adage to differentiate the natives from the invaders.

And the people of the islands. The man who dyed his hair blue with indigo because his son was a fearless warrior. The father and son who had once been sharks and that was why they never smiled, so as not to reveal their pointy teeth. The old woman called the mother of the Pox who had to be fended off with a branch of thorns tied to the front door. The three little ghost girls who had all died on the same day, the day of the great earthquake—or was it poison?—and who visited the garden on occasion and left rose petals in their wake. The fishermen who whistle for Mister Wind to loosen his long hair and allow their boats to go out to sea.

And the treasures seen and unseen. The sea fans in mauve or dark yellows woven as fine as linen. The much-talked-about Coco Palm of the Sea found in a whirlpool in the deepest depths, a black tree or perhaps purple or violet, because underwater black isn't always black. And the creature the children feared the most—"the Leviathan who is too terrible!"

The prayer the island devout chant when someone dies: "'The hundred things' was the name of the lament . . . of which the dead one is reminded . . . a grandchild, a friend, a comrade-in-arms; or his possessions: your beautiful house, your china dishes hidden in the attic, the swift proa, your sharp knife, the little inlaid shield from long ago . . ." A hundred times a hundred things recited. Then they would close with: "oh soul of so-and-so, and ended with a long-held melancholy *ee-ee-ee? ee-ee-ee?* over the water."

Something of the grand yet intimate voice, something of the detailed lists she creates with patience and poetry to summon a place, a time, a state of being, inspire me to pick up my pen and play at being God.

But, *ay,* what a lot of work to write like this! *¡Tanta lata!* Nothing but trouble! Like sewing tiny glass beads with a fine needle in stitches that would drive a nun blind. True. All the same, exquisite needlework to make one marvel and turn over the cloth in admiration and wonder. How does she do it? Perhaps the body remembers. "The hand has a good memory."

Opening *The Ten Thousand Things* is like unlocking a curiosity cabinet filled with rare treasures, just like the ones described in its pages. A woman who fell into the sea and became red coral. A fleet of jellyfish with sails of milk white and a mass of streamers trailing behind in jewel blues and green. Sadness something you can move past only gradually, like rowing a boat through seawater—"She knew that a bay and rocks and trees ending over the surf cannot relieve sadness—can sadness be relieved, or can one only pass it by, very slowly?"

If you wish, open this book at the beginning and read to the end. Or you can select any of the chapters, which read like a short story, and indulge in the Javanese flora and fauna that the author has meticulously cataloged to delight our senses.

The ten thousand things mentioned in these pages pay homage to what was holy to this writer. Dermoût has named her world as she knew it, and in a sense she is reciting her own funeral chant, the ten thousand things that all together made up her life.

To read this book is to be reminded of one's own ten thousand things. Jorge Luis Borges said the same in his vignette "The Witness." He named a piece of sulfur in a desk drawer and the corner of two streets in Buenos Aires as his private legacy, but forgot to mention the obvious—mirrors and tigers.

And I wonder if all storytelling isn't a list, conscious or not, of the ten thousand things tucked inside the special drawers of the brain, a curiosity cabinet lined with old silk scented with incense. A pretty fan of real tortoise with gold inlay from the time of before. A basket woven from orchid roots. A snakestone to suck the venom from a sea wound. From the "land at the other side," Ceram, a plate to detect poison "of rough china, glazed a light even green."

The Author Responds to Your Letter Requesting My Book Be Banned from the School Library

I got a letter from an angry mother in Austin, Texas, that made me even angrier. However, I believe Thich Nhat Hanh has taught me the greatest lesson, and that is not to speak/ write when I'm angry. And so, I waited several days . . . out of necessity since I was traveling, but her letter traveled with me like a burr in my sock. Finally, after a week, I wrote and rewrote this letter. I imagined I was sending it to my father, and this helped me to be more respectful, especially since my mission was to have her hear me. Friends said I was wasting my time, but I have always naively believed in the power of the word, especially when written with love. In the end, the angry mother wrote back and apologized, and we made peace. I am grateful to her for giving me the opportunity to put my thoughts to paper, and doubly grateful she was willing to listen.

Inn of the Turquoise Bear
Santa Fe, New Mexico

Wednesday, November 11, 2009

Dear JP,

I'm sorry I was unable to write back to you until today. I'm traveling on a community-read project, and your letter necessitated more than a hasty response.

First and foremost, my apologies for my writing making anyone ill or ill at ease, least of all a child. My first rule in writing is this—"Do no harm." I always remind my students and readers of this primary rule. To learn my book had caused any disorder was unsettling. It was never my intent.

If you have not yet read the introduction to the twenty-fifth-anniversary edition to *The House on Mango Street,* will you allow me to send it to you? In it I write how and why I wrote the book twenty-five years ago, and that it was dedicated to my high school students, kids whose lives were greatly in need of healing. I wrote because I was only their teacher and didn't know what else I could do to save them.

Nine-year-olds are not my target *Mango Street* audience, though I'm aware fourth graders sometimes read or are read selections from my book. This doesn't alarm me because the parts they shouldn't read were intentionally written in a poetic way that should sail over their heads if they're not mature.

Though I used a middle school narrator to write this book, I wrote about serious topics in a roundabout way only adults would understand. That's why I was surprised by your letter that stated my book had made a child ill. I wonder if this child was suffering from experiences he couldn't talk about, experiences the book may have stirred up—a delicate question that you may not have an answer for, and which may be totally off the mark. I don't know; I'm not a social worker, but I do know this: social workers and counselors often use my book for young people who have been abused, physically, sexually, or otherwise; it allows them to talk about difficult subject matter without having to speak directly about themselves.

Regarding my author bio—"She is nobody's mother and nobody's wife." I meant no disrespect to you or anyone who is a wife and mother. I was stating the personal route I had to take in order to become an author. To be nobody's mother and nobody's wife was not a choice for me, but a requirement; I was poor and could hardly raise a child alone on my salary. And being single was a result of another kind of poverty: my poor choice in men, though in retrospect, I'm grateful for these constraints. They allowed me the solitude and single-mindedness necessary to write.

True, I have no biological children, but I have, as it turns out, become a mother nonetheless. I have over one hundred creative writers I mother directly and indirectly through my two foundations, the Macondo Foundation and the Alfredo Cisneros del Moral Foundation, along with thousands of readers of all ages I work with through my public engagements in libraries and schools across the country. Even though all this is exhausting and takes me away from my desk, I strongly believe the work of community outreach is part of my task of healing and making nonviolent social change in a time of extreme fear and xenophobia.

In addition to my work as a writer, I shelter several stray animals annually and find them permanent homes. All are my children, and believe me, my work, like yours, is never done.

Now, I must address your objection to my book featuring

witches. Your fear is a cultural misinterpretation, I suspect. In Mexican culture we have gifted women who are called *brujas* or *curanderas*. They are healers, herbalists, visionaries, midwives, advisers, and spiritual guides. Women have these same intuitive gifts in North American culture too, but here they're called intuitives, counselors, holistic doctors, therapists, psychics, health workers, social workers, nurses, artists, or nuns.

Brujas are not necessarily the same as an evil sorceress, though they can be if they use people's fear for their own gain. I have known a lot of politicians, media personalities, and religious folks who use people's fear for their own gain, and if you ask me, these are the sorcerers we need to be wary of. In my perspective, anyone who works with their positive, feminine spiritual energy is a *bruja/o,* and we all have the ability to develop this divine gift, just as we all have the potential to turn into public menaces by working from fear.

I believe books are medicine. A library is a medicine cabinet. What can heal one person may not work at all for somebody else. You know when something is healing you, just as you know when something isn't. And if my book isn't doing the trick and doesn't serve you, you're not required to keep reading. But please allow it to remain on the library shelf for someone else who needs its particular medicine.

Further, if you feel the book is inappropriate for your child, you must do what your heart guides you. That too is your responsibility. My own is to write my truth, and I certainly don't insist that children read my books. Personally, I don't think we can make children read anything they don't want to read, do you? True reading comes from pleasure, not obligation. When obliged to read something that doesn't speak to you, you'll ultimately forget it. If, however, it brings the right medicine for whatever ails, you'll remember it. This is the nature of art.

Finally, I don't know where in my book you found prostitution since I don't recall writing about any prostitutes in *House on Mango Street*. However, a reader must bring her own connotations to the text. My book was written in an epigrammatic way since I wanted to write a new kind of novel fusing poetry and fiction together. The stories are there for you to reflect on, like poetry. They are dense and intentionally enigmatic so the reader has something to discover, to savor, since so much of what happens in my stories isn't in what is said, but in what is *not* said.

I agree with you. This book was not written for children, and I often find myself editing my selections when children turn up at my public events. (I read the funny chapters for them.) *House* was written for adults and for children who have lived experiences beyond their years. But children insist on reading my work for some reason, and who am I to forbid what wasn't forbidden to me? I often read books beyond my years when I was a child plucking books off the shelves of the Chicago Public Library. I couldn't take home books beyond the "juvenile" or "young adult" categories, but I could read anything I wanted while I was there. Most adult books bored me back then, to tell you the truth, and I think boredom is censorship enough.

I trust my books will only take flight in the minds of those who need these stories. Those too young or not needing my particular dose of medicine will be bored, and that's how it works best, in my opinion.

May you find the right books to fall in love with and be transformed by, and may those books that don't meet your needs be placed gently back on the bookshelf. I wish you well in your journey of self-discovery.

Sincerely,
Sandra Cisneros

The Girl Who Became a Saint: Teresa Urrea

In 2011 a friend invited me to contribute to a book project on women revolutionaries. I picked Teresa Urrea (1873–1906). Once I even planned to write a novel about her, but her descendant, the writer Luis Alberto Urrea, claimed this project himself, so I stepped aside. Teresita Urrea, like the Oaxacan shamaness María Sabina, is a personal hero. I used strands of both these women's lives to create the witch woman character

Teresita's gravesite

in "Eyes of Zapata," a story I wrote about Emiliano Zapata's wife.

On Wednesday, March 24, 2010, my good friend the film-maker Lourdes Portillo and I drove into the Arizona country-side to search for Teresita's grave, located in a mining town called Clifton. The women at the Tucson AAA office warned us that Clifton was ugly with nothing to see. We didn't tell them we were on a mission and took off from the flat desert of southern Arizona without anticipating the sudden changes in landscape we'd encounter.

In the middle of our yakking, Lourdes and I realized we were driving through great gauzy strips of fog. At first we thought it was a forest fire, and this rightfully scared us. Then we saw the clouds floating alongside us, drunk and slanted and sleepy. I didn't understand. I'd never seen such clouds, as if they'd fallen from the sky. Then Lourdes explained we'd driven to their elevation gradually without even noticing. We laughed about this forever.

The land continued sneaking up on us, surprising us with its changes. The road rose past the drunken clouds through prehistoric mountains, rust-colored, pachydermian, and then descended through a valley giddy with poppies, a hue more vibrant than pumpkins, brighter than the orange stripe divid-ing the road. In the horizon, lavender mountains, and then the green scrubbed hills sprinkled here and there with turmeric poppies. Lucky for us to arrive after the rains.

Clifton surprised us too. A town in the cleft of two huge cheeks of earth like a giant pair of mooning buttocks. Who would build a town in a space where it was destined to flood? And it *had* flooded, even in Teresita's time, to disastrous pro-portions. Oddly placed or not, Clifton is not an ugly town.

Decayed, perhaps, abandoned, like a silk ball gown washed ashore after a tempest, but this is a kind of beauty. Hills fresh and green from the rain, the sky a morning-glory blue. Best of all, the most marvelous air, verdant and crisp.

We walked past the jail, a cave transformed into a cell with iron bars. This is where they incarcerated Teresita's husband of one day, Guadalupe Rodríguez, in June of 1900. We wandered the town's old main street, stopping at the Greenlee County Historical Museum, and met a helpful Mr. Joel Briskly, a local history buff, who connected us to Teresita's great-grandniece, another Teresita—Terry Urrea.

I'd been heartbroken when Terry Urrea didn't answer a note I'd left at her door earlier in the day, but Mr. Briskly, all kindness, called on our behalf and gave her our number. And, miracle of miracles, Terry Urrea did indeed phone us just as we wended our way in our rental car toward the cemetery. Terry directed us as we were driving and patiently stayed on the line until we pulled into the graveyard parking area. And yes, there was Teresita's resting place, just as both Terry and Mr. Briskly had said, to the left as you enter the cemetery, surrounded by a wrought-iron fence, small as a crib, an unmarked slab with pink silk roses, and rosaries and a dream catcher others had left behind.

What a beautiful spot to rest. It was lovely to watch the sunset among the hills. I sniffed the air and tried to discover the scent of roses, which some claim happens when you visit Teresita's grave, but I can't lie. I smelled green plants and fresh wind that whistled through the fence in a moan, but no roses. Such a chipper amber color at that hour of the day, light tethered to long blue shadows. Lourdes sat on a neighboring grave and I on another singing *"Farolito,"* and *"Por un amor,"* and Lorca's *"Son de Cuba,"* because those are the only songs I know all the words to.

Then I asked Teresita to receive our lovely friend, the poet Ai, who had just died. And to open our *camino,* to bless and take care of our family and friends, my textile teacher la Señora María Luisa Camacho de López, who was in ill health, my friends and family with all their needy needs, Lourdes, me, my animals. Bring us peace, please. We left windburned and tired, but thrilled to have discovered what we came for. Someday I'd like to dedicate a story to Teresita. Until then, here's what I know so far.

There was once a Mexican girl so famous she frightened the president of the Mexican republic and had to be exiled. It doesn't seem so outrageous in our times for someone to terrorize a head of state now that we are living in the age of *puro susto,* pure fear, when plenty of people get deported or worse, but it's hard to imagine a woman, a teenager, *una mexicana* capable of such power then or now. Her name was Teresa Urrea, and she was known in her lifetime as Teresita, the Saint of Cabora, a village in northern Mexico, in a region currently overrun by narcos.

Teresita lived and died before the Mexican Revolution began, yet she was certainly part of its volcanic rumblings that warned of the end of the old world order. Her story is extraordinary because she was a woman of color with no formal education who rose to power and fame as a mystic healer in Mexico and in the United States.

Teresita was mixed-race, a *mestiza,* during a time when class and color differences were more pronounced than even today. Her mother, Cayetana Chávez, was an indigenous woman, and her father, Tomás Urrea, was a light-skinned Mexican of Spanish descent. He owned all the lands and ranch where Teresita was born and where Cayetana was employed. Teresita was his natural daughter, but when she was in her mid-teens he recognized her as his offspring and invited her to live with him and his second (common-law) family.

Before this, Teresa had lived in a ramada, a house made of sticks and mud, with her mother's relations. She was said to have been an excellent horsewoman, and she knew how to play the guitar and sing—all this the *vaqueros,* Mexican cowboys, had taught her. She must've been a remarkable child to have caught her father's attention. Girls weren't valued, especially those who were illegitimate and indigenous, and certainly not by a wealthy man like Tomás Urrea. But Teresita was tall and beautiful, as we can see for ourselves from her photographs, as well as charming and clever, by all accounts. Maybe her father recognized some part of himself in her and was proud to claim her as his. Only God knows. But by her mid-teens she was living the plot of a Latin American telenovela by moving under her father's care and protection and moving up in class and color.

It was here in her father's house that she met an indigenous elder who would lead her on her life path. The woman was known as Huila, and she was a *curandera,* a healer and midwife, who knew the powers of native plants. Teresa began working as Huila's apprentice, and Huila shared all her skills since the girl showed aptitude. But something happened that would change Teresita's life forever and give her powers that outreached her mentor's.

They say that Teresita suffered a seizure as a result of a terrible *susto* in her mid-teens. Some say she was sexually assaulted or that there was an attempted assault. Some believe she suffered from epilepsy. It isn't certain what happened exactly, but it was something powerful enough to cause Teresita to go into a coma for several months with her pulse and breathing so imperceptible, a mirror had to be held to her nose to make sure she was still alive. Over time Teresita's pulse grew weaker and finally dimmed completely until her family had to admit death had claimed her.

Teresita's wake was held in the family home, as was the custom in those times. Tomás Urrea ordered a coffin built for Teresita, and Huila bound the girl's wrists together with a ribbon. It was during her *velorio* when the community had gathered to pray the rosary over her body that Teresita's first two miracles occurred. First, she rose from the dead, or at least from her temporary death, and second, she announced that they need not remove the coffin, as it would be needed in three days. Her prediction proved true; her teacher Huila passed away and was buried in the coffin intended for Teresita.

Teresita was reborn, but she was visibly altered, and her life would never be the same. She spoke of having visited the Virgin Mary while she was away, and lived distracted for several weeks, unable to even feed or dress herself. When she finally came back to herself one morning, she couldn't remember anything that had happened since she fell ill. It was as if she'd been alive, but not alive, as if she were paying attention only to things inside her own heart.

Other strange events occurred. After her rebirth, Teresita exhibited extraordinary powers of healing and vision. Teresita claimed she could look inside her patients and see their illness clearly as if she were looking into a window. Sometimes she was able to cure them just by placing her hands on them, and those she was unable to cure, she was at least able to comfort and give temporary relief.

Word spread across the region that a young girl could cure miraculously. Thousands of sick people, rich and poor, came to seek her out. Her father's ranch was soon transformed into a carnival. Although Tomás Urrea tried to dissuade his daughter from doing her work, in the end her piety and dedication won him over. "I believe God has placed me here as one of his instruments to do good." She was fulfilling an obligation.

And so the Urrea family made huge sacrifices on Teresita's behalf. The world as they once knew it turned upside down. Teresita was installed in her own building, where she might receive her patients, and those who could afford to pay for food were charged, and those who could not were fed for free. In the way of a true healer, Teresita did not charge, however, for her healing services.

Teresita's family loved and supported her, but they never claimed she was a saint. Whenever Teresita cured someone successfully, it was the crowd who called out, "Miracle!" and "¡Santa Teresa!"

Teresa did not want to be a saint. Who would want to be a saint? Would you? But sainthood is conferred by others, not by the saint, isn't that so? Savvy businessmen out to make a living printed holy cards with Teresita's image with angels floating about her, and these sold very well and were popular among her followers, especially among the indigenous tribes who claimed her as their patron and who wore Teresita's image on their hats to protect themselves from harm.

"I'm not a saint," Teresita insisted in an interview. Teresita admitted her body was like any other person's, but her soul, that she knew was different. Teresita's family also denied Teresita's sainthood, though they had to admit Teresita had certain gifts even they couldn't explain. For example, when she wanted to, she could make herself so heavy not even her strong half brothers could pick her up, but when she willed it, her slender best friend could lift her in her arms. Even more amazing was her ability to invite her best friend to travel together with her while they dreamt the same dream at night. They could go to Mexico City and walk about there, and then travel back to their bodies and remember the journey the next morning.

A great many theories abounded as to how exactly Teresita accomplished what she did. Was it magnetism, hypnotism, spiritism? Well, what exactly? Not even Teresita herself knew except she knew she was doing God's work, and later in life even expressed an interest in going to Europe or to India for an explanation of her own mystical gifts.

Throughout her life Teresita defended the rights of the indigenous communities, perhaps because she was half indigenous and had lived in their world. Then as now, *los indios* were the poorest of the poor and suffered greatly. Teresita always spoke on their behalf and criticized the abuses inflicted by the government and the church. She encouraged the people to pray directly to God without the intercession of the priests or costly sacraments. Needless to say, the Mexican Church did not look kindly on Teresita's power over the multitudes and denounced her as a fraud.

Eventually Teresita's popularity among the Mayo, Tarahumara, and Tomochiteco communities caused her to become involved in politics, and ultimately exiled from the country. It so happened that the indigenous communities held Teresita in high regard as they recognized in her a person of great spiritual integrity and power. Porfirio Díaz, the dictator/ruler of Mexico, felt she was inciting them to rise against him and had her escorted to the U.S.-Mexico border, where she was booted out of the country. Her father accompanied Teresita and protected her during her exodus, and eventually established a home in Arizona, and later in Texas in El Paso. While Teresita was exiled, several indigenous communities did indeed organize themselves in strikes and uprisings. And though she was no longer a Mexican resident, Teresita was often implicated in these events because her followers wore her image on their sombreros. This caused Porfirio Díaz to fear she was even more powerful than imagined. Maybe the Mexican president believed the stories of Teresita's ability to appear in more than one place at the same time. At any rate, he purportedly sent agents across the border to kidnap Teresita or to assassinate her.

It's with good reason that the Urreas feared for Teresita's safety, and so they were advised to move inland, away from the border and its volatile environment. Tomás sent for his wife and children and settled his family finally in Clifton, Arizona, a beautiful mining town tucked in the cleft between two bluffs. Here he established successful dairy and firewood businesses. But it was also here that he and his daughter would experience heartache.

It seems that Teresita fell in love with a Mexican miner from a neighboring town. His name was Guadalupe Rodríguez, and he was tall and handsome, like her father. Maybe she saw in him a man who could protect her, and she felt safe with him. And after knowing him eight months she married him, though her father didn't approve the match. She was twenty-seven years old when she met Lupe. Did he see in Teresita a beautiful young woman, and not a saint? And perhaps this was something altogether new for Teresita, and though her father cursed her choice in love, women are always brave in the face of love even it means defying fathers.

Lupe had to steal Teresita from her father's house. He came with his rifle and took her away, but not against her will. Maybe she had planned the confrontation, and she willingly went away with him to be married, and was married in the neighboring town of Metcalf, where he lived. But by morning her husband began to act strangely. Many Mexican men act strangely after their wedding night. Maybe he'd been drinking. Maybe he suspected Teresita was not such a saint, and this made him angry. Maybe she had been violated that day when she went into a coma, and this may have made Lupe feel he was cheated and getting damaged goods. Maybe he was hired by Porfirio Díaz. Or maybe he was simply *un loco*. We can only imagine, because we don't know what happened to trigger Teresita's new husband to such odd actions. He went into a rage, Teresita reported, and tore up her things. He made her pack her clothes in a bundle, and then, carrying it over his shoulder, ordered his new bride to follow him.

There were witnesses watching Teresita follow this madman. Was he shouting? Did he beat her? What did he do that folks came out and warned her not to follow him? Maybe they knew he was a crazy man all along. Guadalupe Rodríguez walked on the railroad track, and Teresita was forced to follow behind. Then Guadalupe broke into a run, and Teresita ran after him. He turned around and started to shoot at her. And only then did the bystanders come after him and carry him off to the authorities. They brought him back to Clifton and put him in a jail that had been created from a mountain cave, and there he behaved like a wild creature pacing his cage.

I want to imagine the things Lupe shouted about his bride for all to hear. I want to imagine her pain and her sadness. It couldn't have been more humiliating to have gone against her father's wishes and then return the next day knowing he was right. Her husband frothing in jail spewing out words against her. Now was she a saint?

And what does her father say? And what does Teresita say to him? What do they not say to each other, and what do they think? And if she could see into people's hearts and into the future, why was she not able to see through love? the townsfolk ask. If you ever have lived such a scene in your life, you can fill in the blanks. Perhaps love makes fools of us all.

At the right moment, a Mrs. C. P. Rosencrans arrives and invites Teresita to California to heal her child, and perhaps because of her disastrous marriage, Teresita accepts and leaves Clifton, because she too is sick and needs to heal her own heart.

More than five hundred citizens go to the train station to see Teresita off. I think one person is not there. I think her father refuses to go and goes to work that day and pretends he's too busy with his dairy, with his firewood business. This is how I imagine a man too proud, too hurt, dealing with his sadness. Or perhaps he's there. Does he join the crowd in waving a handkerchief, or does he stand as hard and still as a mountain?

Teresita is lost to him. Her father is lost to her. How powerless her father must've felt when she married, and now when she moves away, does a part of him die too?

And what about her? What must she feel to accept a trip to California that will take her far away? I think of her father sitting watching the sun set in Arizona. I think of Teresita watching that same sunset in California. Each thinking about the other.

Is this the beginning of the saint's loss of her powers? Because in California a medical company will hire Teresita and promise her thousands of dollars to go on a curing crusade, and they will tell her she can travel and heal many people, but they don't tell her they will charge her patients, and because she will be healing Anglos, she will have difficulties because she doesn't speak English. And so Teresita's healing crusade begins in Los Angeles, and takes her to St. Louis, and on to New York. And because she can't find an adequate translator now that she is serving an Anglo audience, she sends a letter to her good friend, her *comadre* Juana Van Order, in Arizona, a Mexican woman who has married an Anglo and has two bilingual boys. The older son is sent to New York to assist Teresita in her work. His name is John Van Order, and he will become the father of Teresita's two daughters.

How could love not develop between a nineteen-year-old boy and a woman of twenty-seven who has very little experience in love? Maybe he tells her things he believes with all his heart, but his heart is the heart of a child. But her heart is the heart of a girl. And though they can't marry, because she is still legally married to Lupe, they promise to love each other as if they were married and to marry when they can. I can't imagine it any other way, because Teresita lived and spoke always by way of her heart.

She can't know that John and she will have nothing to say to each other in a few years. They have little in common. That even though she will seek out the divorce in Los Angeles, by then John will have outgrown his love with the girl saint. Saints don't make good housewives.

It's when she's expecting her child in New York that she hears her father is ill, and finally that he has died. Teresita with life in her belly and with a contract that is keeping her in New York, what is she thinking now?

How is it that Teresita finally becomes aware of the duplicity of her employers and hires a lawyer to cancel her contract with the medical company? She's exhausted. She wants to go home. And she does go home, with her two girls, but not with their father. She has given up being a saint.

With her savings from her touring she's able to open a small hospital in Clifton, and here she lives until she contracts tuberculosis in her thirty-third year and dies. During Teresita's short but extraordinary life, doors opened for her wherever she went even though she was Mexican. She never forgot her indigenous roots and always allied herself with the poor even in the United States. While living in Los Angeles it's said she supported the Mexicans organizing a union. She was a bridge between communities in conflict, and this in a time when Mexicans were even more oppressed than now.

Teresita Urrea was not a writer, so we don't know how she felt about the things that happened to her. We have accounts by witnesses. We have newspaper interviews, but these were translations of her words. We don't have her words directly, we have to trust those who put words in her mouth. And it seems as if everyone has put their own thoughts, their own politics, their own spin on how they see her, including this writer.

But perhaps that's the mystery and power of Teresita Urrea, a woman from both sides of the border. Activists, revolutionaries, historians, writers, indigenous communities, kin, friends, and enemies alike have used her to carry their own words, their own stories across borders. Over a century after her death, she continues to live as an immortal, because those remembered in stories never die.

SUGGESTED FURTHER READING

Teresita, by William Curry Holden

Ringside Seats to a Revolution, by David Dorado Romo

Hummingbird's Daughter and *Queen of America,* both by Luis Alberto Urrea

Chavela Vargas:
Una Mujer Muy Mujer

I was walking along the beach in Miami when the call came: Did I want to write a tribute to Chavela Vargas for *The New York Times*? I said I'd finish my walk and decide. My first response was "I can't do this," not because I wasn't capable, but because I didn't feel I was the best person for the job. But the more I walked I realized if I refused, *The New York Times* would ask the Latino writer du jour, who most probably was a man. This motivated me to call back and accept the assignment. I meant to write about Chavela the woman of self-myth, not Chavela the scandalous. But the space I had was limited, and finally, with all the cuts and edits, my *homenaje* was reduced to *puro chisme*, pure gossip. *¡Ay, Chavelita, perdóname!*

The article appeared in *The New York Times Magazine*'s "The Lives They Lived" issue on December 28, 2012.

Once, when Mexico was the belly button of the universe, Isabel Vargas Lizano ran away from Costa Rica and resolved to make herself into a Mexican singer. This was in the 1930s, when Europe was on fire, the United States out of work, and Mexico busy giving birth to herself after a revolution.

At fourteen, Isabel was busy birthing herself too. Cast off from her Costa Rican kin for being too "strange," she would become Mexico's beloved Chavela Vargas.

It was the country's golden era. Visitors came from across the globe. Sergei Eisenstein, Luis Buñuel, Leonora Carrington. Mexico was a knockout, and everyone was crazy about her.

At first, Vargas made her living doing odd jobs: cooking, selling children's clothes, chauffeuring an elderly lady. She was adopted by artists and musicians and sang at their parties and favorite bars. When she was not yet twenty-five, she was invited to the Blue House of Frida Kahlo and Diego Rivera in Coyoacán. "Who's that girl, the one in the white shirt?" Kahlo asked. Kahlo summoned her over, and Vargas sat at her side the rest of the night. Because Vargas lived all the way up in the Condesa neighborhood, Rivera and Kahlo offered her lodging for the night. Rivera suggested she take to bed some of their *xoloitzcuintlis,* their Mexican hairless dogs. "Sleep with them," he told her. "They warm the bed and keep away rheumatism." Vargas had found her spiritual family.

Eventually Vargas apprenticed with Mexico's finest musicians: the composer Agustín Lara and Antonio Bribiesca and his weeping guitar. She fine-tuned her singing style listening to Toña la Negra and the Texas songbird Lydia Mendoza, among others. The songwriter José Alfredo Jiménez became her maestro with his songs that "expressed . . . the common pain of all who love," Vargas said. "And when I came out onstage they were mine, because I added my own pain too."

With just a guitar and her voice, Vargas performed in a red poncho and pants at a time when Mexican women didn't wear pants. She sang with arms open wide like a priest celebrating Mass, modeling her singing on the women of the Mexican Revolution. "A *mexicana* is a very strong woman," Vargas said. "Starting with la Adelita, la Valentina—*mujeres muy mujeres.*" Chavela Vargas belonged to this category of women-very-much-women.

Even when Vargas was young and her voice still as transparent as mescal, she danced with her lyrics *tacuachito* style, cheek to cheek, pounded them on the bar, made them jump like dice, spat and hissed and purred like the woman jaguar she claimed to be, and finished with a volley that entered the heart like a round of bullets from the pistol she stashed in her belt.

"She was *chile verde*," Elena Poniatowska, the Mexican writer, recalls when I ask. "Chavela was a *tortillera* and flaunted it at a time when others hid their sexuality. She lived and sang *a lo macho.* Chavela sang love songs written for men without changing the pronouns.

"Her big hit was 'Macorina,'" Poniatowska went on. "*'Put your hand here, Macorina,'* she sang with her hand like a great big seashell over her sex, long before Madonna."

In her autobiography, *Y si quieres saber de mi pasado,* Vargas writes, "I always began with 'Macorina.' . . . And lots of times I finished with that song. So that folks would go home to their beds *calientitos,* nice and horny."

Because she immortalized popular *rancheras,* Vargas is often labeled a country singer. But she kidnapped romantic boleros and made them hers too. Her songs appealed to drinkers of *pulque* as well as champagne.

The critic Tomás Ybarra-Frausto remembers the Vargas of the early '60s. "I used to see her at La Cueva de Amparo Montes, a club frequented by the underground in downtown Mexico City. She dressed in black leather and would roar over on a motorcycle with a blond *gringa* on her back."

Someone else told this story. In a Mexico City club, Vargas serenaded a couple. Then she slipped off the man's tie, lassoed it around his woman's neck, gave it a passionate yank, and kissed her.

She had a reputation as a *robaesposas.* Did she really run off with everyone's wife? A European queen? Ava Gardner? Frida? What was true, and what was *mitote*? You only have to look at Vargas's photos when she was young to know some of the talk was true.

In the town of Monclova, Coahuila, go ask the elders. They'll tell you: Chavela came to town and sang. And then ran off with the doctor's daughter. People still remember.

Judy Garland, Grace Kelly, Bette Davis, Elizabeth Taylor . . . She was invited to their parties, danced with the wives of powerful *políticos,* claimed to have shared *un amor* with "the most famous woman in the world," but would not say more.

And then, somewhere in her sixties, Vargas disappeared. Some thought she had died, and in a way, she had.

"Sometimes I don't have any other alternative but to joke about my alcoholism as if it was just a one-night *parranda,*" she said. "It was no joke . . . Those who lived it with me know it."

Before Pedro Almodóvar and Salma Hayek featured her in

their films, there were friends who helped Vargas walk through fire and be reborn. Performers Jesusa Rodríguez and Liliana Felipe invited Chavela to make her 1991 comeback in their Mexico City theater, El Hábito.

"There were only a few minutes left before her entrance, and the place was packed," Rodríguez remembers. "All the hipsters of that era were waiting. No one could believe Chavela was returning to sing.

"She was nervous. Well, she'd never appeared onstage without drinking. When we gave her the second call, she panicked and asked for a tequila. Liliana and I looked at one another, and then Liliana said, 'Chavela, if you drink, it's better if we just cancel the show.' 'But how?' said Chavela. 'There's a full house.' 'Well, it doesn't matter,' we said. 'We'll just give everyone their money back, and that'll be that.'

"Chavela looked serious for a few moments, then she took a deep breath and said, 'Let's go!' We gave the third call, she climbed up on the stage, stood there like an ancient tree, and sang for . . . years, without stopping, without drinking."

Her voice had become another voice. Ravaged but beautiful in a dark way, like glass charred into obsidian.

Vargas's specialty was *el amor y el desamor,* love and love lost, songs of loneliness and goodbyes in a voice as ethereal as the white smoke from copal, but as powerful as the Pacific. Songs that sucked you in, threatened to drown you; then, when you least expected it, pulled down your pants and slapped you on the ass. Audiences broke out into spontaneous *gritos,* that Mexican yodel barked from the belly and a lifetime of grief.

Every nation has a singer who captures its soul. Mexican parties always end with everyone crying, the journalist Alma Guillermoprieto once noted. Vargas satisfied a national urge to weep.

She embodied Mexico, that open wound unhealed since the conquest and, a century after a useless revolution, in need of tears now more than ever.

This summer 2012, at the age of ninety-three, Vargas returned to Mexico from Spain. She was sick. On August 5th, Death came at last and ran off with her.

Chocolate and Donuts

When I've told a story aloud more than once, then it's time to capture it in print. I began this story on paper in April of 2013 and read the first two pages to Franco over the phone, but not the finished version a year later. I hope he doesn't get angry with me for going past the veneer of his house and examining it in a light he might not find flattering. I was trying to examine myself, and, as always, houses help me do that.

Even in dreams I conjure up houses, some from my past, some in invented neighborhoods I return to again and again during a dream series. In the houses of my past I go back to live at an old address with my parents, who in the dream are still alive, and with my brothers as single adults.

Or I dream I've forgotten to feed the animals I keep as pets, goldfish, or once even penguins, and in the dream someone warns me, "Don't forget to feed your penguins!" Then the panic, because I didn't even know I *had* penguins. An overwhelming dread and urge to get home, wondering what I'll find when I get there.

Often I dream I'm living in a hotel lobby, or in a room without doors, or I unlock my hotel room only to find it filled with writers seated in a workshop circle or with guests sleeping in my bed. Then I know the dream is telling me it's time to retreat from society. When I feel safe and alone, but not lonely, I write my best.

We'd just breakfasted on dim sum, but hadn't had enough helpings of talk. Franco suggested we go over to his house for cups of Mexican chocolate and donuts from The Original Donut Shop, a drive-through taco/donut shop on Fredericksburg Road. No one was hungry, but Franco's home is a feast for the senses.

The house once belonged to Franco's great-grandfather, a watch repairer, and later his grandfather, an elevator operator in San Antonio's tallest downtown building, where Franco would work one day as a lawyer. Now their descendant was an international artist living like a Roman emperor in one of the city's humblest neighborhoods—the West Side. Hard to believe this

Getting ready for the house's close-up; I'm seated far right.

bungalow, four rooms without doors, had once been home to a family of nine.

Now chandeliers illuminate the front porch, the garden, every room inside, including the studio next door and the aviary, enough to dub this house the West Side Versailles. Blue maguey and prickly pear sprout from massive mosaic garden planters. Plaster cherubs and Greek goddesses do war with Aztec gods and Cantinflas. A glass gallery with paintings big as doors.

Interior walls are lacquered black as Mexican Olinalá jewelry boxes to better showcase the art, antiques, pottery, sculptures, and pastry. Outside galvanized watering troughs with water lilies and koi fish serve as water garden. And about the grounds, turtles, stray cats, fancy chickens, white doves, and handsome gardeners strut about like the peacocks Franco also keeps. It's a fusion of worlds, Old and New, of high and low art, of Roman middle class meets Tejano working class.

Franco grew up in Boerne, a small town now practically a San Antonio suburb. In his former life, when he was a high-paid lawyer, he lived in a minimalist glass house in San Antonio's swankiest neighborhood. Now he finds living in the West Side romantic. Who am I to argue?

So it's Franco's idea to install a bed in the living room, the way my family did growing up. For him it's aesthetics. For us it was necessity.

From the kitchen the sound of coffee cups clinking, Mexican chocolate being whisked with a wooden *molinillo,* the voices of my friends gossiping and laughing. I lie down on the living room bed, a chocolate faux-mink blanket spread over me. And it's then it comes.

The fear I always live with, gone. A sense of remembered well-being. As if I'm no longer in my woman's body and am pure spirit. A comfort and security surrounded by the overflow of lives and voices and shouting and footsteps of those I love, those who love me, that overcome all the dangers and terrors of the outside world.

Because I've lived alone for too long, I want to savor this. I'm floating among the sounds of the wooden churn whirling against the pot, the murmur of voices from the kitchen receding and then increasing now and again as sleep comes in like the tide and takes me.

In Turkish there's a word for when you're blessed and *know* you're blessed: *kanaat*. I feel this now in Franco's living room, lying on the narrow bed covered in fake mink. Once on a beach off the coast of Quintana Roo, I felt this same joy, as if I was connected to everything in the universe. A sense of belonging, unity, peace.

Thunk, thunk, thunk, thunk! Someone pummels the front door like he means to bring it down with his fists. When I open it, standing on the porch is a carnival strongman in a Spurs T-shirt.

"Franco here?"

"I'll get him. Want to come in?"

"Naw, I'll wait."

Franco attends to the door, and I climb back into bed and try to recapture that state of rapture before the door thumped me awake, but it's hard to find nirvana with Franco and Hercules arguing on the front porch. I try to ignore them, but their voices grow louder.

"No, you *didn't,*" Franco says. "No. You. Did. Not! Do you want me to call the police? Because if you don't get off my porch, I'm calling 911, and you don't want to go back to jail."

The door slams.

"Who was *that,* Franco?"

"Just one of my ex-employees who stole from me. Don't worry about it."

"Franco, he was pretty mad! Aren't you afraid he'll come back with a gun?"

"Oh, I'm not scared. I have this really butch new assistant, Peppermint Patty. She can handle him."

Franco goes back to pour the chocolate and lay out the donuts. A coward, I slink after him to the kitchen, the room farthest away from the front window, remembering how I spent the New Year's Eves of my youth. My mother herding us into the basement before midnight to protect us from the passion of neighbors. A rock, a word, a bullet, a bomb. Overflow from the Vesuvius called the heart.

Is home the place where you feel safe? What about those whose home isn't safe? Are they homeless, or is home an ideal just out of reach, like heaven? Is home something you move toward instead of going back? Homesickness, then, would be a malaise not for a place left behind in memory, but one remembered in the future.

Immigrants and exiles know this art of mental acrobatics for a lost home. Their homesickness causes them to storytell until they've created an "imaginary homeland," as Salman Rushdie named it, where sweets are sweeter than any reality.

Even the Chicago neighborhood of my youth, with its self-imposed curfew at dusk, drunks crashing their cars on our curb, abandoned vehicles set on fire in our alley, rats scurrying under Mother's hibiscus bushes after garbage collection was cut from twice a week to once a week despite the fact that the neighborhood population doubled. But we were people of color and thus didn't need our garbage collected twice a week like the white folks who, once gentrification occurred, had their garbage reverted to twice-a-week collection. That's my Chicago! Even with all this, there was safety in numbers, among your own, a tribe who might not understand or know you. But you were theirs; you felt safe belonging. A feeling hard to re-create once you left home.

Now, under fake mink, I'm suffering from *comezón;* roughly translated, the heebie-jeebies. Along with familiarity comes the deluge of doubts. Life is as tenuous as the coat-hanger television antenna, the light fixture repaired with electrical tape and aluminum foil, the kitchen cabinets lacquered a Coca-Cola color to better ignore the amber-shelled nightlife.

At any moment bliss might be interrupted by the last word sent through the window in a ball of fire. The flick of a light switch could trigger an electrical-short explosion, a reminder never to hire the cousin studying to be an electrician. How much truth exists in a drunk man's gossip; during Franco's last fiesta, an artist claimed he'd seen real fur, alive, four-footed, footloose among the faux. And what of the handsome gardeners circling about—hyenas waiting for the lion to falter? Santa María Virgen Purísima, *soy la más miedosa de toditos los pobres infelices del mundo de la misericordia.* Cover me with your faux-fur mantle, Virgencita, keep me in the dark. Pray for me, keep me safe. Bless this humble home.

Akumal

When I wrote the previous story, "Chocolate and Donuts," that memory jogged another memory—a moment I told few people about. It was a visit to a place in the Yucatán Peninsula I'd been to for only a few minutes, but what happened there stayed with me a lifetime. I realized after writing the other selection, it was time to visit Akumal again, if only in print.

I have yet to return to Akumal in the forty years since that first visit, though I borrowed from the experience for a chapter in *Caramelo* (but nobody would know that but me). My friend the designer Verónica Prida passed through Akumal and was surprised to see my photo in a Texas newspaper clipping taped under the gift shop counter. "But why is this news story here?" she asked. "Well, I don't know," the cashier said. "Someone put it there." What is the connection between Akumal and me? *Sólo Dios*, as the Mexicans like to say, only God knows.

It was the last time I'd travel with them, or so I thought. I was twenty-one, the end of my childhood. Too old to be traveling with my mother and father, I told myself. Yet, out of love for Mexico and my father who'd invited me, I said yes.

It was the summer between undergraduate and graduate school. Am I remembering or inventing here? In my memory it's just before I go to study at the Iowa Writers' Workshop. In my mind I've settled this summer like a jade bead before the dull two years to come working in that foreign place Iowa City.

The trip is Father's idea; so is the idea that I'd be coming along with them. Most probably he didn't ask Mother before he invited me; he doesn't think about that. Or she doesn't care yet, but will later when she has one of her famous tantrums. Then it's him and me against her, always against her.

Every trip has low points, just as it has its highs. I want to talk about the highs, a few only, the ones I remember now, today, thirty-seven summers later, as brightly as the day they waltzed away with me.

The trip was to take us to the Yucatán, Quintana Roo, and finally Oaxaca. Father's choices. We were traveling to states where his father, a military man, had been posted. Because of his father's meandering career, Father was born in Oaxaca instead of at home in Mexico City. Maybe the ancestors were calling Father back, but if so, he wasn't listening. He talked about new beaches and good food, and that was enough to convince us.

We flew from Chicago to Mexico City, then Mérida. After the lulling drone of the plane, I glanced out the window and was amazed to see, standing alongside us, an enormous mountain with snow on top and a little cloud snagged on its peak like a beret. It took my breath away. I could only nudge and point.

"Popo," Father said. Popocatépetl, that was it. Our Mexican Mount Fuji. One of the twin volcanoes seen from the rooftops of Mexico City when I was a child. I'd never seen it from this altitude. Our plane's shadow swept across like a mosquito, the great mountain as solid and still as a Buddha.

In Mérida we rented a sky-blue VW Bug, Father at the wheel as always, and drove into the jungle headed for Chichén Itzá, a Mayan pyramid we'd only seen on television. The blue Bug was zipping along the two-lane highway, all of us jabbering like macaws when we came around a curve and there it was. We were left with words dangling from our mouths. Chichén Itzá rising from the jungle. Brilliant, white, enormous, as impressive as Popo.

How had we not known Chichén Itzá would be . . . stupendous? Chichén Itzá was as magnificent as the Parthenon, or the Egyptian pyramids, or the Eiffel Tower, or any other world wonder. Here again was a "How come nobody told me?" moment.

Chichén Itzá might have been enough for the whole trip, but we had to drive on before nightfall to a new resort called Cancún, the place where Mayan kings had supposedly wintered, or so the ads wanted us to believe. It was just a few hotels then, with sacks of cement and piles of sand and loose boards lying about, a town so new it had no charm. But the waters, ah! They were the most beautiful beaches I'd ever seen: fine white sand like talc and water more shades of turquoise than I'd ever dreamt.

We stayed only a night and then aimed the Bug toward the Mayan ruins of Tulum, down the coast of Quintana Roo, syllables so lovely to the mouth and ear Joan Didion stole them for her daughter's name.

Tarantulas skittered across the highway, making their trembly way from one part of the jungle to the other. Father stopped at a place called Akumal so we could rest. It was nothing more than a few thatch-roofed *palapas* with hammocks strung up and a quiet lagoon rimmed by palm trees.

I was lucky enough to be wearing my swimsuit, or I might not have ventured in. The water was calm and still. I lay down at the shallow lip of water and land where the sand, ridged and soft and firm at the same time, settled into the contours of my back and neck. The water, warm as a body, lapped at my earlobes, and the trees set a dappled light waving the sunlight gently over me as if giving me a cleansing. The waves, slow and calming, murmured things I didn't need to understand for now. I shut my eyes.

And I felt something that has come and gone in my life at odd times without my asking. A sense of detaching from myself, of sliding out of myself and connecting with everything in the universe. Of being empty so I could fill up with everything.

And I wondered if dying was like this, and if so, why was everyone so afraid of it? All the while the water lap-lapped at my earlobes, saying and saying things softly.

This was only for a moment, maybe a few seconds, a few minutes at most. I was living in dreamtime, like when you're in love. There's no such thing as time, just being, unhitched from a body, that tractor trailer. I was fearless finally. Infinite happiness.

"*¡SANDRA, YA VÁMONOS!*" my father shouted, reeling me back to the world of the living with its minutiae of petty obligations.

"Let's go," Father shouted, impatient to get us to the next destination on his list, not knowing how far away I'd just traveled. How could I explain?

It was gone as suddenly as it had come. But it belonged to me, it had been given to me.

I kept it a secret inside the car and inside my heart, as if I'd unearthed an exquisite artifact that might be confiscated at the border. Something ancient yet new, something of great value, like a coin I would have to hide under my tongue.

A Borrowed House

I once gave a lecture called "Quiet as Snow" at a librarians' conference where I told the story of my many childhood libraries and mentioned a much-borrowed book. Why did that little book from so long ago stay with me all these years? Writing is the tug of a question, but you don't know the question until after you've written the answer.

This essay was one of two written for the Thomas Wolfe Lecture, the University of North Carolina, Chapel Hill, and delivered on October 21, 2014.

M y first crush was over a book, and not just any book, but a book about a house. Virginia Lee Burton's *The Little House.* My brother Kiki and I were wild about this picture book as kids and checked it out of the Chicago Public Library seventeen times. Okay, maybe I'm exaggerating, but what I remember for sure is that we memorized its pages, we fell asleep with the book, we wanted to keep it, and we even planned to steal it. Can you blame us? Like many inner-city children, we had no idea you could *buy* a book. For a long time I thought books were so valuable they were issued only to institutions and not individuals. We'd never seen a bookstore or books that didn't have a stamp in them that said "Property of Saint Mel's" or "Chicago Public Library."

One exception. My cousins had a collection of books behind a glass cabinet in their apartment thanks to Aunty Lily, who worked at a book-binding company. I read bits and pieces of Charles

Kingsley's *The Water-Babies*, fascinated by the illustrations, but was never able to read more than a page or two at a time, because I was told it was rude to prefer books over cousins.

The only books we owned as children were the glossy cardboard ones you could get at Woolworth's or the supermarket, but these didn't count as real books to me. As a kid, I'd never seen a store that specialized only in books. In our neighborhood anything that mentioned books was prefaced with the word "exotic," and that meant for adults only. Nowadays with bookstores disappearing the way of the dodo bird, I bet there are plenty of kids who haven't seen a bookstore either.

We may not have known where to buy a book, but we did know the price of *The Little House* by checking the cards tucked inside the front cover pocket. Back then library books came with two cards tucked into a manila pocket glued onto the front page. This card had the name of the book and price on it, and it also had a rubber-stamped date that told you when the book had to be returned. It stated in clear letters along the border there would be a twenty-five-cent fine if you lost the cards. I touched these cards over and over to make sure I wouldn't lose them, and blame the Chicago Public Library for the beginning of my obsessive-compulsive anxieties.

Kiki and I got a fifty-cent allowance each Sunday. If we pooled our money and saved for a few months, we could own our favorite book. We meant to tell the librarian we'd lost it and pay for it, so it wasn't technically a theft. But the idea of lying to a librarian was infinitely more difficult than stealing a book, and we gave up on the plan before carrying it out.

The Little House is the story of a house set on a pretty country hill. The landscape changes as the years pass, but the house is solid and constant. All the while, lurking beyond the horizon is the faint glow of the city, growing steadily closer with the decades. We see the horse-drawn carriages giving way to automobiles, the country roads paved over with steam shovels, the clothes of the home-owners changing with the times. Only the house remains the same as everything around it is altered, the city gobbling up the countryside, replacing it with tall buildings and elevated trains, so that in the end, the house finds itself no longer in the country but in the middle of a busy downtown street, neglected and shabby, but still as good as new deep down inside. Finally, at the climax of the book, the house is rescued by the original owner's great-grand-descendants, who haul the house away on wheels and drive it out into the countryside and place it on a beautiful hill spangled with daisies just as when the story began.

The Little House arrived at a time when my life wobbled. My brother Kiki had been my best buddy while our older brother, Al, was away in military school, but I found myself alone on Al's return. It was hard for me to make friends. I was not pretty. I had asymmetrical bangs thanks to my mother, who invented the Vidal Sassoon look years before Vidal Sassoon. My school uniform, a plaid skirt, was patched in the front because Mother had scorched it accidentally while ironing. At school I was convinced everyone who saw me was staring at the patch on my skirt. I knew what it was like to feel like the Little House when it was sad, afraid, and run-down. I needed to know that, though the world around me was often frightening, I would be all right in the end, especially in my family, where things happened nobody told you were coming, or they told you and you weren't listening.

I remember climbing into the backseat of our Chevy once and asking, "Where we going?" "Mexico," my mother said. I looked out the rear window and caught a last glimpse of our apartment, 1451 West 63rd Street, second-floor rear. It was just another grace-

Fifth grade

less Chicago building whose best feature was its fifty-dollar-a-month rent. Four rooms with linoleum floors. Nothing to love, but it was home. My heart sank.

The story of *The Little House* gave me courage. It opens with the man who built the house declaring, "The Little House shall never be sold for gold or silver and she will live to see our great-great-grandchildren's great-great-grandchildren living in her." No wonder this book was a favorite! Why couldn't my own grandfathers make such a promise? Why couldn't Father? He traveled back and forth to his hometown, Mexico City, almost every year the first six years of my existence, or at least that's the way it felt to me. Could it be Father was homesick even when he was home with us?

My Mexico City grandparents lived at Fortuna, number 12,

in the neighborhood officially named la Colonia Industrial, but more commonly known as la Villa or Tepeyac for its most famous visitor—la Virgen de Guadalupe, in 1531. If only Abuelito Cisneros had declared that the house on Fortuna would never be sold, not for Mexican pesos or U.S. dollars, so that I wouldn't have had to live long enough to witness its mint-candy facade painted a fecal brown. Even if it hadn't been sold, how could Abuelito have bequeathed the Fortuna house to eighteen grandchildren scattered across two countries.

My mother's father, Grandpa Cordero, was a widower before I even began grade school. In Chicago's Lawndale neighborhood, Grandpa shared his dark and dreary two-flat at 3847 West Grenshaw with four of his grown children. Uncle Maño, who didn't work for reasons we never thought to ask; Aunty Lily, thrice married (and twice divorced from the same man!); Aunty Margaret, raising two daughters alone; and upstairs, Aunty Lupe, her husband, Pete, and their three kids. No room for any more guests there, that was for sure.

We whirled about Chicago from apartment to apartment in neighborhoods where we were able to find a flat on the cheap. Father's forays back to Mexico kept us constantly broke, until finally Mother, born the year of the stock market crash, figured out we needed a house for stability. Like so many working-class women, Mother knew a house meant safety from the wolf at the door.

Maybe Father never would've followed Mother's advice if Divine Providence hadn't stepped in and given him a good kick in the pants. In January of 1966 the pipes in our old brownstone froze, burst, and forced us to haul water up four flights of stairs in glass milk gallons. When Father saw our icy coat sleeves, shoes, and mittens, he realized it was time. He sold his beloved new Chevy station wagon for three thousand dollars, borrowed money from any relative who would trust him, and placed the down payment on our first home, a two-story bungalow in Humboldt Park on Chicago's Near North Side.

At our old address we lived on the top floor of what was once an elegant one-family brownstone at 2152 West Roosevelt Road. It was already divided into three-flats when we moved in. We told everyone we lived on the third floor, but technically it was the fourth, because of a raised basement. Behind a hidden door on the second-floor hall, you climbed up a narrow flight of stairs to what were once the servants' quarters. That was our flat. You entered by way of a middle room, but this room outfitted with two beds served as a bedroom for my four younger brothers and me.

Imagine how overjoyed we were at our new address to turn the faucets and have water gush out. We could walk easily to the nearest public library only five blocks away instead of the five-mile hike to the library on Madison off Western Avenue. And best of all, I no longer had to sleep with my little brothers. I had a real bedroom—the size of a closet, but I wasn't complaining. That closet was mine.

The Little House sparked a lifelong hunger for a house of my own, a place to restore yourself from the world that might rough you up a bit now and then. A house meant a lot for a girl who lived with too many people, in run-down neighborhoods, who talked to trees, whose family thought she cried too much because she did. A house, even borrowed for a little, but all your own, would mean a place to imagine and be safe. All my life I've dreamt and dream about a house the way some women dream of husbands.

When my father was sick and knew he had only a few months to live, he confessed to me in private, "I wanted to leave each of you children a house. But I've failed." And then he started to cry.

It astonishes me even now to think Father's idea of success was leaving each of his seven kids a house! Father had given us so much by not giving us much.

Necessity. That's what he gave us. Necessity taught us to value what we worked for, to recognize others who, like us, didn't have much, to be generous to others *because* we hadn't had much. When you haven't had much, you *never* forget what that feels like. Compassion. That's what Father gave us.

In my life because of my poor choices, men came and went, but mainly went. I couldn't rely on them to buy me a pumpkin shell. I bought my house with my pen. All by myself. Without having to borrow from my father and mother for the down payment. I bought my first house in San Antonio with tremendous fear, in a neighborhood so beautiful I didn't think I belonged. Could I meet the mortgage on a freelance-writer's income? Two women in my life convinced me I could. My literary agent and my then accountant, Pam Hayes.

When the Brooklyn writer Betty Smith finally earned some money with *A Tree Grows in Brooklyn,* she went out and bought herself a house in Chapel Hill, North Carolina. For her, for her mother before her, for my mother, for so many working-class women, a house is a life raft to keep you afloat when the storms sweep everything else away. Maybe things have changed, but back then, that's what a house meant to women. For Betty Smith it meant something she could give her kids to make up for the hard times her writing had caused all of them to suffer.

Smith once wrote, "Serene is a lovely word. It means to me, a walled garden with a gate in it and end-of-the-day sunshine and peace and sanctuary."

One of the first things Smith did with her new house was pull down the front porch and build that wall about the garden. The neighbors were aghast. I understand. A front porch is supposed to be for waving at neighbors and chatting. But for a writer it's when you look like you're not doing anything that you're actually writing; people who don't write don't understand this.

I'm reminded of something the novelist Helena María Viramontes shared. When she was young and still living at home, her mother would see her writing at the dining room table and say, *"Mi'ja, ayúdame, no estás haciendo nada."* Daughter, help me, you're not doing anything. Her mom worked so hard physically that Helena would feel what she was doing in comparison wasn't really work. She'd sigh, get up, and help her mom.

When I was young and still living at home, my father would call me *vampira* for writing at night. I couldn't tell him the night was my own private house.

In grad school we were assigned to read Gaston Bachelard's *The Poetics of Space* for a seminar. It left a wrinkle in my brain then, and rereading it all these years later wrinkles me now. He said: "If I were asked to name the chief benefit of the house, I should say: the house shelters day-dreaming, the house protects the dreamer, the house allows one to dream in peace." He forgot to add: but only if one lives alone and can afford to have someone else clean it.

My first house was my invented Mexico. I painted, decorated, and built it according to the Mexico of my childhood memories. (Only now as I write this do I realize that my house in San Antonio is painted the same shade of pink as the Little House of the storybook. We'd found a historic house in the neighborhood that had originally been pink when it was built in the 1880s. Its original owner, it turns out, was Cuban. Maybe he was homesick too.)

When I added an office to my house, I chose a Mexican Bauhaus style that reminded me of Mexico City, a building with *un lavadero,* an outdoor laundry sink, and a spiral staircase leading up to a rooftop terrace. I built it with the idea of taking care of others—my mother, my fellow writers, a space for an assistant or houseguests.

And now I'm searching for my last house. I imagine one with

a high wall. Someplace to protect me from folks who want to interrupt my writing. At sixty I want a house pared down to what nourishes my own spirit. I want a wall for privacy, *un zaguán*, a vestibule between the outside and inside areas, and again *un lavadero*, an outdoor sink, so I can wash under the sky and think and think. I want a house to take care of me.

The Little House planted a seed without my knowing it all these years. What I've longed for is a refuge as spiritual as a monastery, as private as a cloistered convent, a sanctuary all my own to share with animals and trees, not one to satisfy the needs of others as my previous homes have done, but a house as solid as the Little House, a fortress for the creative self.

The day I announced I was leaving my house in San Antonio, March 31, 2011

Epilogue: *Mi Casa Es Su Casa*

Why would you want to buy an old house?
It's like choosing to marry an old man!
—MY FATHER

I came to Guanajuato because they sent for me. My mother's
people. Grandfather José Eleuterio Cordero Rodríguez and
Grandmother Felipa Anguiano Rizo, and perhaps their people as
well, spirits all. I wake in the middle of the night and receive their
message.

In the fifty-sixth year of my life, I'm invited to speak at a writers' conference in San Miguel de Allende. I'd visited the town only
once, twenty years prior, a visit so brief it barely left an impression. This time I accept the conference invitation because it's the
only way I can be sure I'll have a Mexican vacation. I've decided
in advance I won't like San Miguel—too many expats—and am
ashamed and surprised when I do. I like the people, both native
and foreign, and I come back of my own accord a few weeks after.

This happens, then, on the return trip to San Miguel that fifty-
sixth spring. Walking down one particularly steep alley in the Atascadero neighborhood, beneath a bright canopy of bougainvillea, I
pause. I'm reminded of my island in Greece and am overwhelmed
with happiness. I remember the dream I had while living there, of
swimming with the dolphins even though in real life the sea terrifies me. But in my dream I felt at home in the ocean, at peace.
Does home mean being unafraid?

On this visit to San Miguel, a friend invites me to accompany him to an Alcoholics Anonymous meeting. I go out of curiosity, as I've never been. It's not much different from a literary reading, except here the storytellers are reeling their tale right in front of you, dangling like spiders with no safety net. There are testimonies of incredible pain, of humiliations that would knock out anyone. I'm almost afraid to watch. I too perform the death-defying act, and I know how tricky and dangerous it is. But I give birth to my stories in the privacy of my office, then wash them clean before presenting them to the public, without the messy placenta and afterbirth in view. These speakers weave their story without a script, tossing out filament after filament into the audience, words that must arc and reach and snag us, and boy—and how! That night I go to bed wobbly and weepy for reasons I can't explain.

It's as if a tooth has been pulled I didn't realize was loose. After I had listened to the testimonies of shame at the AA meeting, an old shame bubbles and resurfaces in me. It wakes me in the middle of the night, and this is when the spirits speak. Not through words, but through light driven through my heart. And what they have to say to me is this: "You are not your house."

This seems elemental, ridiculously simple, but it's a major discovery for me at fifty-six years of age, even though I discovered this same truth in Iowa City years and years ago. Do all major truths have to be learned and relearned like a spiral?

I am not my house. Therefore, I can walk away. I can let go everything I've built, the art collections purchased to take care of painter friends, the office I created to please my mother, the foundations for fellow writers, the house I thought I would leave upon death.

What strikes me about Mexico is the fluidity between the physical and spiritual world, a porous border where the living and the dead cross without papers. It's a culture of profound spiritual knowledge, but with no superiority over those who are spiritually innocent. In the deepest spiritual tradition, humility is a state of grace, misunderstood as inferiority by those who don't have it.

In the First World, Mexico is considered a Third World nation. But in order to create that hierarchy, certain values were put into place. Money. It appears to me the countries with money created this hierarchy where they would come first.

Are communities who have suffered the most, the cultures with the most spiritual wealth? Is there a correlation between *aguantando,* enduring, and soul? Is the transformation of pain into light the alchemy that creates soul?

If that is the case, then by the measurement of soul spirit, Mexico would be a First World nation.

———

It's a magnificent heaven, the sky of Guanajuato. Like the Virgin Mary's cloak. A pure, buoyant blue, bright as the Pacific. And drifting upon this sea, a fleet of clouds wide as galleons sailing so close, you think if you stood on a chair you could maybe touch them.

One of the main attractions of this region is that you can look out and see undeveloped land, hills and countryside like a Mexican *taquería* calendar.

But for how long?

I have roots in these lands centuries old, but though we drove through neighboring Querétaro often on our way to visit Father's relatives in Mexico City when I was a child, we always bypassed Guanajuato. There was no one, after all, we knew. Mother's family had all fled north during the time of violence, the Mexican Revolution, with stories they wish they could forget. They took with them only what could fit inside a shawl, only what they could haul with their own bodies.

Now, one hundred years after that migration north, I find myself returning in their place. Again, during the time of violence.

I'm going back to a region where we came from—Guanajuato; to a town founded seventy-nine years before the Pilgrims' *Mayflower* landing.

———————

Since before the conquest, Mexico has been a world of haves and have-nots. And even though there was more than a decade of bloodshed in the revolution of 1911, things have only gotten worse since then.

Citizens in rural Guanajuato have on the average less than a handful of years of education, and sometimes they have none at all. If they know how to write, it's only print, as script isn't taught anymore. The school supplies and uniforms and extras at the "free schools" are so expensive, it often obliges students to drop out. The suggested daily wage for domestics in San Miguel de Allende is about $20 a day, but the women I interviewed earned half that sum. Many of the people here who are responsible for paying these inhuman wages can well afford to pay more. They own land and houses, dine in restaurants, go on expensive vacations. What do they choose to see and not see if they love so much this country?

The young girls can only imagine love as the greatest accomplishment of their small lives. I watch them chewing on the lips of their boyfriends on the park benches in front of the church, and wish I could tell them—tell them what?

———

Most of the cabdrivers have worked up north, and admit the pay is good; here they earn a *miseria,* but they want to be near their families. They count themselves lucky even though San Miguel is inundated with foreigners taking the best of what is best from here, including the natural resources. The locals are grateful they have employment at all.

Instead of sombreros, the humble Mexican men of today wear baseball caps. Instead of baskets, the humble women of today carry plastic buckets the color of Easter eggs. Everywhere you see *nopalitos,* prickly pear, gathered from the wild countryside; *nopalitos* offered from these bright buckets, cleaned and de-spined with a sharp knife. A way for women with great need and no education to try to make ends meet.

Police, there are too few, but they give priority to protecting the wealthy, the center of town, not the *colonias* where the poor Mexicans live.

It's an apartheid existence. Over there in San Antonio where I once lived. Over here in San Miguel where I live now. Perhaps this is a universal truth.*

———

Walking the dogs, I come upon two men hauling a wheelbarrow filled with three boulders the size of cement sacks, a delivery for someone's garden. They're hauling these as a beast with a

---

* A friend reminds me the town benefits from the philanthropy of its foreign guests, and this is certainly true. Expat pioneer Sterling Dickinson created the public library and fine arts center to integrate foreigners and to teach them to appreciate and respect Mexico and its citizens. But a San Miguel driver recently told me he feels these venues are exclusionary by being beyond the budget of most locals. As anthropologist Ruth Béhar said, "We try to fix injustice and inequality as best we can, but we are also complicit with the system that lets us live out our dreams while others suffer."

cart would, one pulling and the other pushing, with all their might.

It's February, the time for the Feast of the Candelaria, and Juárez Park is filled with vendors selling plants. I meet the two men in the Balcones neighborhood, at one of the highest points of the town, a neighborhood of huge houses with huge vistas, as if the larger the house, the larger the slice of sky to go with it.

These two *pobres infelices*, unhappy souls. One, an older man, just a piece of gristle on bone, hauling the wheelbarrow. A face like a sock stretched from overuse, slack and baggy. The other, thick from a bad diet, has tied a yellow *mecate*, a plastic rope, round and round his waist, and is pulling the wheelbarrow uphill like a workhorse.

"What do you have there? A pyramid?" I ask.

"We've brought it all the way from Juárez Park," the grandfather says proudly. "The cabdrivers refused to take us."

"So we've had to walk," the chubby one adds.

"What a Calvary!" I say. "I hope you'll mention you came walking all the way so you'll get reimbursed for your efforts."

"We hope so," they say, and after resting only a moment they continue upward, tugging beyond their strength, *aguantando* beyond anyone's imagination.

————

After walking into town to buy a baguette, I sit to rest on the way back at los Arcos de Atascadero. The walk to my house is uphill. Los Arcos is a series of arches by a wild scrub of land I call *los duendes,* where mulberry trees were planted to feed silkworms back in the time of the dictator/president Porfirio Díaz. It's here I find myself talking to a lanky, dusty boy with a skinny dog, both the color of coffee with not enough milk. He sits next to me and tells me all about his pet, whose name is Bacha, which I at first mistake for Russian, but later in the conversation he explains Bacha is named after the stub of a marijuana cigarette, what we would call a roach. He tells me this calmly. I say, "Be careful." "I only smoke at home," he says. I suggest meat for his dog to fatten her up since she's skinnier than any of the town's street dogs. But he tells me he doesn't have money for meat. I ask if I can give her a piece of my bread. "Yes," he says, and I tear off a piece for him too and some for me, so he won't feel bad. And we eat and talk and then say goodbye. I feel sad about his not having money to buy meat, and then sadder I hadn't given him more bread or at least the whole loaf. And I felt I was as bad as San Martín, who gave away only half his cape—but I didn't do even that. Am I even worse than San Martín?

––––––––––

When I was in high school, I took a class for Spanish speakers. One of the assignments each week was a list of vocabulary words. One of the vocabulary words was *ametralladora*, machine gun. *When will I ever need to use that word?* I thought.

Now that I'm living in Mexico, I'm startled by the ubiquity of machine guns the local police carry as calmly as if carrying plastic shopping bags. At the downtown street corners, in every national parade, at the Office Depot. Even now with no machine gun in sight, I can't go into the Office Depot without experiencing an involuntary shudder.

When Aunty Baby Doll was alive, she had to go into Mexico City regularly to collect the rents on a building she owned.

"But, Aunty," I asked. "Aren't you afraid?"

"Oh, no," Aunty told me over the telephone. "Not at all. I stay over by the military school where they have policemen everywhere carrying *ametralladoras*. I feel nice and safe."

Where is the country where a woman can feel safe? Is there such a country?

When I was living in Europe I often cited Virginia Woolf: "As a woman I have no country, as a woman, my country is the whole world." I would amend that to the current times: "As a woman I have no country, as a woman I'm an immigrant in the whole world."

The Texas poet José Antonio Rodríguez says writers have "the power of just the right words."

I have the power to make people laugh. That's a power, isn't it? And to have it here in Mexico is a gift I can give daily, often, and generously, like handing someone a flower or a piece of bread. My father often handed out these *flores*. He liked to give people something even if it was only a kind word. "Oh, she was polite and beautiful, just like you."

When I make people laugh in English, it's wonderful. When I make them laugh with something I've said in Spanish, it's pure glory. I walk with a higher step. I'm at peace with myself. I go to bed feeling I've improved the world. Maybe not by much, but just enough.

I have no place in Mexican society as a woman who has borne no children. If I were young I might have a future purpose. But as I'm past childbearing years, well beyond being *una señorita,* the town doesn't know what to think of me.

Calixto and Catalina, my employees, insist on calling me *señora,* out of respect, but as I am no one's mother, how can I answer to that? Besides, *señora* smacks of a prissy church lady. I don't ever want to be *una señora.*

One morning when walking into town, I salute two laborers on the street near los Arcos. They're country people wearing baseball caps, resting along the side of the road where the natural springs spout and the cabdrivers like to park to wash their cars.

"*Buenos días,*" I say to them both.

"*¡Buenos días, señito!*" they reply buoyantly.

They use the country word that is neither *señora* nor *señorita,* but something like a cross between the two, like "ma'am."

"*¡Buenos días, señito!*"

It occurs to me then and there, that's who I am here in Mexico. I'm *señito.*

———

A dog barks. In the distance the drums from the Matachines dancers who have been drumming and dancing all day for today's fiesta like a tribe announcing warfare. At night the town echoes with boleros, mariachi, Banda music. Fireworks. A rooster. Always add a rooster. Church bells. I think of Emily Dickinson's recipe for a prairie. "To make a prairie it takes a clover and one bee . . ." To make a pueblo it takes a church bell and a rooster . . . Fireworks will do if roosters are few.

———

I feel lucky to have at my side my assistant, driver, dog trainer, handyman, and jack-of-all-trades, Calixto, a San Miguel native. He's a young man who was once in a rock band but now works to support his family as a domestic, or an electrician, or a mason, or a bartender, or whatever it takes. He's only twenty-eight, but already has a family of two, a wife, and too much responsibility.

Calixto insists I go see the house his grandparents are selling once he hears I'm house hunting. Not at once. It takes me a while to understand that I'm going to live here. It seems I'm the last to know.

Calixto says I need to see his grandparents' house as it's in the neighborhood I want. We arrive in the late afternoon before dark falls. It's a narrow house with an open door like a mouth saying "Ahhh." In the doorway there are a few vegetables in crates, just a few, like in a store. It's then I realize this *is* a store. A tiny neighborhood convenience store, but with only four tomatoes, some dried *chiles,* a few onions. That's it. Like many locals, a table is set up in the doorway to sell one or two items—maybe mangoes on a stick served with chili and lime. Or fried pork rinds. Or a small sign might be taped along a corridor announcing tortillas *hechas a mano,* homemade. A way to earn a few needed extra pesos. So why shouldn't Calixto's grandparents sell a bit of produce?

Calixto introduces me. The *abuelo,* dark and dry as *machaca,* beef jerky, sits in a shadowy corner. We exchange *"Buenas tardes."* He nods and shakes my hand and asks me how I am, as courteous as only Mexican country people can be. The house is as dark as he is, with only a bare bulb illuminating the room, a yellow light that can't quite flush out the darkness in the corners. I can make out a series of mismatched furniture, a dresser from the 1930s, a bed in the same room, a television murmuring in the corner like someone praying a *novena.* A *"Buenas tardes"* bubbles up from the grandmother seated on the bed, but she can't tear her face from the telenovela as she says this. She talks to us as a blind person would, without turning her head, without looking in our direction.

The house we're in is just one big room like the old-fashioned houses, like the modern houses imitating the old-fashioned one-room houses. Outside there is a narrow courtyard, a passageway open to the sky, cluttered with caged birds, crates, potted plants, and a wringer washer. The bathroom must be reached through this vestibule.

It's a terrible business staring at other people's homes, peering into cupboards, investigating private areas, like sniffing someone's armpits. I'm both repulsed and compelled to poke my snout everywhere and sniff.

We climb up to the *azotea,* the roof terrace, a space that is used for many things in Mexico, and here it houses the several little dogs who have speckled the roof with *caquita,* turds shaped like donuts and *churros.* Calixto tells me the unmarried uncle lives in the little room up here beyond the glass door; it's he who watches over the grandparents, though I suspect not much, just as he doesn't do very much cleaning. "Where's your uncle?" I ask. Calixto says with disgust, "Out drinking, no doubt."

"It's like *un palomar*—a dovecote," Calixto says of the narrow tall house of his grandparents.

"To me it's like many of the downtown houses," I say. "Narrow as a slice of birthday cake. But if I buy this house that your grandparents so desperately want to sell, I'll be displacing *viejitos,* old people."

Calixto says, "Anywhere you buy a house in town you'll be displacing someone's *viejitos.*"

It's a truth that hurts to hear. I am part of the gentrification.

———

Though it's easy for me to come south, I'm told the story of a woman wishing badly to come north, and it stays and stays with me. Who tells me this story is Servando.

Servando Bustos Ybarra: an intelligent, respectful, green-eyed Mexican who is about forty but looks younger because of the baseball caps he always wears. Originally from a farming community on the outskirts of town, now he lives and works as a concierge/

gardener for a boutique hotel catering to tourists from Canada and the United States. Servando is fully bilingual in Spanish and English and, as he is smart, easily picks up current slang. He's popular among the hotel guests because he shows them deep deference, and therefore confirms in their eyes their feeling of racial and economic superiority. His Don Quixote subservience is typical of Mexican hospitality and often misunderstood by foreigners, who see it as the propriety of a servant and not the generosity and good breeding of a social equal. Servando is especially Mexican in that he often invites his guests to sunset cocktails and appetizers at his own expense, not his employer's, though he earns only modest wages. For Mexicans like Servando, it's important etiquette to offer his guests everything. From the halls of Montezuma, this *"Mi casa es su casa"* philosophy has been misinterpreted by entitled foreigners as permission to help themselves to more than what is intended.

Servando has a handsome square face like an ancient Olmec stone head, but he confesses he dislikes his Indian nose. Servando's face is creased from working under the sun, which makes his agate eyes more pronounced, a reminder of the history of foreign intervention in the Guanajuato area, including the imposition of Archduke Maximiliano, who was put to death by firing squad in nearby Querétaro.

Servando's grandparents spoke Otomí, but within two generations this language has been all but forgotten. From his Otomí ancestry he has inherited the sturdy body and strong limbs of the locals. Often Servando is seen climbing up and down the hilly streets about town several times a day ferrying groceries or doing errands for hotel guests, and like the worker ants who carry items five times their size, Servando is always ready to comply. This is the story Servando tells me:

We traveled by bus to the U.S. embassy in Guadalajara, two dozen of us wanting our visas. But truthfully, in my heart of hearts, it was more for la Señora, *my boss, who keeps asking me to come. My visa application cost 10,000 pesos* [$673].

I sat across from an old couple: humble country people you could tell by the way they dressed. He in cowboy clothes, and she a chubby shorty still wearing her kitchen apron under a pale blue sweatshirt. She was talkative and told me her name was Señora Concha and that she wanted to go to the States to visit her two sons who live outside Dallas.

We left at one in the morning and got to Guadalajara at dawn. First they took us to the Mexican consulate and we had to wait four hours till they opened, standing outside in the street, and there was already a line at 6 a.m. Five hundred people in front of us! Who knows when they got there. First you freeze, then you're burning up when the sun comes out. Finally they take your photo, your fingerprint, and that's it. Five or six hours and it's over.

They put us up at a one-star hotel so ugly I slept with all my clothes on. Then to the U.S. embassy at eight in the morning. Another line of a thousand people. Three more hours of standing. Then they interview you in two seconds.

You stand behind a thick window with la cónsul *on the other side talking through a mike. She asks you questions in front of everybody, because behind you more than a thousand are all listening.*

—Why do you want to go to the U.S.?

—I just want to go on vacation.

She looked at my papers. —Who invited you?

—My employer, she has a house there. I want to get to know Disneyland, because I've read about Walt Disney.

Then she looked at her papers and said, —Por el momento no aplica. At the moment, you do not qualify.

—Gracias.

I felt [and here he makes a sound of exhaling deeply] . . . *I felt,*

Okay, it doesn't matter. On the contrary, I was relieved, because in my mind I was calculating the cost of the trip, and I can't afford to stay but a couple of weeks.

When la Señora Concha came out of her interview, I could see on her face she hadn't been granted a visa either.

—*I so wanted to see my sons. It's been twenty years. This is the third time I've tried. Sometimes we phone my grandkids over there, and they answer us in English!*

—*Señora, I know your children can't come and see you because they don't have papers, but can't their children who were born in the States come and visit? They won't have problems crossing. Why don't they try to do that? You're spending money you shouldn't spend.*

And I thought, this señora, so humble and poor, trying not to over-spend too much when we were out and about. To make her feel better I told her about my uncle.

—*My uncle went to visit his relatives, and he felt like he was in jail. He didn't drive or speak the language. If they didn't take him out, he couldn't go out. It's not easy over there.*

—*Well, maybe you're right.*

But I didn't convince her, because she's a mother. Her kids are her kids, and she wants to see them.

————

Mexico breaks my heart on a daily basis. The men and women who ring the bell looking for work. The man with too many teeth asking if I need a gardener. The Central American selling candy bars trying to make his way across yet another border. The honey-voiced *anciana* who rings my bell each Sunday needling me with small requests one after another, one at a time like rosary beads, forcing me to run up and down nineteen stairs to fetch a pair of shoes first, and then some clothes I might not want, perhaps a little food left over from lunch, any loose change, till I no longer feel generous and compassionate, I feel like strangling her, and then I feel miserable at my lack of humanity.

And the old ones downtown folded into little rag piles on the sidewalk, like bags of collapsed laundry, who bless me. *May la Virgen protect you. May she look after you always. La Virgen will pay you back. May she keep you under her mantle of stars.*

What must it be like to come from this town where so many of the houses are empty days, months at a time? Imagine you don't have a house, or your house is something not worth inhabiting. What must it feel like to walk by these houses worth a million, two million, three, when one's own home has no heat except firewood?

The wealthy Mexicans like to live in houses that resemble the future. The expats who live here like to live in houses that resemble the past, or houses that are the Mexico of their imagination. Houses that allow them to feel like *hacendados,* hacienda owners.

Where do I fit in as a U.S. Latina who wants to live in a convent without the nuns?

———

Breakfast in the kitchen with Catalina and Calixto. The talk is about how sometimes when you go into a restaurant here in San Miguel, and they don't want to serve you, they say the restaurant is full.

"Is this true? Has this really happened to you?"

"*Sí,*" Calixto insists.

It reminds me of what my friend the Mixtec poet Celerina Patricia told me about how indigenous people are treated in Mexico. How in the Zona Rosa in Mexico City, when they don't want to serve her, they tell her the tables are all reserved.

"But how can this happen in this day and age?"

"It does," Celerina assures me.

Catalina and Calixto both tell me about going to the cheese store Luna de Queso on an errand for me. How the salesclerk took care of all the foreigners and light-skinned Mexicans first before finally attending to Catalina and Calixto, who had been there before anyone else.

Even Calixto, as pale as Ranchero Queso, is snubbed, possibly because he dresses in T-shirts that say "That's How I Roll" with a drawing of a roll of toilet paper. He doesn't have the inclination or funds to buy button-down shirts. Calixto with his *mestizo* Euro-skin, but almond *indio* eyes. The shopkeeper ignores him and his *mulata* wife, Catalina, with her night jaguar beauty. At the Luna de Queso shop on Salida de Celaya they serve first and foremost those whose skin is as white as the waxy Brie moon.

On May 7, 2014, at 6:30 p.m., I take my friend Norma to a restaurant *named* "The Restaurant," on Sollano Street, a high-end foodie's delight, which I go to only when out-of-town friends make reservations. I'm just as happy, if not happier, eating at the market. I don't need fancy. I never think of it. But it's May, the slowest month in this town. My favorite, El Correo, is closed, as are many businesses this season.

Norma and I decide to dine at The Restaurant. I run ahead because Norma has a bad hip. I'm hoping we'll be lucky and get a table without a reservation since we're dining between lunch (2 to 4 p.m.) and supper (8 p.m. or so). When I get there I'm thrilled to see the restaurant is empty.

"*Buenas tardes,*" I say to the hip young thing serving as hostess. "Do I need a reservation for dinner?"

"All our tables are reserved," fashion model tells me.

"Really?"

"But you can sit at the bar," she says.

"Oh, but can't you try to seat us in the main courtyard?"

A waiter comes by as I make this request, and he ushers me to a table in the main courtyard, all cordiality. Finally Norma hobbles in, out of breath and in pain, and she asks the waiter if she may smoke. Only at the bar, is the reply. I'm a bit disgruntled by all this, after all the trouble I went through to get a courtyard table, but okay, fine by me.

It's an expensive, delicious, but forgettable meal. Norma is happy, and I'm happy she's happy, and that's all that matters. When we exit, we walk through the main courtyard, where all the tables but two are still as empty as when we arrived.

I find the manager. I ask him if the tables are reserved, and why were we told they were reserved when there's still no one here? He sputters something about having a talk with the hostess, but I know she's only following management policy. I tell him I'm a writer and confess it will be an interesting story for me to write about.

It occurs to me I've passed as a local. I'm refused a table at The Restaurant, and now I know why. It's filled with gringos, it's a restaurant that caters to them, and it makes them feel like they're in Beverly Hills when they're really in Mexico.

Welcome to Mexico. *México lindo y querido.*

———

When my uncle Baby died recently his children had no idea where to spread his ashes—in Mexico City, where he was born, or in Chicago, where they lived. During the last decade of his life, when he was a widower, Uncle Baby chose to immigrate back to Mexico and live outside Guadalajara. But his children didn't like his choice of a new life—a wife younger than any of his kids, a baby younger than his own grandkids. *Pobrecito* Uncle Baby. Where's home? In his life, he lived in his shop. And now in death, his ashes are in an urn in the same Chicago shop where he worked as an upholsterer. His kids have decided to share the ashes and send half back to his "widow" in Mexico. They're pleased with having come up with this diplomatic solution.

———

Last month I went back to the United States to close up the house I'd lived in for two decades. When I first bought the house, my father was furious. He couldn't understand why I'd chosen a hundred-year-old house when I could've easily have bought a brand-new one. But I love old homes. Their *duende,* their soul/ spirit.

Father's first concern was that I wouldn't be able to take care of a house by myself. One of the first things he did when he walked in was bounce on the floorboards. *"Mira,"* he said as he jumped. The planks squeaked and moaned as if he were hurting them. This was proof enough, he thought, to show me how foolish my choice had been. But after a few weeks, Father saw I had a team— handyman, yardman, housekeeper—attending to the needs of my elderly house. He sighed and finally admitted I'd done well.

Now, twenty years later, I am selling the house I said I'd never sell. On my last night, I wake at 3 a.m. for a 4:30 taxi pickup to the San Antonio airport. The driver arrives a half hour early, but my bags are already waiting on the front porch.

Before locking up, I look around at the empty rooms. I think about all the creative folks who have passed through this house and my life. Filmmakers and painters, designers and writers, architects and activists, politicians and poets, organizers and educators, musicians and dancers, singers and scientists, performance artists and feminist nuns. A writing workshop was born in this dining room and went on to become the Macondo Foundation. Here began los MacArturos, the caucus of Latino MacArthur fellows; here they gathered and celebrated. So many *locos*—local and from far away—passed through these rooms. Twenty years' worth.

I pull the door firmly behind me, lock it for the last time, and ask myself this:

—*How do you feel?*

I say to myself, *I feel . . . gratitude.*

This house in San Antonio no longer brings me joy. It grew from a grande dame into a grand pain in the you-know-what, a curmudgeon constantly banging a stick on the floor for my undivided attention. "You don't take care of me anymore," I want to confess to my house, but I don't want to hurt her feelings. For too long I've felt my solitude and concentration invaded now that the River Walk has been extended behind my back fence. Pedestrians trot on the other side at all hours, even during the night, setting my dogs into pandemonium and my heart leaping. Condominiums, under construction on the opposite bank, roar and growl and sputter into life, setting off dust storms. I don't want to admit this, but my house makes me feel afraid.

I think about what my Mexican friends and employees said recently when I told them I was traveling north to the United States: "Aren't you afraid?"[*]

This is exactly what U.S. friends said to me when I told them I was moving to Mexico. "Aren't you afraid?"

Soon after 9/11, on a radio talk show in Mexico, a caller gave

[*] When I remind Mexicans of the abductions and disappearances in their own country, the political corruption, human rights violations, and drug wars, they counter, "Yes, but we don't have to send our children to school with fear they will be assassinated by other children."

The empty living room of my San Antonio house,
January 2015

the United States a new name. Instead of "los Estados Unidos," the United States, he referred to it as "los Asustados Unidos," the United States of Fear. We are living in the age of *susto,* fear, on both sides, on all sides, on all borders, across the globe.

The paradox is this: fear unites us, fear divides us. In a post-9/11 United States, with so much vitriol allowed in the media toward people who look like me, I no longer feel at home at home. You shouldn't feel afraid in your own house.

Often in interviews I'm asked how it is that I identify as both Mexican *and* American, and I reply, "Well, you have a mother *and* a father, right? How is it that you can love both? Loving one doesn't cancel out the other."

I've been living in the Fatherland for a long time. Now it's time to explore the Motherland, for what is Mexico if not a matriarchal society, even if matriarchs do sometimes create monsters. Isn't a macho another word for a mama's boy?*

I peer out the cab window at the house while the driver rearranges my bags in the trunk. The porch lights shine cheerily through the punched-tin Isaac Maxwell fixtures. The magueys and cacti I planted are doing a beautiful flamenco dance in the dark; look how big they've grown. The pecan and the mesquite trees, the house sentinels, *se despiden* without sadness. I look at the house I've called for so long home. I *am* grateful.

I tell the driver, "Let's go."

February 16, 2015
Casa O'Leary
San Miguel de los Chichimecas

---

* I have complete faith that mothers and grandmothers are the solution to the violence not only in Mexico, but across the world. There can be nothing that is more highly revered in Mexican culture than a mother, except perhaps a mother's mother, and beyond that the holy mother of mothers, the goddess Guadalupe.

Once on San Antonio television, a live TV camera followed the tense exchange between a sniper holed up in his house and the San Antonio police. In the middle of the drama, the sniper's grandmother came home and asked what was going on. When it was explained, she tore past the yellow police tape, went in herself, and came out with the young culprit dangling from her arm as she swatted and spanked him with her *chancla*. What the world needs now are the grandmother brigades to shame, swat, and spank the *meros* machos of *el mundo*.

Pilón: Infinito

There was once a woman who longed to live in a house all her own, where the rooms would be clean and quiet, and she could work. She fell in love with houses because of their silence as well as their light. But she did not have a house of her own.

She rented cheap rooms in buildings built for cars, where rooms for people were only an afterthought, though cars didn't even need to be sheltered, for it was a land where it was never truly cold. The heat came in through the tin roof, and cockroaches, lacquered as Egyptian scarabs, marched in through the cracks as if they were Egyptian royalty. Desperate "rodentia" scrambled between the walls.

The sun shone hard and harsh in this land, and the *nopalitos* and the flowers bloomed most of the year. And when they did not, pecans crunched beneath shoes. In this season, rowdy grackles shook out their feathers, black and shiny as the skin of night rivers, and gathered in the skeleton of winter trees.

Sometimes this woman lived in borrowed homes, but these have their own poison. They were not for keeps, and to fall in love with them and to know eventually you had to give them up was as terrible as falling in love with someone else's husband. To fall in love like this is nothing short of torture.

Houses came and houses went, flirting with her, but they were not to be hers. Until one day, a wise woman arrived and asked for water. The woman who owned no houses remembered that to give water is a way of being blessed, and so, *con ganas,* with desire, she gave water to the wise woman.

—I want to give you something in return. What is it you wish for more than anything? A husband?

—Oh no, not anymore.

—A new car?

—Not worth the price. I always buy used.

—What about shoes?

—I don't have room to store the ones I have. What I really want is a house of my own.

—Who wouldn't? the wise woman said. —Just you wait. See you later.

And so it happened that a house did appear, not only one she fell in love with, but one that was for sale and at a price she could afford, without even a realtor. She was terribly frightened, but her agent and her accountant gave her *ánimo,* which is like courage but with a push.

It was a house with a mesquite tree alongside dancing an arabesque and a pecan tree in front that dropped its fruit on the roof in the autumn like coins—*plunk, plunk*—and a river behind snaking into a graceful S. Well! It was such a fine house, every time she put the key in the lock, she had to laugh.

This house she painted violet because of her overwhelming love, and oh, what an uproar this caused. Who would think violet would cause so much pain to others? But people who have no life of their own like to meddle in the lives of those who do.

More sooner than later, the sun faded this violet house to blue, and the next time paint was due, the woman knew to paint it a darker shade of pink, so that it would fade from pinker to pink.

This house, though it was big at first, became small in time as she grew and grew, so that near the end of her time there, she felt like Alice in the illustration by Sir John Tenniel after she has drunk from the "Drink Me" bottle. To make matters worse, she had filled the house up with furniture, dogs, a man, and a lot of clutter. Because she was industrious, she built another little house beside the first, the color of the thousand-petaled marigold, *xempoaxóchitl.* And here she put her books and her desk, and the guests who visited overnight.

In time, a third house, across the street, came to be hers, and inside this house, which she painted blue, she decided to put all the things that got in the way of her work—writers in residence, workshops, tax receipts, and even the man she now lived with, who was as sweet as burnt-milk candy but as untidy as *un remolino tejano en agosto,* a Texas dust devil in August, and eventually would be asked to leave.

But, oh, how the houses wailed and cried, and were worse than little children.

—I need a spiral staircase so as to reach the roof and look at the stars, said the Marigold House.

—But look at me! I need lights so that folks at night can see I am now pink, said the house formerly known as Violet, because she had gotten used to fame.

—But I haven't got fresh paint at all, said the Blue House, and my roof needs repairs, and my doors need mending, and my glass is cracked. Compared to you two, I look rather raggedy.

Well, the woman who owned these three houses had no idea they would keep her up nights with their whining. They were as spoiled as courtesans, as vain as hothouse flowers, as demanding as trust-fund children, and they needed things now, or they would hold their breath and collapse under the weight of seasons.

The woman who owned the three houses sat at her desk and tried to set to work dreaming daydreams, because this was her profession. But because fear is great and courage small, she could not dream a single dream.

Finally, she decided to take a nap and listen to her night dreams. And so, in her dream she saw all around her were stories, some that the neighbor parking his car in his driveway gave her, one that was brought to her by the cleaning lady, one that her gardener plucked as perfect as a Fragonard rose. Well!

To think! They had been whirling and flying all about her all along, and they were free for the taking. You only had to sit still, and down from the skies they fluttered and landed in your hair. Stories without beginning or end, connecting everything little and large, blazing from the center of the universe into *el infinito* called the great out there.

Resting Place/*Descanso*

Ai

María Romualda **Felipa** Anguiano de Cordero

Gloria Anzaldúa

Enrique Arteaga Cisneros

Gertrude Baker

Gwendolyn Brooks

Ronnie Burk

Reverend Tom Chavana

Carolina Cisneros Cordero

Estela Cisneros Beamonte

Alfredo Cisneros del Moral

Edna Cisneros del Moral

José **Enrique** Cisneros del Moral

Jorge Cisneros del Moral

Luis Gonzaga Cisneros y Guillén

Efraín Cordero

José Cordero

Manuel Cordero

Tomasa Cordero Alcalá

Guadalupe Cordero Cabrera

Elvira Cordero Cisneros

José Eleuterio Cordero Rodríguez

Eulalia Cordero Rosen Gómez

José De Lara García

Trinidad del Moral de Cisneros

Maria Dermoût
Marguerite Duras
Federico Fellini
Carlos Fuentes
Eduardo Galeano
Alejandro Garza Fuentes
William Geyer
Cynthia Harper
Oscar Hijuelos
Rick Hunter
Ryszard Kapuściński
James Patrick Kirby
Danny López Lozano
Salem Malović
Eugene Martínez
Jerry Weston Mathis
Isaac Maxwell
Craig Pennel
Astor Piazzolla
Victoria Rizo de Anguiano
Mercè Rodoreda
Luis Omar Salinas
Mario David Sánchez
Antonios Stavrou
Studs Terkel
Chavela Vargas
Senator John Vasconcellos
Mariana Yampolsky

Acknowledgments

I once complained to Eduardo Galeano that I felt homeless. His reply: "You have many homes at once." Well, this was true, I realized, after giving it some thought. Many doors have opened in the past and taken me in when I had nowhere else to go or didn't know my next address. Sometimes it was a room of my own that was offered, and sometimes it was the whole house. I thank all who have generously sheltered me.

Borrowed Houses: Cavanaugh O'Leary and Blanca Uzeta O'Leary; Sara Stevenson and Richard Queen; J. Frank Dobie Paisano House; Foundation Michael Karolyi; the Mabel Dodge Lujan House; Arturo Madrid and Antonia Castañeda; Juan Ríos and Estévan Rael Galvez; Rosemary Catacalos; Norma Cantú and Elvia Niebla; Alfred and Julie Cisneros; Tey Diana Rebolledo and Michael Passi; Denise Chávez and Daniel C. Zolinsky; Ruth Béhar; Dennis Mathis; Tracy and Teresa Boyer; Phyllis López-Kirby.

Home-Sweet-Home Publishing Houses: Gary Soto and Lorna Dee Cervantes's Mango Press, Norma Alarcón's Third Woman Press, Joni Evans and Julie Grau of Turtle Bay, and my current home, Vintage and Alfred A. Knopf. *Mil y un gracias.* Belated gratitude: Back in the day, when *Woman Hollering Creek* first appeared, Ann Beattie gave me one of my first blurbs. I want to thank her here finally in print since I was too shy to write and thank her back then.

Construction workers: Macarena Hernández, Yvette DeChávez,

Erasmo Guerra, Ruth Béhar, Norma Alarcón, Dennis Mathis, Liliana Valenzuela.

Good Cents: Nely Galán, Tracy Boyer, Marie Silverman. Good Sense: Ida Roldán.

Feng Shui Expert: Gayle Elliott.

Literary *Curanderas:* Dr. Sonia Saldívar Hull and Dr. María Herrera Sobek. Art *Duendes:* Tey Mariana Nunn and Ceserero Moreno.

Contractors: Dr. Tey Diana Rebolledo and Dr. Carla Trujillo.

Home Team San Antonio: It takes a village to move a writer. My thanks as always to Bill Sánchez, Alejandro Sánchez, Roger Solís, Josephine (Josie) F. Garza, Macarena Hernández, Ray Santisteban, Natalia Treviño, Miguel García, Jessica Fuentes, Irma Carolina Rubio, Juanita Chávez, Daniel Gamboa, Dave the Cowboy Chávez, Nancy Barohn, Roger Vásquez, Ann Van Pelt.

Equipo México: Ernesto Espinoza López, Eunice Chávez Muñoz, Francisco Ramírez Arzolar, Benjamin Huerta García, Rodolfo Ybarra, Cyndy Severson, and especially *madrina* Mary Katherine Wainwright, who nominated me for the San Miguel Writers' Conference 2011. *Brujas:* Diana Phillips and Gaby Vidrio. House midwife: Susan Rensberger. *Divina Providencia* House Seller: Karen Reyes.

Home Inspection: Josie F. Garza, Macarena Hernández, Ito Romo, Liliana Valenzuela, Gayle Elliott, Norma Alarcón, Susan Bergholz, Ruth Béhar, Charlie Hall.

Foundation Work: David Kepes, Susan Bergholz, Bill Sánchez, Roland Mazuca, Orlando Bolaños, Olivia Doerge Mena, the Guadalupe Cultural Arts Center, Eve Porter, K. T. Whitehead, David Rodríguez, John Phillip Santos, Richard Blanco, Ruth Béhar, Josie Garza, I'rene Lara Silva, Moises Silva, Kristin Naca, Francisco Aragón, Kathy Sosa, Miryam Bujanda, Cynthia Pérez, Dr. Ellen Riojas Clark, and Ramiro Salazar.

Animal Wranglers: Yvette Benavides, David Martin Davies,

Christianna Davies, Betty Padilla Beck, Debra Múñoz-Bratina, Rebecca Martínez, Monica Riojas Wozniak, Macarena Hernández.

Documentation: *Visual*—Thanks to all the photographers who gave permission for us to use their images. See the illustration credits for the long list of people I am indebted to. A special thanks to Diana Solís, Lourdes Portillo, Ester Hernández, Josie F. Garza. *Audio*—My thanks to Scott Cresswell and Daniel Garcia for guiding me through the audio recording of this book. It was a lot of work, but a lot of fun.

Archivists: Josie F. Garza, Roxanne Rose Peña, Bibi Lobo, and especially Ray Santisteban.

Landscapers: Cassandra Pappas and Stephanie Ross, who designed this book exquisitely.

Architect: Robin Desser, who gave me a wonderful blueprint and inspiration as the house went up. Thank you, *corazón de melón*, for your *ojitos*. *Gracias* is due as well to Robin's assistant, the diligent, ever efficient Jennifer Kurdyla, for custom, quality craftsmanship.

All-Around Handypersons: *Amor, gratitud, y más amor a las hermanas de mi corazón*, Josie F. Garza and Macarena Hernández, who worked weekends, evenings, and holidays on this book as lovingly and tenaciously as if it were their very own. *¡Qué suerte la mía!*

Madrina de las Letras: la Santa Susan Bergholz, a candle with a flame like a conflagration. *Eres mi protectora. Bendita sea.*

To all, those here with me now and those who are spirit, my friends, teachers, and ancestors, who opened the path that I might be here this moment, *gracias*.

Virgen de Guadalupe, estoy aquí para cumplir.

Illustration Credits

Unless otherwise noted, all photographs are from the author's personal collection. We have tried to identify all copyright holders; in case of an oversight and upon notification to the publisher, corrections will be made in subsequent printings.

The following pieces first appeared in these publications:

Elle: "Vivan Los Muertos" (October 1991)

Granta (Chicago): "*Ofrenda* for My Mother" (December 2009)

House & Garden: "*Que Vivan Las Colores*" (April 2002)

Los Angeles Times: "An *Ofrenda* for My Father" (October 26, 1997) and "*Un Poquito de tu Amor*" (February 22, 1998)

Los Angeles Times Book Review: "My Wicked Wicked Ways" from *My Wicked Wicked Ways* (Knopf, 1992), first printed as "Poem as Preface" (September 6, 1992)

The New York Times: "Who Wants Stories Now" (March 14, 1993) and "To Seville, with Love" (November 16, 2003)

The New York Times Magazine: "Chavela Vargas" (December 28, 2012)

Tonantzin: "Luis Omar Salinas" (January 1984)

The Washington Post Book World: "Marguerite Duras" (February 2005)

Many of the stories were originally published in the following:

"Eduardo Galeano" from Introduction to *Days and Nights of Love and War* by Eduardo Galeano (Monthly Review Press, 2000)

"Mercè Rodoreda" from Introduction to *Camellia Street* by Mercè Rodoreda (Graywolf, 1993)

"*The House on Mango's Street*'s 10th Birthday" from *The House on Mango Street 10th Anniversary Edition* (Vintage, 1993)

"*El Pleito* / The Quarrel" from *Moctezuma's Table: Rolando Briseno's Mexican and Chicano Tablescapes* by Rolando Briseno (Texas A&M University Press, 2010)

"Infinito Botánica" from *High Pink Tex-Mex Fairy Tales* by Franco Mondini Ruiz (Distributed Art Publishers, Inc., 2005)

"A House of My Own" from *The House on Mango Street 25th Anniversary Edition* (Vintage, 2006)

"Resurrections" from *Have You Seen Marie?* (Knopf, 2012)

A NOTE ABOUT THE AUTHOR

SANDRA CISNEROS was born in Chicago in 1954. She is the author of two novels, the internationally acclaimed *The House on Mango Street* and *Caramelo,* awarded the Premio Napoli, nominated for the Orange Prize, and shortlisted for the International IMPAC Dublin Literary Award.

Her awards include National Endowment for the Arts fellowships for both fiction and poetry, the Lannan Literary Award, the American Book Award, the Texas Medal of the Arts, the Thomas Wolfe Prize, and a MacArthur fellowship.

Other books include *Have You Seen Marie?;* the story collection *Woman Hollering Creek;* two books of poetry, *My Wicked Wicked Ways* and *Loose Woman;* and two books of children's literature. Her work has been translated into more than twenty languages.

Cisneros is the founder of the Alfredo Cisneros del Moral and Macondo Foundations, which serve creative writers. She lives in Mexico.

Find her online at www.sandracisneros.com.

A NOTE ON THE TYPE

This book was set in Monotype Dante, a typeface designed by Giovanni Mardersteig (1892–1977). Conceived as a private type for the Officina Bodoni in Verona, Italy, Dante was originally cut only for hand composition by Charles Malin, the famous Parisian punch cutter, between 1946 and 1952. Its first use was in an edition of Boccaccio's *Trattatello in laude di Dante* that appeared in 1954. The Monotype Corporation's version of Dante followed in 1957. Although modeled on the Aldine type used for Pietro Cardinal Bembo's treatise *De Aetna* in 1495, Dante is a thoroughly modern interpretation of the venerable face.

Composed by North Market Street Graphics,
Lancaster, Pennsylvania

Printed and bound by R. R. Donnelley,
Crawfordsville, Indiana,

Designed by Cassandra J. Pappas